P/114/24 1/3 ⁹/₉

Eleanor Merrifield OP
May, 1970

$45 ⁰⁰

0038 ~~774~~

07/15

BEYOND
THE
COUCH

BEYOND THE COUCH

Dialogues in Teaching and Learning Psychoanalysis in Groups

Alexander Wolf, M.D., FAGPA
Emanuel K. Schwartz, Ph.d., D.S.Sc., FAGPA
Gerald J. McCarty, Ph.D., FAGPA
Irving A. Goldberg, Ph.D., FAGPA

Science House
New York
1970

Library of Congress Catalog Card Number: 70-110256
Standard Book Number: 87668-029-5

FORMAT BY HARVEY DUKE

Manufactured by Haddon Craftsmen, Inc.
Scranton, Pennsylvania

Introduction

My interest in analytic group therapy was activated in the early 1940's when one of the authors of this book, Dr. Alexander Wolf, reported on his experiences with an assemblage of patients suffering from a variety of neurotic and personality disorders treated analytically in mass. His enthusiasm with this group analysis was in my opinion at the time the chief instrument for his success. For without faith in what he was doing, on the parts of both therapist and patient, I was convinced that little movement in therapy could have been achieved. In the next few years, my confidence in faith as a prime therapeutic agency did not dwindle, but in experimenting with some of the procedures Dr. Wolf advocated, I soon realized that his conviction was inspired by much more than faith. Indeed the sheer truism is that group analysis has great reconstructive potentials—potentials not only as an adjunct to individual analysis, but as an analytic process in its own right.

Back in 1929, as a student in medical school, I was assigned, as an extern, to one of the medical clinics of the Boston Dispensary. An innovation in the dispensary had been initiated by an old-time clinician, Dr. Joseph Pratt, who, disappointed with the results of traditional methods of dealing with chronic medical outpatients, had initiated a weekly meeting of the oldest clinic habitués who had in vain desperation sought relief from their physical suffering through regular attendance at the dispensary outpatient clinics. Despite their eloquent complaints that they were not being helped, these frustrated recipients had insisted on reporting regularly for visits, often sitting about for hours chatting happily with each other about their physical misery. During this vigil they cluttered up the clinic rooms and aisles so that there was hardly any room for new patients. Dr. Pratt had a theory that if he could gather these hopeless specimens of suffering humanity and bring them together into a weekly congregation, he might accomplish two things: First, he would provide an outlet for their social and dependent needs; and second, he would free seats in the waiting rooms for less chronic patients.

To the surprise of many, including medical students like myself, Dr. Pratt's theories proved fruitful. Indeed, no Lourdes boasted of greater miracles than were brought about by this dedicated physician through his simple group procedures. Even the most dubious observers were soon convinced that Dr. Pratt's inspirational talks and relaxing procedures were far more helpful to this conclave of chronic sufferers than the tons of medications that had been wasted on them during the years when they futilely exhausted all of the tests and methods of classical medicine.

It was this experience that actuated me as a resident officer at the Kings Park State Hospital in the early 1930's to employ supportive group approaches among the mental patients who populated the wards to which I had been assigned. It was my opinion at that time that group therapy had an important but limited function in helping mentally sick people achieve an adaptive equilibrium. No reconstructive impact could possibly be registered on the deeper strata of personality.

Alexander Wolf's insistence that analytic procedures could be employed within a group framework to influence the intrapsychic structure itself was a challenging revelation, and when my personal analytic training had been completed, I decided to experiment with psychoanalytic group tactics. Around 1945, my wife and I organized a small mental health clinic which soon expanded into a larger Postgraduate Center for Mental Health. Around 1946, Wilfred Hulse founded a group therapy department at the center, and with

Alexander Wolf, Edrita Fried, Helen Durkin, Asya Kadis, and Emanuel K. Schwartz (another author of this book), developed it into an exciting and innovating division, which to this date has continued to play a pioneer role in the field of group therapy and group analysis.

Our observations of the groups at the center, particularly when the Group Therapy Department came under the direction of Asya Kadis, quickly established what Alexander Wolf had so often accented before, namely that it was possible to do good psycho-analytically oriented therapy in a group setting. The manifold kinds of interaction among the group members, clarified by proper inter-pretations of the leader, quickly cut through resistances and defenses. Exposure to the verbalized problems of other patients, and the experiencing of hostility, criticism, and a variety of transferential projections, enabled motivated individuals to become increasingly perceptive about their own unconscious emotional processes. This was particularly helpful in dealing with rigid character defenses and imbedded ego-syntonic traits. Each patient identified with certain members of the group and rejected others; he developed multiple transference reactions with re-created sibling and parental figures. He was in this way often enabled to work through distortions that had resisted individual psychoanalysis. Some patients, by allying themselves with selected members, gained the strength to challenge authority figures and to express impulses previously repressed. More-over the objective reactions of the other participants provided a forum for reality testing. Patients became more and more capable of tolerating criticism and hostility that were directed toward them, and to distinguish projections based on transference from realistic accusations.

We were so impressed with the potentialities of group analysis that we made some training in group methods a part of our fellowship program. Emanuel Schwartz, creative maverick that he was, who had become our dean of training, helped to institute some unique methods in communicating principles of group therapy. While evolving these pedagogic tactics, he co-operated with Alexander Wolf in experimenting with supervision conducted by telephone with supervisees many miles away. The rationale for this approach was in part expediency. Many professional people of high caliber were being denied essential learning experience because they practiced in areas of the country that lacked proper educational facilities. This put severe limitations on their acquiring the expertise required for the effective practice of group analysis.

To many psychotherapists, steeped in the tradition that personal supervision is the *sine qua non* of good training, there is no substitute for face-to-face supervisory confrontation. Supervision through mere graphic or verbal reporting would seem to lack among other things the ingredients of nonverbal communication, as well as potentially rich transferential and countertransferential vectors without which the supervisory process would be relatively barren. Movies or videotapes of a student working with a group, reviewed by a skilled supervisor, might provide some interesting dimensions that could possibly be of value as a supplement to or substitute for personal supervision. However, the expense involved, apart from the mechanical skills required for the operation of the essential apparatus, would militate against the use of these devices. The telephone would appear to be a much more practical instrumentality. If there were any validity in telephonic supervision, this would surely constitute a remarkable contribution toward expanding educational horizons. It is because of this that the present volume, reporting on an experience in telephonic supervision, is so interesting.

The fact that each supervisory session was tape-recorded, transcribed, and distributed to the participants, and that the supervisory process was implemented over a four-year period, makes this an extraordinary study. The observation of how an intensive interpersonal supervisory involvement, including transference and countertransference, may take place in the absence of face-to-face contact has many important research implications that suggest a number of potentially fruitful hypotheses. But even more important is the finding, so vividly described by the authors, that good supervision may be done expediently through telephonic communication. For busy practitioners, isolated from centers of training, this constitutes a vital means of continuing education. Finally, one may read the cognitive content and didactic aspects of this form of supervision with the assurance that it can supply information that will enable us to understand better the supervisory process as a whole.

Drs. Gerald McCarty and Irving Goldberg should be congratulated for devising the experiment and for the courage to participate so fully and so freely in the exchanges. Their contribution to the contents of this volume is illustrative of the kind of involvement that other students might well emulate. The four authors are to be congratulated in making available to us a document that may be continually mined for riches that go far beyond the goals toward which they originally organized their experiment.

Lewis R. Wolberg, M.D.

Contents

Introduction *by Lewis R. Wolberg, M.D.* vii

1 Conceptual Perspectives and Current Constructs 1
2 The Training Experience 27
3 The Alternate Session 35
4 Socialization, Activity, and the Alternate Meeting 53
5 Models, Roles, and Individuation of the Patient 73
6 Interaction as Associational Flow 81
7 Autonomy Versus Ritual 95
8 Violence and Sex 111
9 History Is Tradition-Forming 123
10 Oedipal and Pre-oedipal Derivatives 145
11 A Psychotic Episode 155
12 Lateral Transferences in This Training Group 169
13 Elaboration of Feeling of Participants 177
14 The Borderline Patient 187
15 The Nature of the Analytic Contract 209
16 Effect of Absence of Face-to-Face Cues 217

17 Supervision: Education or Treatment? 237

18 The Physical Structure of the Treatment Setting 259

19 Transference Theory: Excerpts from the Later Years 279

20 More Transference Theory: Excerpts from the
Later Years 309

21 Termination 337

References 357

Index 361

BEYOND
THE
COUCH

1

Conceptual Perspectives and Current Constructs

We plan briefly to review the history of the development of the kind of group therapy that has become identified as psychoanalysis in groups.[51] This history is in a sense the odyssey of one of us, Alexander Wolf. In addition, we will try to explain in a new way the assumptions and constructs implicit in this form of treatment and to provide a theoretical and practical basis for distinguishing it from the other group therapies. Finally, we make a statement about what we might call the therapist's philosophy of life. In all forms of psychotherapy this is an operational force that too often remains recondite and unexplored. We have tried to expose ours for consideration.

History

Early in the 1930's Wolf became interested in the field of group psychotherapy and read whatever was available at that time. He studied Trigant Burrow, Paul Schilder, and Louis Wender. He visited Moreno and participated as a performer at one of the psycho-dramatic meetings. In 1938 he proposed to five men and five women in his practice that they work together in a therapeutic group.

This was the period of the Great Depression. It was also a time of much group activity, of collective struggle, when many people from all walks of life were in financial distress and tried to solve their problems by concerted endeavor. There was no overt resistance to Wolf's proposal, in contrast to what he experienced when recommending group therapy after the Second World War. There was in fact such an enthusiastic response that within a year he had four groups of men and women. In 1940 he organized a group of five married couples.

At first the therapist was probably himself as anxious as the patients, and he spent several sessions lecturing to the group on procedural matters. He learned before long that his concern that group members might not interact was inappropriate, and found it unnecessary to start a group with lectures. He also discovered that structuring sessions by asking members to "go around" was unnecessary; although this method turned out to be useful, there was enough spontaneous interaction in each group not to have to build in this kind of forced interaction.

Another development proved quite interesting. After the group had their meeting in the therapist's office, the patients would proceed to a cafeteria or restaurant to spend sometimes as much as a full hour continuing the mutual interaction and self-examination. The therapist would hear subsequently something of what had happened at these postsessions. Occasionally a member would complain about the lack of privacy and the embarrassment of being observed or heard by neighbors at other tables or by a waiter. The therapist then proposed that group members meet at each other's homes to maintain privacy. The suggestion was picked up, and these meetings subsequently were referred to as alternate sessions.[52] The therapist had the group meet with him in his office three times a week and alternately without him at patients' homes twice a week.

Before long some group members began to complain of the length of time spent in group therapy and suggested that the number be reduced to two regular and two alternate sessions. But even such frequency brought complaints from some members, and the time was later reduced to one regular meeting with two alternate meetings. The reduction in frequency of sessions also resulted in part from the number of therapists who began to seek an experience of their own as patients in group therapy. It was largely these professional persons, all of them with heavy schedules, who pressured to curtail the number of meetings each week.

This is still true today. Patients who are nonprofessionals generally seem to be able to make more time. One of us has two patient groups with alternate sessions in which there is not a single professional. He has two other groups without alternate meetings in which more than fifty per cent of the membership are professionals who tend to resist devoting more time to being patients in a group. Schizoid or schizophrenic patients, very frequently isolated, seem much more free and eager to have frequent meetings than patients who are married and have children or have an active social life. Two of us at the present time lead groups that have two regular meetings and one alternate each week; three of us have groups in which there is one regular meeting and two alternates. All of us have groups with one regular and one alternate session.

It is reality, then, that a good deal of time is required in group therapy with regular meetings of an hour and a half and alternate sessions of between one and a half and three hours. But factors of resistance on the part of therapists against being patients in the group probably play a role that in some instances should be analyzed. For example, one of us went into the army in 1942 and sent his groups to therapists none of whom had any experience in or commitment to group therapy. After working with these groups from six months to a year, all but one therapist returned the patients to individual analysis. Only one continued to work with groups and is still doing group therapy.

World War II gave great impetus to the development of the group psychotherapy movement. So many soldiers suffered combat exhaustion that it was impossible for therapists to handle them on an individual basis. The number of patients even in general hospitals which were farther from the front, was too large. Combat exhaustion centers were formed, and there were hundreds upon hundreds of patients for whom it became necessary to initiate group psychotherapy. As a result of this experience a great many therapists turned to group therapy and sought training in the field. While before the war some therapists had expressed interest in and curiosity about group therapy and sought to join groups as observers, later a considerable number of them wanted instruction and sought a personal group therapy experience. Group psychotherapy was introduced into the curricula of various analytic training institutes. Specialty training programs were initiated for analysts who wanted formal training as analytic group therapists.

In 1947 Wolf began to give seminars in psychoanalysis in groups at the New York Medical College. In 1948 a similar seminar was introduced by him at the Postgraduate Center for Mental Health. At about the same time he began a private workshop in psychoanalysis in groups, which continues to the present day. In 1947 he had in his private practice as many as thirteen groups and three workshops. In 1949 he had his first experience in treating simultaneously an entire family as a group.

All of us have participated in workshops and institutes throughout this country and in many foreign lands to help professionals upgrade their skills in group therapy and to instruct them about psychoanalysis in groups. We have also participated in elective courses and group experiences for candidates in analytic training and for psychiatric residents, as well as training programs specifically for specialists in group therapy. We have also developed experimental and laboratory group procedures.[26, 36, 53]

At one point the members of Wolf's private workshop in psychoanalysis in groups constituted themselves as a separate training institute for group therapists. At about this time (1954) a specialty training program specifically to prepare psychoanalytic group therapists was started at the Postgraduate Center for Mental Health, which has since certified more than fifty specialists in analytic group therapy.

No attempt is being made in these pages to write a definitive history of the development of psychoanalysis. No claim is being pressed as to the origin of psychoanalysis in groups or group therapy in general. Statements are often made that the beginnings of group therapy are to be clearly found in the activities of one therapist or another. One might just as well attempt to demonstrate that group therapy began in the meetings at the Greek marketplace where disciples gathered around such philosophers as Socrates and Pythagoras, or that it began in the gatherings of the Apostles around Jesus and that the first analytic group session was the Last Supper. In fact, Ernest Jones in his biography of Freud suggests that psychoanalysis in groups began on board the ship that brought Freud, Jung, and Ferenczi to the United States in 1909. Jones describes the passage as follows: "He [Freud] evidently enjoyed the voyage and they had discussions and pleasant laughter all day long. They had good weather but for fog. Freud asserted he was the best sailor of the three. During the voyage the three companions analyzed each other's dreams—the first example of group analysis—and Jung told me afterwards that Freud's dreams seemed to be mostly concerned with cares for the future of his family and of his work."

Furthermore, we are not suggesting that group therapy began in the 1930's. We are pointing out, however, that there was a climate in society during those years that was particularly conducive to the development of collective activity, of social groups, of group spirit for a variety of purposes. It is true that the foundations for psychoanalytic therapy in a group had already been indicated by the work of Trigant Burrow in the 1920's. But the period of the Depression, the atmosphere around FDR, the wish to help people, to consolidate various groups into such activities as the WPA, with its theater and arts projects and its education and counseling services, all helped set the stage for an upsurge of group therapy in the 1930's in the United States. The kind of group therapy that was being done or could be done then was different from what can be done today. In contrast to those days of group rebellion against domination by the establishment, the current scene is one in which the way to rebel against the establishment is to withdraw, to go into one's self, to find one's solution through isolation, loneliness, and trips into fantasy.

In surveying the history of group therapy, it becomes obvious that patients with social and emotional problems have ever been brought together under the aegis of educators, physicians, psychiatrists, and counselors of one sort or another in order to help resolve these problems. The use of a group as a treatment modality has had sporadic beginnings everywhere.

The exact origins need not be determined. It is sufficiently clear that the traditional psychoanalytic approach led to a rejection of the group as a treatment milieu.[39] Psychoanalysis demanded noninteractivity on the part of the therapist, passivity on the part of the patient, privacy, regression, inturning, a focusing on the intrapsychic rather than on the interpersonal, a pursuit of history, anonymity on the part of the participants, and emphasis largely upon one person, the patient. The traditionalists tended to deny that the values, the personality, the commitments of the therapist had an influence upon the results. They emphasized the mirror quality of the therapist's functioning.

It is no small wonder therefore that the early forms of group therapy were largely nonanalytic, experiential, educational. It was not until Trigant Burrow that an attempt was made to understand the nature of individual neurosis on the basis of social role and social behavior.[35] He was the first to apply psychoanalytic psychology to a group of persons who sought the resolution of deeper internal conflicts. It is this kind of therapy, psychoanalysis in groups, that we are discussing in this book. We have a strong commitment to psychoanalytic psychology and an equally strong conviction that psychoanalytic methods can be successfully applied to treatment in a group setting. Our focus is on an understanding of unconscious processes and motivation, the significance of resistance, transference, and dreams, the importance of historical determination in current behavior, the necessity for working out and working through of psychodynamic and psychopathological mechanisms. These are the concerns of the psychoanalyst whether he works in the individual situation or in the group. The additional dimensions and modifications necessary to treat ten or a dozen patients simultaneously in a group constitute what follows. We shall try to analyze the essential characteristics of group therapy and those special elements required if the therapist wishes to do psychoanalytic work with patients in a group setting.

The Nature of the Group Therapies

There are four basic ingredients of analytic group psychotherapy. They are:

1. a triad, only one of whose members is a therapist;
2. multiple interaction among the group members, the interpersonal;
3. exploration of the intrapsychic, that is, unconscious processes;
4. limits.

Three of these are integral parts of all group therapies. One, the exploration of unconscious processes, is essential to the practice of psychoanalysis. It is what distinguishes psychoanalytic group therapy from all other forms of treatment in a group. If the therapist structures treatment without including the exploration of unconscious processes, he will be doing a form of nonanalytic therapy.

It is obvious that we cannot specify all of the characteristics of good psychotherapy. It must be assumed that most psychotherapists treating emotionally disturbed persons share a frame of reference. An example of such common agreement is that in any psychotherapeutic encounter the needs of the patient are central to the relationship. Another, which we expressed in earlier writings, is that at least one person in the therapeutic relationship should be conscious of what is going on, hopefully the therapist. Psychotherapy is planned experience, flexibly directed by the therapist, a process with beginning, middle, and end phases. In all forms of treatment the therapist is interested in the patient's making a healthier and more wholesome adaptation to reality. Moreover, all therapists must acquire professional training, which equips them to work effectively. Such training consists of an internship or residency and subsequent training in some specialty of psychotherapy. No one should undertake the practice of psychotherapy who has not had extensive preparation, including a personal experience in the process. Having accepted certain values and commitments, like those just described, as basic to all forms of psychotherapy, we proceed to a discussion of group therapy.

There are certain essential ingredients of group psychotherapy. The first of these is that there be a group. A therapist and a patient do not constitute a group. A psychotherapeutic group requires a minimum of three persons—two patients and a therapist. Two therapists and a patient constitute not a group therapy setting, but individual therapy in a group setting. No matter how many therapists there are, unless there are at least two patients there is no group therapy. A triad of two patients and one therapist provides structurally for the simultaneous presence of both hierarchical and peer vectors. The presence of the therapist fills the need for a responsible authority figure, and the presence of at least two patients affords the opportunity for peer relatedness.

We have the impression that in the dyadic relationship it is more difficult for the patient to affirm himself. Once another peer is introduced, they tend to support one another and their respective egos in the face of the therapist-authority. A therapist working with a single patient is in a position to impose more control, more authority, over the patient than when there are two or more patients present. The presence of several patients can even sponsor a tendency on the part of the therapist to deny his own status or authority. This denial may represent a yielding to group pressure, self-questioning about his own activity or his role in the face of assembled criticism. It may represent a countertransference problem: In the presence of his projected family he becomes somewhat immobilized and intimidated. Perhaps this is one reason for using a co-therapist. In any case, group members seem to support one another in ventilating more deep-seated attitudes towards the therapist than any one of them alone might express in an individual session.

In the triad the focus moves from one patient to another. We have referred to this elsewhere as the principle of shifting attention. When there are two patients, no one has exclusive possession of center stage. Attention shifts from one to another. The more patients there are, the more dispersed will be the attention from the therapist as well as from the patients.

Another consequence of the triad is the phenomenon of alternating roles. The patient is required by the structural circumstances to listen to someone else, to try to understand the other. By virtue of the fact that he is present with other patients, persons who are in a position similar to his own, new kinds of activity and of responsive feelings are induced. He would not ordinarily experience these if he were the only patient present. He listens, advises, feels sympathetic, becomes angry, and gets appropriate and inappropriate responses. He helps and seeks help. He experiences peer interaction of an order that is missing when there is only one patient present. In the latter case, the difference in status and activity between the therapist and the patient is so broad, the roles are so clearly marked, or should be, that the patient has less opportunity to modify his role or activities. The moment another patient is introduced into the situation, the role limits, the role dimensions, are augmented considerably by new kinds of activities.

The second essential of group therapy is multiple reactivity, or multiple interaction. This is found only in group psychotherapy. Multiple interaction involves patients with one another and the therapist emotionally, intellectually, behaviorally. It is sometimes described as a network of communication or relationships. The nature of the interaction at this level is largely a dealing with the manifest content. It is characterized by considerable acting and some acting out of a verbal nature. The emphasis is on the here and now rather than the there and then. Group dynamic phenomena are evident, such as the development of group cohesion. If topics come up for discussion, patients may protest when a member departs from the subject under review. A group climate develops.

Some groups are productive of much interaction; in others there is more reticence, reserve, caution. Some members may be silent; there may even be silent periods. In most groups, however, there is considerable interaction. The anxiety of the beginning group therapist that there will be no verbal interaction has not been confirmed by our experience. In group psychotherapy it apparently makes little difference how we begin the first session. Interaction among patients takes place with occasional individual exceptions. Some of the group dynamics that emerge with interaction are the establishment of group roles, group rituals, group traditions, and a group history. These determine to some extent the ways in which the members of the group and the leader conduct themselves over a period of time.

When there was absence of activity or silence we used to call on a patient to "go around," that is, to give his impressions of and reactions to other members of the group, who in turn would respond. More recently, such formal arrangements have been used less and less frequently. Multiple reactivities vary for each patient. Some patients relatively inhibited in the individual session or perhaps showing only one kind of behavior exhibit another in group. What occurs as a consequence of multiple reactivities is that group members demand participation of one another and generally force interaction so that there is no necessity to impose a formal going around. While some members are more active than others, the more passive or silent members are observed and responded to for their nonverbal communications.

In the course of multiple reactivity there is a kind of homogeneity in which group members tend to go along with the prevailing theme or climate. There is more concern for what is going on at the moment, and attention may shift rapidly from one member to another without examination in depth. At this time group members play counseling or advisory roles and suggest alternatives to one another's current problems. There is also more emphasis on the group than on the individual. A group that is led by the therapist to function in this way remains not only homogeneous but non-analytic. Group members are encouraged to identify with one another. As a result, the group becomes more cohesive as therapeutic activity emphasizes the similarity among the members, whether or not the group was originally constituted along more or less homogeneous lines. This push for homogeneity is often therapeutic in that it sets up group conventions to which the membership generally tends to conform. Deviant behavior is frowned upon and not rewarded.

Most group therapy is characterized today by these essential elements: the first, the presence of authority and peer vectors, and the second, the presence of multiple reactivities. Such therapy centers on the phenomenology and the sociology of the group, the manifest behavior and verbalized communications of the members. The therapist leads in exploring the nature of behavior as it appears, as it is spoken, as it is observed by the members within the context of the group.

To these characteristics of group therapy, psychoanalytic group therapy adds another. It is this third dimension that differentiates psychoanalytic group therapy or, as we call it, psychoanalysis in groups, from all other forms of group therapy. This fundamental ingredient of psychoanalytic group therapy may be identified as working with unconscious material, or the exploration of intra-psychic processes. Group therapy with this additional dimension works not only with the phenomenological, the manifest, but it searches for an understanding of what is latent in patient interaction and function. Here the therapist leads the exploration of unconscious processes by using free asssociation and the analysis of dreams, resistance, and transference.[27] Seeking for unconscious processes and motivations and exploring projected behavior lead necessarily into history, away from the emphasis upon the here and now. Only when the third element is added, namely the investigation of latent, unconscious, intrapsychic material, do we convert group therapy into analytic group therapy.

This kind of therapy sponsors individuation and heterogeneity. When the group and the therapist explore each patient in depth, they discover how each person differs from the next in his history, development, and current psychodynamics. A working out takes place, making the group members more interesting to one another, exposing not only their differences in pathology but their differences in healthy resources as well. There is a complementation in difference, a novelty that stimulates all the participants to try to understand and accept their differences. At the same time, this searching in depth may incidentally show members certain areas of commonality as well.

Nonanalytic group therapy promotes similarities with less concern for differences. In psychoanalytic group therapy, increased emphasis is placed upon the differences, the uniquenesses of the members. This is in part a consequence of the necessity to explore individual history and pursue psychodynamic formulations. Both kinds of group therapy permit the presence and recognition of similarities and differences among the patients. It is a matter of where the emphasis is placed as a result of the kinds of operations. The greater the exploration of the manifest, the greater the likelihood of emphasizing similarities, homogeneity. The greater the exploration of the latent content, the past, history, psychic determinants, the greater the likelihood of emphasizing individual differences, heterogeneity, diversity.[34]

It is relevant here to discuss for a moment the question of inhibition in the development of neuroses. Perhaps it is useful to regard in some degree the problem of neurosis as one not so much of inhibition as of compulsive conformity. The patient in childhood has been subjected to a series of verbal and nonverbal directives that have shaped his character. He has then conformed to the demands of the mother, father, and siblings, to certain ways of adapting himself for emotional survival. In nonanalytic group therapy, he is encouraged to continue to act out this kind of conformity. Through the exploration of intrapsychic processes, he begins to see in more detail the nature of his conformity. He tries to find his way out and to recover his repressed ego. Analytic group therapy then sponsors nonconformity, individuation, recovery of the lost self.

Since heterogeneity and individuation seem to be characteristic of psychoanalytic group therapy, the question may be asked whether the constitution of the patient membership needs initially to be heterogeneous as well. It is our experience that both manifest and latent heterogeneity exist in all groups. The therapist may consciously organize his groups, however, along specific lines, selecting patients for certain similarities. But even in that event, unless homogeneity is demanded by the leader, the chances are that the group will become more and more diversified with the passage of time.

There is also the question whether psychoanalytic group therapy can be done at all with a group of patients who are constituted along homogeneous lines—for example, patients in a psychiatric hospital, or inmates of a prison, or a group constituted entirely of homosexuals, or a group made up exclusively of males or of females. As we have indicated, such a group, unless it is forced to maintain this original identity, will tend to become more and more diverse. But once it is conceived along homogeneous lines, limitations will be placed on the extent to which analytic exploration can be done. If a therapist who had a group made up only of men did analytic therapy, a time would come in treatment when the men would demand that women be introduced into the group. This has been our experience. Group members request that the other, the diverse, be brought into the group. This could be one indication that the therapist was doing analytic therapy.

A new kind of activity is added in analytic group psychotherapy. Not only is there interaction between the therapist and patients and among the patients, but now the therapist introduces to the group his role as interpreter of the nature of unconscious processes. Members of the group soon learn to add this to their repertory of activities. The therapist interprets fantasies, dreams, free association, slips of the tongue, identification, transference, resistance, defensiveness, displacement, and neurotic alliance. The patients soon became aware of these phenomena in themselves and in others and interpret such manifestations to one another, sometimes correctly, sometimes incorrectly. This is a new kind of work that takes place only in psychoanalytic group therapy. It is not only a period of working out but a period of working through, of insight that enables the patient to understand his disorder so that he can struggle to resolve his problems with the affirmation and support of the therapist and group members.[50]

The following is a comparison of the differences in emphasis in the two categories of group treatment:

Nonanalytic group therapies	Analytic group therapies
1. the group as a whole	1. the individual
2. the here and now	2. the there and then
3. bipersonal psychology	3. multipersonal psychology
4. manifest behavior	4. latent content
5. group dynamics	5. unconscious motivation
6. homogeneity	6. heterogeneity
7. similarity	7. difference
8. conformism	8. individual uniqueness
9. adjustment	9. insight and freedom
10. interaction	10. self-examination
11. interpersonal processes	11. intrapsychic processes
12. less anxiety	12. more anxiety

Although many of the characteristics of analytic group therapy may be taken over by the nonanalytic group therapist, unless the emphasis is placed upon the exploration of the latent, it is not analytic group therapy. This does not mean that the analytic group therapist emphasizes only the unconscious manifestations, unconscious processes. In fact, we would consider a person who emphasized only unconscious processes to the neglect of manifest behavior to be a therapist doing individual psychoanalysis in front of the group. In order to do psychoanalysis in groups, we must heed all three ingredients, horizontal and peer relations, multiple reactivities, and working with unconscious material—but with an emphasis upon the exploration of intrapsychic processes. However, this does not mean that group dynamics, individual similarities, and manifest behavior, for example, are neglected or denied.

In all group therapy there is one additional essential ingredient that is most necessary to analytic group therapy. The more committed the therapist is to an analytic approach to the patient, the more this element will have to be included in his technical and theoretical considerations. This does not in any way imply that this element is not essential also for all other forms of treatment, individual or group. We are referring to the ingredient of limits.

Everything in life has its limits, and therapy is no exception. Therapy needs to be limited in time, in frequency of sessions, in the duration of a session, in activity, in participation. One of the qualities of pathology is limitlessness. The demand for absolutes, for immortality, is an attempt on the part of the individual to overcome his anxiety in an inappropriate way. A commitment to limits, then, is a commitment to reality. Limitlessness is related to unreality, to omnipotence.

Limits do not imply inflexibility and rigidity, but provide the opportunity for change, re-examination, and revision depending upon the development of new insights and new experience. We are discussing an attitude toward and the recognition of the necessity for limits.

Limits are difficult to define. For example, a particular therapist may find it difficult to work in a group larger than six or seven. For another it may be possible to work effectively in a group of ten, twelve, or even fifteen. It seems unlikely to us, however, that one can practice psychoanalytic therapy in a group larger than twelve or fifteen. We have already established a lower limit for the size of the group, an inexorable lower limit of three. Elsewhere we have said that the upper limit should be eight or ten.[51] But this is not inflexible. We know one analyst who works with groups of twelve. Some of us have worked with groups of eleven and a group of fifteen. So far as we know, there are no analytic group therapists who have groups larger than fifteen, and we doubt their advisability.

It is also relevant to consider the length of time that a single session should last. In recent years there have been "marathon" group sessions going on day and night for seventy-two hours with alternating therapists or with the same therapist. We have heard reported that some marathon group sessions have gone on for six consecutive days. We believe this to be inappropriate and not in the patients' or the therapist's interests. We do not think analytic therapy can be done in this kind of setting. Although we limit our own group sessions to an hour and a half, we can see that such time might be extended appropriately. Similarly, the alternate sessions should be limited in time. While some groups have an occasional alternate session that is longer than usual, sooner or later they set time limits. It is sometimes necessary for the therapist to limit the length of the alternate meeting.

It is wise also to limit the length of time a patient remains in any one treatment group. Among many patients who continue in psychoanalytic group therapy for more than four years, there tend to be stagnation and diminishing returns. Pelz discovered that highly skilled research men working as a team can be increasingly productive for up to four years; beyond that time their co-operative endeavor deteriorates.[30] Moreover, if a patient does not seem to move, make change, or progress in a period of six months to a year, a time limit ought to be placed upon his stay in that treatment group. Such a patient might be more happily referred elsewhere.

Limits ought to be considered also with regard to patient activity. The therapist needs to take a stand against sexual acting out and physical aggression among group members. Limits may also have to be put on verbal acting out—for example, with a monopolist, or with a masochist who invites repeated group attack with his compulsive assumption of a scapegoat role.

We take the position that one cannot do psychoanalytic therapy in a group made up of family members, including couples. It is possible, of course, to do group therapy with families and couples; it is possible for the therapist to play an interpretive role, a mediating role, but it seems to us inappropriate for the therapist to make children aware of unconscious processes going on in their parents or parents aware of unconscious processes going on in their children. This is equally true of husbands and wives.[20, 38]

There are certain patients who should be excluded from psychoanalytic group therapy. Among these are severe alcoholics who cannot come to meetings sober, drug addicts who come to sessions under the influence of drugs, severe stutterers, patients with low intelligence quotients, epileptics, hallucinating psychotics, the actively delusional, suicidal, or homicidal cardiac patients with anginal spasm under emotional stress, patients over fifty or sixty years of age, adolescents under eighteen years of age, and the very severely depressed or manic. All such patients can be helped best in nonanalytic group therapy.

Should the therapist impose limits on himself? We think so. He should end sessions on time. He should not keep patients waiting significantly beyond their appointed time. The therapist needs to stay with reality. He must deny himself sexual or aggressive acting out with a patient. The limits that hold for the patients hold for the therapist as well. Moreover we do no think the therapist should come to sessions highly agitated, intoxicated, drugged, hallucinating, delusional, severely depressed, suicidal, and so on. To these we add an additional limit upon the therapist; namely, that he not be an active homosexual. The therapist should be a trained person and should not go beyond the limits of his training. Psychoanalytic training must be required of him, including successful experience as an analysand in individual treatment as well as in a group.[53]

We should like now to discuss some additional ingredients that may or may not be essential to psychoanalytic group therapy, depending upon the values, theoretical position, and clinical experiences of the therapist and patients involved. We think these features need to be considered in the light of the four essential elements already described. There are many central as well as peripheral issues regarding group therapy that have not yet been thoroughly explored. We can only share our clinical judgment and theoretical commitments about a variety of them in order to indicate that we have considered them and have ruled them out as essential to psychoanalytic group therapy. It may turn out, however, that we have eliminated some elements that ultimately will also prove essential.

Should a therapeutic group be homogeneous or heterogeneous? Should it contain men and women? We have always practiced psychoanalytic group therapy with the simultaneous presence of men and women. Our clinical experience has been that more of the unconscious psychodynamics and psychopathology as well as healthy components of the personality emerge in such a mixture. Variety of all kinds within the limits described above promote mutual interest in one another, diverse stimulation, multiple transference, and a healthy striving to cope reasonably with different kinds of people.

One of the issues that arises about psychoanalytic group therapy concerns the question of the transference neurosis. It is our impression that a deep transference neurosis is not likely to develop in a group. The willingness on the part of the patient to play the game according to the rules laid down by the therapist, to submit, to regress, to accept frustration, is less apparent than in individual treatment. Also, there is very likely less tendency to submit to the therapist when there are alternate meetings or when routine private sessions are not provided. The presence of other patients as auxiliary egos tends to attenuate the development of a deep transference neurosis. We are not saying here that the development of a transference neurosis is good or bad. We are sharing our clinical judgment and suggesting that it be kept in mind.

Is it essential to have one preliminary individual session, or several sessions, or concurrent individual sessions? One or all of these may be desirable but not essential. In our experience a limited number of preliminary individual sessions is useful. They enable the patient and the therapist to get acquainted, explore whether they wish to work together, establish a fee, make a diagnosis, find what time the patient has available and what openings the group therapist has. Preliminary sessions enable the patient to develop some security with the therapist, which is useful as a bridge to joining the group. If a patient cannot be prepared for a group in six to ten or twelve sessions, the therapist ought not to regard further sessions as preparation for a group, but work with the patient in individual therapy. It may be that when the patient has had sufficient individual therapy, either he or the therapist may raise the question again and the patient may show less resistance or opposition. There are some group therapists who always have concurrent individual sessions. It is a serious question whether they do analytic group psychotherapy. It is our impression that under such circumstances the group is used as an adjunct, and that the analytic therapy is really individual.[35, 51]

In addition to the issues we have raised, there are a number of other elements that seem to be consequences of a group therapy situation. Again we are not certain that these elements are essential. However, in any comprehensive view of group therapy, especially psychoanalytic group therapy, consideration must be given to a large number of derivatives of our theoretical assumptions and technical innovations.

One of the consequences of a group therapy experience is that there is less opportunity for prolonged dependency on or gratification from the therapist. Some patients come from extended individual therapy elsewhere and with a deeply entrenched transference neurosis or psychosis to the previous therapist. Such patients attempt to set up concurrent individual sessions, which the group therapist must resist in order to enable the patient to develop some independence, a stronger ego, and some responsibility for himself. The patient's increasing self-reliance is in part a consequence of the group's demand that he function with them, and of the therapist's resistance to the patient's wish for exclusive individual attention. One result of this kind of operation is that the patient adopts a more secure relatedness with his peers, who encourage him to be more independent of the therapist. The patient soon becomes more relaxed in social situations of all kinds. A derivative of group therapy experience is that each member is more ego-oriented, in contrast to the individual session, where the patient is more id-oriented.

There are more stimuli in a group. The question is whether multiple stimuli lead to more diversion, more shifting of attention, less scrutiny, and less focusing than in individual treatment. It is possible for this to occur; it depends upon the leadership of the therapist. Diversity may be used to enrich whatever the patient presents, whether fantasy, dream, conflict, external problem, or reality. There may be in the group less focusing on minutiae than sometimes occurs in analytic dyads.

An outcome of therapeutic group formation is that more activity of all kinds occurs, whether acting or acting out, more expressed warmth, affection, helpfulness, hostility, and attack. The therapist is mainly required to step in and interrupt by interpretation, by insight, by analysis of the nature of acting out. In some instances, all else failing, he may have to interdict acting out by firmly forbidding it. While at first there may be some resistance to this, such control generally brings the patient relief and is therefore appreciated. We regard some of the activity that is not acting out as a healthy consequence of the group therapeutic process. Acting out is probably a product of the large amount of interstimulation and pressure for change, but under the therapist's leadership, analysis, and interpretation acting out can be limited. Even in the most active group where acting out takes place, ultimately the group sets its own limits. Sometimes the members turn to the therapist and ask for his help in setting limits for them. There is such inevitable frustration consequent upon acting out that the patient usually turns to group members and the therapist for understanding and control. Members who act out at an alternate meeting frequently come to the therapist for help when they cannot control their acting out.

Some group therapists believe that the introduction of the alternate meeting encourages acting out. There may be some truth in this. There are, however, many advantages to the therapeutic use of the alternate session. It was clinical experience of the spontaneous mutual support among group members that led us originally to suggest and promote the alternate session. It was discovered that as a result of these meetings thoughts, feelings, and behavior emerged when the therapist was absent that were different from those at regular sessions when he was present. A comparison between patient behavior at alternate and regular sessions demonstrated certain qualitative and quantitative differences, which could then be examined productively to throw light on the nature of the patient's psychodynamics and psychopathology.

We have indicated elsewhere that group therapy cannot persist and succeed if there are only peers, that is, if there is no leader. Our use of the alternate session does not mean that the authority vector is not present even though the therapist is not there physically. The alternate meeting of a group of patients exists only by virtue of their relationship to the therapist. A leaderless group is not a psychotherapeutic possibility. The alternate session is not necessarily an essential ingredient of group therapy, but is a very practical asset.[51]

Where does treatment take place? Treatment takes place in the individual session and in the regular group session. Systematic intervention is less likely to occur in the alternate session because patients are usually not being therapists with one another. They may try to carry out an interpretive role, but they tend simply to interact spontaneously. They have no plan for therapy. The therapist has an idea, a plan of where he wants to go with the patient. There is more of a push to work, to do analytic work, at the regular session. This means not that the alternate meeting does not provide insight, but that it is not so well focused. That is, help may be obtained in the course of the alternate session. Helping may also go on in this unfocused way even in the regular session, but under the therapist's demand there is a greater tendency to work analytically with him, for him. He is the source of information and inspiration, of therapeutic pressure, that impels the patient to work harder.

The patient used as a "co-therapist" is being misused by the therapist in countertransference.[37] If the therapist promotes a patient as a co-therapist, the patient may continue to play this role at alternate sessions. This is not the patient's function. This does not mean that the co-therapist role cannot be a helpful one. In fact help comes from the patients as well as from the therapist. But the patient's repeated use of himself as therapist or co-therapist is resistance to being a patient. An effect of group therapy, nevertheless, is that patients do turn to one another for help in distress. At the alternate session, or when the therapist is on vacation or otherwise unavailable, members are obliged to look to one another for answers and support. And this help is valuable, even in some instances psychoanalytically insightful. In regular sessions, patients get their first experience in mutual interpretation of one another's psychodynamics. Such offering of insight is acceptable so long as it is not done compulsively, resistively.

Another mainspring of group therapy and especially of the alternate meeting is increased socialization among group members. The traditional analyst regards socialization as a manifestation of resistance. It can be resistance in group therapy as well. But socialization that is resistive is subject to scrutiny and analysis. Socialization is a part of all group therapy and is probably one of the largest aspects of the multiple interaction that takes place in nonanalytic group psychotherapy. Only analytic group therapy raises the question whether the value of socialization facilitates or impedes the process of analysis. There is no doubt that socialization has human and remedial benefits. It is also probable that socialization acts as a force for resisting the exploration of unconscious motivation. It is for these reasons that the group analyst must be continuously aware of the uses to which the postsession kaffeeklatsch or other unscheduled encounters of members may be put. Such meetings need to be reviewed for their resistive possibilities.

In group therapy more fulfillment of one another's transference demands and expectations occurs than in individual sessions. Sometimes attempts are made at meetings to bring in food or drink. Some members feel obliged to provide a meal for group members at an alternate meeting. This is rare, but it occurs. In a group there is more scapegoating of certain masochistic members as well as more mutual support. A member seldom stands alone. If certain patients do not give him support when he needs it, the therapist does so, for support from the therapist is important to the members.

The analytic therapist leads the group from the level of multiple interaction to the level of investigating unconscious motivation. In this way the genetic determinants of the experimental data of behavior become available for exploration. On the other hand, multiple reactivities may support resistive and defensive behavior, whether in the course of interpersonal or intrapsychic exploration.

Interpretations by patients are not systematically timed. A therapist will consider when to introduce an interpretation to a patient, but a group member will generally not do so.

As noted earlier, Pelz has demonstrated—at least in a group of sophisticated research workers—that if the group remains together beyond four years, their work becomes less and less productive.[30] Assuming this is true of a closed therapeutic group and even assuming that we set a time limit of four years for group therapy, it might nonetheless be practical to open the group up after two or three years to introduce strangers to the membership in order to revitalize it. It is likely that closed groups should not last too long. A closed group, if it is at all desirable, should be limited to not more than a year or two at most. There is a serious question as to whether closed groups or open groups are appropriate for different kinds of group therapy. If we are doing analytic group therapy, it is preferable that the group be open rather than closed. For other forms of group therapy, it may be appropriate for time-limited, closed groups to be organized.

A committee of the Group for the Advancement of Psychiatry has reported "that confidentiality is essential to psychiatric treatment."[9] In our experience it is not true that absolute confidentiality needs to be maintained; otherwise, we could not do group therapy. On the other hand, we have had patients who assert they cannot expose themselves to others in the group. Our experience is that they can if we analyze their anxiety and resistance. It is necessary to keep confidences in the group among the members. If a patient talks outside the group, there is a good deal of indignation. We always try to analyze the resistive gossip. A breach of confidentiality is a resistive leak, an acting out that may threaten the life of a group unless it can quickly be analyzed.

One of our patients, a young woman of eighteen, reported that she talks to her older sister and her sister to her as a way of resisting. As a result they tell their respective analysts and therapeutic groups less than they should. Group members talking to one another in private dyads apart from the group, cliquing, is a similar example of resistive leakage that is not in the patients' interest. But it is a breach of confidentiality if a member of a group talks outside the group to a person who is not a member. We encourage patients to expose one another within the group. A mutual confidence between two members is bilateral resistance so long as it is secret from the rest of the group. It is an acting out, a resistance that defeats therapy. We urge them to "betray" one another's confidences only within the therapeutic group.

Termination is an encouragement and inspiration to others. Only in group therapy is the patient a witness to another member's improvement. The discharged patient induces other patients to struggle more to effect their own recovery. He may inspire them in a period of relative hopelessness. He may make them more curious and exploratory in order to learn how their peer achieved his aims. He may make them more competitive with the "graduate." He may of course make them competitive in a resistive way; that is, if one patient is discharged, another may claim he too has recovered, when he is not in fact ready to leave treatment.

A Point of View

After many years of working analytically with patients in individual and group settings, we have come to the conclusion that therapy is more than a series of hypotheses concerning the development and functioning of personality, the nature and origination of psychopathology, the cause of anxiety and the defense mechanisms used to deal with it, and the ways in which the patient relates to illusion and reality. We have come to the conviction that in addition to these theoretical and technical constructs, which are applicable to doing psychoanalytic treatment with a patient, the therapist as a person, as a human being, enters into the treatment situation as an important factor. The development of psychoanalysis in which emphasis has shifted from focus upon the patient to focus upon the relationship, and more currently to focus upon the person of the therapist, is in part what we are talking about here.[35] It is more than theoretical persuasion and the technical know-how of the psychoanalyst that effect changes in the persons who come for treatment.[51] There is more communicated in an analysis than the historical origin of a patient's intercurrent behavior or a consciousness of unconscious processes within the self.

These additional facets have sometimes been called the educational aspects of psychoanalysis, but we feel that this is a derogatory label. We are, rather, committed to the idea that the psychoanalyst as a person enters into the analytic relationship. This does not mean that he gives up his objectivity, his neutrality, his commitment to listening and exploring the patient or making the patient's needs central to the therapeutic experience. What it does mean is that the personality of the psychoanalyst enters globally into the relationship and that there are transtherapeutic experiences that the patient has in the interaction with the person of the analyst. We should like briefly to describe these para-analytic experiences—coming into contact with another person and being privy to his values, his approach to the human condition—as an exposure to a philosophy of life.

It is not only necessary for the therapist to have a philosophy of life, a set of values; whether he knows it or not, he surely has a point of view, a style of life. His way of functioning communicates itself to the patient regardless of any manifest commitment. His attitude toward life may be reflected in the way he decorates his office, how his desk looks, the clothes he wears, the kind of art he has around him, the color of the paint on his walls, the tone of his voice, the way he answers the telephone, even whether or not he answers the telephone during sessions. Certainly it is to be experienced in the kinds of things he chooses to interpret and what he chooses to ignore, whether he "thinks big" or is petty, whether he opens the door, shakes hands with a patient, says "Good morning" or "Goodbye." His value system is exposed by his optimism or pessimism, by whether he concentrates on what the patient says or follows his own inclinations and associations, and by whether he writes letters or books while the patient is talking. His commitments are manifested in whether he puts the patient on the couch or has him sit up, whether he sees patients individually or in a group, whether he sees other members of the same family or not.

The therapist communicates to the patient willy-nilly what he thinks is right and wrong, what he thinks is appropriate and inappropriate. Like the parent, he conveys this to the patient not so much by what he says as by the way he acts. The therapist should encourage the patient to participate in his group, but he should also be dedicated to each member's developing his own style of life so long as it is reality-oriented. The therapist is not a dictator. He does not consciously plan or unconsciously hope to direct or control the patient. He is more interested in opening doors and helping patients to open doors for themselves to the recovery and development of their own egos. He does not believe that there is only one way of living. He appreciates the healthy, creative differences among his patients and supports their imaginative and realistic differentiation one from another. In this respect he is a promoter of diverse and individual freedom. Every good analyst is a promoter of freedom so long as he analyzes resistances and transferences, and obsessive-compulsive behavior.

Does the therapist have any influence over and above analyzing psychodynamics and psychopathology? Yes, he does. Where does this extra-analytic influence come from? It comes from the therapist's philosophy, his value system. For example, do we see in the average psychoanalytic textbook any discussion of patience on the part of the therapist? Yet the therapist needs to be patient, he needs to listen, he needs not to lose his temper, he needs to hear the patient out. His patience cannot be limitless. Limitless patience is impossible. Limitless patience may mean limitless therapy. He can therefore have patience only within limits. This does not mean that he must become impatient but that at various points in the therapy he must push the patient to take some action. He cannot sit by patiently while the patient is forever silent or forever passive. If the therapist does, he is probably an angry man, or indifferent or hostile to the patient.

Another important influence on the patient is the therapist's acting as if he knows everything. The therapist needs to accept as realistic that he has uncertainty, that he does not have all the answers, that no one does, that no one ever will.[40] The patient, even though he may be alarmed or may be made anxious by the therapist's uncertainty, finally begins to accept as realistic the abandonment of his own absolute certainty or absolute uncertainty, his own omnipotence and impotence, and elects instead to accept as appropriate his partipotence.[42]

It is important for the therapist to recognize the constructive potential in the patient, to see the positives, to make them apparent to the patient. The therapist searches for the creative, the curious, the exploratory, the expansive, the questing side of the patient. The therapist also gets glimpses of the patient's yearning for sexual fulfillment. He calls to the attention of the patient these assets so that the patient can have a better and more wholesome view of himself. He looks for the positive and the problem-solving component in the fantasy, in the dream, in the patient's dealings with another group member. He is not exclusively preoccupied with the patient's psychopathology. It is this commitment that is probably the most important therapeutic aspect of his work, the commitment to the growing edge in the patient. While a group member may say to another member only what is wrong, for example, the therapist can also see what is right, and what is right for one patient may not be right for another. It is the therapist's appreciation of these differences in reality that enables group members also to accept one another in difference, for the male patients to accept the female patients and vice versa, for the older members to accept the younger, the younger the older. Patients experience the fact that the solution for one is not necessarily the solution for another.

It is the therapist's acceptance of his limitations that frees the patient from his compulsive search for certainty, his compulsive aspiration for perfection.[40] The therapist's freedom from having to be perfect, right, and omnipotent helps to free the patient to give up his own absolutism. The therapist is an open-minded person; there is no final end in view for him about anything. By this we do not mean that treatment is endless, or that there is no end to life. We mean that while therapy ends, life goes on, development goes on, change goes on, improvement can take place, even without the help of the therapist. The patient can grow and develop still further. It is in this sense that we mean open-endedness.

Another aspect of partipotence is flexibility. The therapist is ready to listen, bend, and yield. He does not rigidly adhere to an original commitment. He is open-minded. He is ready to hear another's point of view. He can change his mind and his hypotheses about a patient as new evidence comes in. While he adheres to certain tested traditions, he leaves the door open for new points of view and experience. If he is flexible, he welcomes novelty rather than dogma; and he is careful not to turn novelty into dogma. In this respect he is life-affirming rather than life-denying, for dogma leads to emotional, psychological, and intellectual strangulation and depression. He is optimistic about his patient's recovery as well as about himself and about life. He has hope, believes in change, in innovation. He loves life and people and experiences. He does not regard, however, everything in himself or in nature as not anxiety provoking or not fear provoking. He is not ashamed to be afraid when it is appropriate to be afraid or to weep when it is appropriate to weep, but he enjoys life as well and enjoys his patients and his family and his experiences outside of his work. He can play. He can tell a good story, a good joke, and enjoy one. He sees life as multifaceted, and while he may concentrate on certain aspects of his work, he nevertheless can appreciate other kinds of work and play.

Although we are committed not only to working with the individual patient but to helping him find his way with other human beings, to a socialization, to a gregariousness, to his commitment to working and living within a group, we are nevertheless aware of the importance of his personal growth and development and his ability to think and stand on his own two feet. In spite of the fact that this is a work on psychoanalysis in groups, we wish not to ignore the fact that for each patient his own personal development is central.

We cannot conclude with any better expression of our own position than the words of Joseph Wood Krutch in his "Epitaph for an Age": "The more we teach adjustment, group activity, getting along with a group, and so forth, the less any individual is prepared for the time, so likely to come in any man's life, when he cannot or will not call upon group support. Ultimately security for him depends upon the ability to stand alone or even just to be alone. Belonging is fine. But to belong to anything except oneself is again to give a hostage to fortune."*

* *The New York Times Magazine*, July 30, 1967, p. 10.

2

The Training Experience

From 1961 to 1965 the authors undertook an innovative supervisory experience in psychoanalysis in groups. The treatment method itself has been described in the preceding chapter and elsewhere.[51] The supervisory procedure involved the use of the conference telephone, since teachers and students were separated by 3,000 miles.

The Telephone

There are some precedents in the literature for the use of the telephone as a medium for training. Attempts were undertaken in the Nebraska state hospital system[4] and between the California state and the Washington state hospital systems[45] for the teaching of psychiatric staffs by means of phone circuits and closed-circuit television. In most instances such endeavors have been a didactic form of teaching without opportunity for interaction, although recent developments may add this dimension.[2, 46] It is becoming increasingly possible to teach at a distance not only without serious loss of interpersonal contact, but with additional benefits.

Usually the use of telephone communication for instruction in only one direction has prevailed. There is, to be sure, a single published report of a psychoanalysis completed over the telephone.[32]

In this case, treatment had begun originally in a conventional setting, but the patient's need to change his residence to a locale at a considerable distance from the analyst resulted in an agreement to continue the analysis over the telephone on a daily basis. The telephone was the only medium of treatment until the termination of the analysis. Recently electronic devices are becoming more frequently used in treatment[3] and in training.[19]

To our knowledge, the literature contains no reports on the telephone as the principal medium for supervision. Undoubtedly the use of audiovisual aids, videotape, television, radio, and, in our undertaking, the telephone for teaching at a distance represents a movement in the direction of new frontiers. We want to discuss the quality of such teaching and learning.

In the specific experience under discussion two trainees met together in an office in Seattle and used a speaker telephone for supervisory sessions with two training analysts who met together in an office in New York, also using the speaker telephone. Each session was tape-recorded, transcribed, and distributed to the participants prior to the subsequent meeting. It was agreed that supervision would take place once each week for one hour. This procedure was followed for approximately four years. For a brief time during the third year an additional trainee participated in the sessions by telephone from Atlanta.

A major consideration that arose in supervising via the telephone was whether the complex interpersonal processes and subtleties of the affective exchange between supervisees and supervisors might be attenuated by the intermediation of the telephone and without face-to-face contact. Though it was known that some gestural and nonverbal cues had to be lost, it was unknown in advance whether the emergence of significant material and its discussion would be impeded or expedited. It was questioned whether the absence of information from other sensory modalities would intensify the need to listen. With the stress on one sensory modality, a larger amount of attention and concentration might be demanded. Obviously, the use of the couch, face-to-face contact, or an instrumentality like the telephone or videotape can be either threatening or helpful to different persons, depending upon their character structure.

It is our intention to contrast some of the forces, pressures, and coping mechanisms that are mobilized as a consequence of the increase and diminishment of anxiety resulting from the deprivation of visual cues with those that arise in face-to-face situations. Experiences in the treatment or training of the blind are not directly pertinent to our discussion.

Nature of Supervision

Ekstein and Wallerstein[10] state that there are at least two principal views regarding supervision of the psychotherapeutic process. One is that supervision is didactic, a learning experience that does not investigate the emotional problems of the student; such difficulties are to be referred to the personal analyst, as Fleming and Benedek[13] and Bibring[5] suggest. Another and more classical view is that supervision is a continuation of personal analysis.[25] A third and intermediate position is that training requires the communication of information in a context of overt affective exchange.

Effective learning is not purely intellectual. Learning how to work with patients must include an awareness of transference and countertransference, understanding and frank exploration of the transactions between supervisee and supervisor, as well as a co-operative effort to overcome learning blocks. In analytic training programs, it is considered essential that the student have a personal analysis, in addition to supervision, to deal with the deeper levels of his real and illusory involvements.

Supervision should provide the free discussion by the student of his reactions to the patient and to the supervisor. These exchanges constitute the groundwork for the learning of theory, techniques, and the clinical management of the patient. Supervision is sometimes provided for several students simultaneously in a group. At the Postgraduate Center for Mental Health in New York City, for example, group supervision has been for more than fifteen years a required part of the analytic training program.

In the group supervisory process the students' reactions to patients and to each other as well as to the supervisor form the matrix for theoretical discussions and for the presentations of clinical and didactic material. The opportunity for interaction with peers in group supervision has been shown to be an invaluable asset in training, because students seem to learn much from one another about how to work with patients in the individual as well as in the group setting. Schwartz and Wolf[37] and Menninger[27] have pointed out that the experienced analyst may be helped in dealing with transference and countertransference problems by developing a trusted relationship with a colleague.

Absence of Visual Cues

In the learning-teaching experience described here, we observed among other things that when the participants were deprived of sensory evidence in reality, anxiety arose that provoked defensive maneuvers in many directions. The participants did not have the usual visual cues and nonverbal reactions, such as facial expressions, gestures, and other forms of feedback, including the furnishings of the office and waiting room, to which one would normally have access in a face-to-face supervisory situation. They were deprived even of a range of sounds, masked or obliterated in the telephone exchange. The emphasis and focus were on the voice only. In this monodimensional procedure, whispers between participants at either end of the line, for example, could be heard but not understood. Mainly what was spoken directly into the microphone was clearly received at the other end.

As a consequence of these conditions, transference reactions and fantasy elaborations were stimulated. At times the interaction took on a quality of the magical play of the child who creates a telephone out of old tin cans and waxed string in order to communicate with another child at a distance. An example of a shared fantasy occurred during a session where there was some joking about the use of Telstar as the medium for communication; outer space would be employed to conquer inner space.

Even the peer relationships occasionally had a fantastic, playful quality similar to the secret societies of children. This was evident in the reluctance of the students to accept a new student from another city and the resistance of the teachers to the introduction of another telephone supervisor. The supervisory group sometimes felt like a closed society.

The telephone sessions occasionally took on a spontaneity, a freedom and playfulness, in contrast to the seriousness that is more customary in supervision. There may be some similarity here to the alternate session in group therapy.[51, 52] The great distance, the feeling of separation, and the use of an instrument for contact may have contributed to the attenuation of the vertical vector, as does the physical absence of the therapist during the alternate meeting with the group.

Affective Aspects

The supervisors observed that they became more rapidly aware of their real and projected feelings about the students. The discussions involved some exploration of transference and countertransference reactions of the supervisors to each other, to the trainees, and to the patients being treated by the trainees.

The telephone lent itself easily to the projective coping mechanism of blaming. It was the fault of the equipment when the trainees did not hear a supervisor's reaction or comment aimed at the penetration of transference or countertransference problems in the management of patients.

The tendency of one of the students to focus on the telephone instrument, to move his chair up close as if he were going to crawl through it, seemed to be a substitutive defense to relieve the anxiety of the distance and bring the supervisors into the room. An unconscious reaction of one of the supervisors to this problem of distance and isolation was that he rather constantly found himself talking loudly to make sure that his voice was being heard so far away.

Another compensatory mechanism based on a fantasy was the conviction of one of the supervisees that the supervisor with whom he identified most was sitting on the edge of his chair enraptured with the discussion. It was subsequently revealed that the actuality was quite different.

The fact that the trainees had face-to-face contact with each other, as did the supervisors, had a somewhat countering effect in that the proximity of the trainees somewhat lessened the anxieties of isolation from the authorities. In addition, face-to-face contact tends to increase awareness of reality factors.

At the outset, the trainees had a variety of responses to the supervisory process. Clinical summaries of patients in group treatment and transcripts of group therapy sessions were prepared and presented in a competitive and rivalrous attempt to woo the supervisors. There were attempts to struggle about time and its equitable distribution between the supervisees. Resistance to the exploration of feelings often took place behind a formal presentation or a demand for the discussion of theory. Sometimes it took the form of trying to focus exclusively on the patient and to solicit from the supervisors the kind of direction that would constitute treatment of the patient through the supervisee.

As the search for structure and the competitiveness began to be better understood, they diminished. A more spontaneous interaction developed, which was less related to time considerations; the quality of interaction improved.

The trainees tried to avoid feelings of anxiety. One trainee, for example, accused the other of failing to set up the recording device properly. This accusation seemed to be motivated in part to show up the co-trainee in front of the authority figures. Once when one of the trainees requested that the session be held at an earlier hour, the second trainee overslept and failed to appear for the meeting. Another time, both trainees felt that they had been hostile to the supervisors the previous week, and one of them began the subsequent session by singing a childish "Good morning to you" in an attempt to undo the anticipated hostility.

Cognitive Content

We have so far described affective parts of this learning experience. It is important to emphasize some of the cognitive content and didactic aspects of the supervision. Problems of time management during group sessions, financial arrangements, seating plans, patient selection, and group composition, as well as other structural matters, were repeatedly discussed. Theories of psychopathology and psychodynamics were evaluated at length. Clinical problems and their attendant technical implications were part of each supervisory session. The supervisors had the impression that more information was communicated per unit of supervisory time than seemed generally to be the case in face-to-face supervision. The reader will have the opportunity to judge this for himself as he observes the actual interactional experiences in the dialogues that follow.

The supervisees made substantial changes in the techniques they utilized in group treatment. In keeping with the theories of psychoanalysis in groups as explicated by the supervisors, both trainees discontinued the routine use of individual sessions and made the group the central medium for treatment. They introduced alternate sessions and focused on dreams, interactive associative material, resistance, and transference with a depth of understanding not discernible prior to the telephone supervision. Time was spent in clarification and discussion of the literature of psychoanalysis, with particular reference to such concepts as transference, transference neurosis, regression, and the observance and interpretation of these phenomena in the treatment sessions with patients. As a consequence of the discussion of individual cases and group treatment necessities, and the introduction of metapsychological and practical issues, considerable development occurred in the trainees' clinical orientation and sensitivity.

The effect of the presence of visual cues in the horizontal vector between the two trainees and between the two supervisors needs to be called to attention. The existence of two distinct psychological fields, one with and one without visual cues, allowed for the discussion of comparisons similar to those that exist between behavior in the regular and in the alternate session. It also led to an exploration of the development of what might be called cliquing behavior, or the over-identification of one participant with another. During the brief time that a third supervisee participated, this kind of over-identification or pairing was brought more clearly into focus. While the earlier arrangement of two trainees and two supervisors produced a situation that resembled dyadic relationships, the new member at a distance from both pairs created a triangle. This condition may have contributed to the reasons why the third supervisee dropped out.

It is possible that the positive reactions of all the participants toward their joint experience were partly determined by both the supervisees' and supervisors' prior experience as colleagues and friends, although the two supervisors had only one contact with the two supervisees before beginning supervision. Some of the results may be different if the experiment is repeated with four strangers as participants. The breakthrough to projection and fantasy material and to countertransference problems might under such circumstances take longer.

Should the necessity arise, it is obviously possible to set up an advanced program of supervision over the telephone. Such training can achieve depth and breadth in the examination of the trainees' countertransference problems with their patients and transference problems with the supervisors, as well as what we might designate "supertransference" reactions of the supervisors toward the supervisees and their patients. There can also be ample opportunity for the discussion of didactic material with theoretical and clinical content.

This kind of supervision can be undertaken with individual or group psychotherapists. It is possible to increase psychotherapeutic skills through training without face-to-face contact with the teacher. Variations in student-teacher contact can and should be experimentally tried and evaluated. Many professional persons may be able to refine further their knowledge of specific therapeutic techniques where training is not available on a local basis, if they are willing to forego face-to-face contact. And even where face-to-face supervision is the prevailing condition, an additional dimension can be added by a supervisory experience without visual cues.

In the following chapters we present edited segments of the transcripts of training sessions, mainly from the first year. We have not attempted to analyze the dialogue. As a reference point, however, we have made a brief comment at the beginning of each chapter to identify the problem or issues with which that particular exchange seemed to be concerned. The reader can learn much about group treatment as well as about the teaching and learning experience from the ideas that were discussed and explored.

The problems and anxieties of the supervisees were ones that are common to those who are learning about or engaged in the practice of group therapy in general and the psychoanalytic variety in particular. Sometimes the selection of the manifest content of the training session can be seen as determined in part by latent ideas and feelings of the supervisees. While there are, then, certain parallels between what occurs in the training experience and what occurs in treatment, the phenomena are of a different order.

3

The Alternate Session

Most people experience anxiety about the unknown. Beginning psychotherapists are not exempt when they contemplate what will occur as they enter into the psychotherapeutic contract with a patient. It is no surprise, then, to say that the beginning group therapist will have anxieties when treating more than one person at a time.

Each of the trainees in this instance had considerable experience in doing individual and group therapy. Consequently, their anxieties in regard to the unknown became focused on what was for them a new dimension in the therapeutic process—having their patients meet in alternate sessions without the therapist present.

The reader may recognize in these interchanges that within the manifest communication about introducing the alternate session is a covert anxiety about treating patients in a group. An additional factor is the supervisees' anxiety about the new technique for learning, namely, telephone conversations.

A first concern in introducing the alternate session is often fear of losing the patients; the group may learn it can get along without the therapist. There may be also some residual anxiety about separation and symbiotic fusion. A typical defense is the therapist's fantasy of his own omnipotence and the patients' helplessness. The alternate session challenges such a magical attitude.

Problems of domination may be other determinants of the anxieties besetting the therapist when he contemplates introducing the alternate session. Specifically he may fear that the members of the group will act out aggressively or lose impulse control because the therapist is not there to restrain them. The alternate session gives the patients an opportunity to struggle for distributed leadership. If he anticipates that the patients will take over the group, the therapist may experience discomfort, which may be related to residual oedipal problems in the therapist.

Some therapists have to know everything that goes on in the treatment matrix as well as everything that goes on in the patient's life outside of therapy. To some extent, such a compulsion reflects the therapist's voyeuristic needs, which will be frustrated by his absence.

For the beginning therapist these anxieties are frequently condensed into such defensive transactions as intellectualization, seeking didactic information, or demanding the theoretical rationale for a treatment procedure from the supervisors.

Whether one undertakes to do group therapy or not, whether one introduces the alternate session or not, whether one allows the alternate meeting of the patients to be held in the patients' homes or only in the therapist's office, will usually reflect the anxieties, fantasies, and reality concerns of the therapist in regard to community acceptance of his practices in treating patients in a group, even encouraging them to meet without him.

The therapist beginning group treatment who is confronted with the alternate session will, of course, experience a variety of anxieties depending upon the nature of his psychodynamics. He might expect that the patient's anxieties will be greater than his own even if of a similar dynamic origin.

The following transcript comes from one of the earliest supervisory sessions and deals with concerns about the alternate session.

Gerry: I suggested an alternate session to a group. They were very interested in the idea and talked it over and they are going to start by having one on Sunday. Nicky, of course, didn't react to this. The group "went around" and talked about it.

There were mixed reactions, but they were interested. Then the others asked Nicky if she could go with them afterwards to talk about setting up such a meeting. She said just four words, "I don't think so."

Al: But perhaps she did go anyway.

Gerry: No, in individual sessions afterwards, a couple of them said Nicky didn't come. They had asked her after the session but her mother met her in the lobby of the building. The group saw the mother and thought maybe they ought to go over and tell her about it, but they didn't. Then I saw Nicky on Friday and she sat the whole hour without saying a word. I thought it would be good for her to attend. I said, "Maybe you are not able to get to meetings unless your mother brings you; maybe this is necessary at this time. The fact that you are here tells me that you are not altogether resisting the idea." Finally I indicated that I expected that she would attend the meeting, and if she was not able to get there on her own, then I would take it that she felt it was necessary for me to let her mother know where it was to help her get there. At the end of the meeting I said, "I'll get a piece of paper and write down the address and time for you." And she said, "Never mind, I've got a paper." She opened up her purse and took it out and wrote the information down. It is the first time she has talked to me in about two months.

Al: Then she is looking for an escape from mom.

Gerry: Well, she reacts to this with some facial expression, but you can't tell what she is thinking or what is going on inside.

Mannie: But she wanted the address.

Gerry: Yes, she wrote it down, and she was saying she didn't think she could go, but she took it.

Al: I have a thought that I'd like to give you on this. This is really too specific, but I want to share it with you anyway. In the event that she needs someone to take her or she doesn't go, you might think of using one of the co-patients rather than her mother to—

Gerry: Go pick her up?

Al: Go pick her up or accompany her or even to give her the name and address of the next meeting and so on, rather than for you to do it. Sooner or later she must relate to the peers as a way of escaping the parental authority. You might begin to encourage it in this way.

Gerry: I was wondering what I ought to do at this point. I was going to wait and not even give her the address yesterday but talk it over first with you today. Then I decided that the best thing was to give her the information, see what happened, then talk to you and find out what I might do next.

Al: Is Nicky an only child?

Gerry: Yes, she is an only child. She is in her twenties.

Mannie: I would like to ask you to go back for a moment, Gerry, and review some of the feelings that some of your patients had when they responded to your suggestion about an alternate session.

Gerry: Well, Harry in this group, Harry is a patient in his late twenties. He is a very withdrawn, isolated, paranoid person who has been in treatment a couple of years, and he was never able to participate except when he takes on a quasi-therapeutic role, questioning other people about what they think. He expresses very strongly his feelings about this to me and says that I'm like his father. His father was a very punitive man; they lived in a farm area.

Mannie: How did he feel about the alternate session? Come on. . . .

Gerry: He said—well, I was giving you some buildup.

Mannie: Why give us so much buildup?

Gerry: He said he thought it was a very . . . oh, well, . . .

Mannie: What's the matter, Irv? I hear you laughing there. How do you feel about this, Irv? It sounds like an alternate session going on.

Irv: I'm in an alternate session by myself.

Mannie: I see, well, what do you think?

Gerry: I'll tell you, Mannie, what Harry said was that he liked the idea very much. He thought that he would be more able to talk when I wasn't around.

Mannie: What were some of the others' feelings?

Gerry: Another, Peggy, who is about twenty-six, is a pretty weak person also. She said that she liked the idea. She was anxious about it. She did not know how it would be without me there. She has repeatedly expressed the feeling that I'm a kind of a god with clay feet, which is her impression of her father, too. Still she was favorably disposed. Ethel, a twenty-two-year-old married woman, who is promiscuous, thought it was a real good idea. She was a bit concerned. Harry said, "Well, what's the matter, don't you want to invite me over to your house?" She said, "I don't think I do," and then she laughed about it, but was in favor of the idea. She was worried about herself and whether she would function appropriately in such a situation. She did not know whether it would work, but she wasn't opposed. Harry had some thoughts which he brought up in his private session, but not in the group. He was afraid Ethel would stay around and then he would seduce her. But he hopes that it will not work out that way.

Al: Did you suggest he say that in the group?

Gerry: Well, I didn't suggest it to him at the time, no.

Mannie: It is something to be considered. Go ahead—what other feelings? It's very important, Irv, to listen in, because you're next.

Gerry: Tim has had a stuttering problem. He is very compulsive and quite paranoid. His father is a coach. He idolizes the old man and he hates his guts. He said, "Oh, this is crazy, what the hell, meet without Doc there and it would just be a whole bunch of superficialities." But he went along. He isn't resisting the idea, he's toying very pleasantly with it. I think he likes it, but he is always saying in the group that they are not saying what they really think, what they really feel, that "this is a bunch of shit, a bunch of bullshit. We're not really talking about our feelings," and he felt that meeting in an alternate session this is all that would happen. They would just talk nonsense and never really get down to business. I think business for him is some sort of onslaught on the authority figure and anyone in the vertical vector. With the horizontal only, he has some feeling of loss of opportunity.

Irv: I concentrated a little bit on George in the last session. He is a patient who sits in silence most of the time. I think someone was talking about how he felt on his way to the meeting. That gave me an opportunity to ask George what he felt on the way to the session. He said he felt pretty good until he came to the meeting; then he began to feel pretty bad and didn't like it.

Mannie: That's your regular session?

Irv: I don't have alternates as yet.

Mannie: Well, we want to get to that, too.

Irv: Then I asked him why he felt so bad when he came here. Did he think that it would make any difference if I were or were not in the meeting? He thought it would make a big difference, that he probably would behave differently if I were not around. Then some of the other group members began to talk about it. Flora began. Incidentally, Flora has quieted down quite a bit and is really taking a back seat, listening and looking. Anyway, Flora said, "Well, I don't know how I feel toward Doctor Goldberg. I wonder how I feel without him or with him around." This led to the others participating as to how they felt about meeting without me. At no point had I directly suggested an alternate session: I was just exploring the feeling.

Mannie: You did?

Irv: No, I had not suggested that they meet without me. But I explored with them their speculations as to how they would feel if I were there or if I were not there.

Mannie: That's wonderful. That's a great idea. So what happened?

Irv: So then George began to talk. Now this is a point where I have some questions. You say it is not good to try to isolate one person in the group and do psychotherapy with him. This is a very difficult concept for me to understand.

Mannie: Come on now, Irv, don't change the topic. What happened with the alternate meetings? You had a wonderful buildup. I am impressed. What happened? Did you say to them, "Well, how would you like to meet without me?"

Irv: No, I didn't follow through at that point.

Mannie: Why not? Let's talk about that. Gerry, listen in.

Gerry: I'm listening.

Mannie: Why not, Irv?

Irv: I did not talk about that at that point because I still wanted to work with both of you on some of my own feelings about the idea of alternate sessions before I followed through with the group.

Mannie: So you did not respond or take advantage after having really handled, magnificently I think, a way of introducing it?

Irv: That's right. I had a good opportunity, but I sort of chickened out.

Mannie: All right, at this point you have some feelings. . . .

Irv: Well, I have had feelings all along. As a matter of fact, I even had that dream I said I would have.

Al: Is that so! Tell us the dream.

Irv: This was following the meeting we had last Saturday. I told you that I was frustrated and in conflict. I dreamed that Gerry and I were in New York City and we had bought a new car and it was supposed to be serviced for us. It was being serviced that day, but the people we bought the car from were about thirty miles from us . . . or something like that . . . in Connecticut. They were supposed to bring the car to us in New York City, but they didn't do it, which meant that we had to go to them. It was very complicated to get there and we were thinking of taking a bus to get there. It would take a long time and finally I suggested, "Let's take a cab. It will only cost a few dollars and we can get there in about half an hour!" So we got in a cab and I guess we got out there. That was the gist. In other words, the feeling I had when I woke up is that I was wondering about the kind of servicing I was getting.

Mannie: It depends, you know, upon what kind of servicing you want. We don't have to go into that. But apparently you did not chicken out in the dream. Why did you chicken out about suggesting the alternate sessions?

Irv: The reason I did is because, well, I suppose a lot of it has to do with my feelings about my own analysis, which probably colors a lot of my thinking about therapy at this point.

Mannie: Are you telling us your analyst is opposed to group therapy?

Irv: Well, I would say that he is. My feelings would be that he is, although he has never said so. Gerry and I are among the few in town that actually do group therapy and are the

only ones doing analytic group therapy, and I know what
the analytic community feels about it.

Mannie: Sounds like you are looking to have your car serviced.
Sounds like you want to do something with your analyst;
you are trying to change his mind. My association is that
the car is not really your relationship to us, but your relationship to your own analyst. But this is my association and
not yours. I think you are probably struggling between
two sets of authorities.

Irv: Well, there's no question about it, no question about it at all.

Mannie: Regardless of how your analyst feels about it, you will
never solve this problem until you discover your own
feelings about the alternate session. I would like to know
more about how you feel about the alternate session and
what your anxieties are. Gerry was giving us a rundown
on what were fairly characteristic, typical reactions of both
patients and therapists in anticipating alternate sessions.

Irv: I might add that both Gerry and I have had groups meet
without us before, but they have not been structured on
a regular basis. When I have gone out of town and times
like that, I have had my groups meet without me, although
I have had them meet in the office.

Mannie: So you wanted to have some control even though you were
not there.

Gerry: I want to interject here at this point. One of the members
of the group, Tim, the one who felt that it would be all
superficiality without me there, said he thought the alternate idea would be good, but it should be here in the office.
And also Ethel, the girl who acts out a lot, thought it would
be good. Why couldn't they have the meeting here in the
office when I wasn't here? They wanted to keep me in.

Al: Do you recognize the anxiety underlying that kind of
wish?

Gerry: Yes, the wish was to keep me in the group and in alternate
session.

Al: No, the anxiety was to get your support because they are
afraid of the peers. They want to get as close to you as
they can.

Gerry: At that point I asked, did they feel that if they had an
alternate session and I were not there that I would not

be there? And they responded very favorably to that too. They all said that they guessed that after all, their feelings about me would be there anyway.

Mannie: Fine. If you don't mind my structuring this a little bit, I think both Gerry and Irv at this point ought to talk about their own feelings about the alternate session before we get into any of the technical or management problems that might be involved. What do you say? Who's gonna take off? Gerry, you heard all of their feelings about their doubts and anxieties and wishes. . . .

Gerry: I don't think I heard all of them. I heard some of them.

Mannie: What I meant was, you heard the patients' reactions. How about yours? What are your doubts and anxieties, wishes and fears and fantasies?

Gerry: Well, I have a lot of wishes about it. I am hopeful that it will work adequately and that it will liberate Nicky from her silence. In fact, I wonder how it will work with this fellow, Tim. I don't think he is able to cope with the disturbing thoughts and feelings that he has when he is with me individually or even in the group with me. As far as negative feelings about it, I have a lot of doubts, but I think I am influenced somewhat by the people around here in the community, even by Irv and how he reacts to it. I told him on Monday that I had brought it up with the group, and he kind of smiled at me. I thought, well, am I sticking my neck out—what am I doing? But I felt like—again this conflict of authorities—that you people have been doing it successfully and that it is an idea that you feel contributes significantly to treatment in the group. I thought, I don't really have an adequate argument for or against it and I don't know how I feel. The only way I will know is if I go ahead and see what happens and begin to look at the feelings I have as they come up in relation to the fact rather than the hypothesis.

Al: Gerry, you said something about sticking your neck out. You wouldn't have a fantasy that this is a dangerous activity you are embarking on?

Gerry: Oh, yes.

Al: Do you want to tell us about the fantasy you have, your feelings and the dangers you anticipate?

Gerry: Well, I don't know. I can associate to it; that's all I can do. All I can say is I feel that Ethel is a very blatant, ebullient person and I am concerned about her. She is promiscuous anyway. This doesn't influence . . . I don't expect I can control her in the bar or anywhere else, but I am wondering about how her husband will react to it should she go out and get impregnated by one of these men after an alternate session. How am I going to preserve myself from his retaliation, say his legal retaliation, or something like that. . . . I don't know that it will ever occur, but I have the feeling and fear nevertheless. And I think I certainly would not be getting any support from other authorities in the community.

Irv: Yes, I think that is the main factor. We are more or less on our own in this community. Most of the analysts in town look down upon group psychotherapy, and the idea of an alternate session is even more crazy as far as a feeling of support in the community—we just do not have it.

Mannie: Both of you told us you were low men on the totem pole anyway. What have you got to lose? What is your anxiety here? What is your fantasy?

Irv: My fantasy about being low man on the totem?

Mannie: Yes, what is your doubt?

Irv: I have the same kind of feelings Gerry has about the fear that someone in the group might impregnate somebody's wife, and that really would be a complication. Someone might say to me, "Well, look here, a person comes into treatment and you put him in a situation where you stimulate his acting out or you give him an opportunity to act out." The fact that these patients are in a treatment situation where they developed intense transferences to each other encourages acting out which ordinarily would not occur. I placed them in a situation where there were no ordinary restraints.

Gerry: Yes, but I have also the feeling, regarding treatment of any kind, that it is my responsibility to try to help them understand what they are doing, not to influence or direct their behavior. I feel I can defend myself in this logically and intellectually. Yet there is a danger involved here because of other people. I don't think that anybody in the community is going to initiate that kind of thing themselves, but I concern myself about the group itself. I feel that with the alternate session Ethel is just more likely to go out to a bar and be promiscuous, which I don't have responsibility for or control over. However, it is a contingent possibility. And I wonder, since I have set up the alternate meeting as a part of treatment, and I think that that is the idea of an alternate meeting, that it is a part of treatment. Even though I am not there, my responsibility and, I don't know about accountability though, extends to the alternate meeting as well. This is the anxiety that I have about it. Yet at the same time I have the kind of wishful fantasy of really developing skill as a group therapist and being top man on the totem pole instead of bottom man in the community.

Mannie: Gerry, did you ever stop to think that what you have said here this morning must reflect some anxieties unrelated to your practice? Did you ever think that the kind of concern you have is more personal? Irv said he agreed with you; maybe he has the same questions.

Irv: Gerry is echoing my sentiments.

Mannie: The question that I'm asking is, Why is it that the sexual implications are the ones that you are most concerned about?

Irv: Well, I think two factors. One, that we have impulses in the same direction and probably we might be tempted to do the same thing if we were in a group.

Irv: Yes, but you probably also have some fear, quite unrelated to the group, that you are going to be punished by the husband or by the community.

Mannie: Well, it goes back to an oedipal kind of thing. I am sure that our own oedipal problems are—

Gerry: Now I see what you wanted to hear about my sticking my neck out.

Mannie: I didn't want to hear about it. I only wanted you to think about it.

Irv: I know that, and it's quite a sado-masochistic fantasy to have. I can see that it would tie in with all the other sado-masochistic fantasies I have and would be a little bit more grist for the mill.

Al: Can I give you a few associations?

Irv: Could you speak a little louder?

Al: Can you hear me?

Irv: Now we can, yes.

Al: In the first place I think it is important for each member of the group to have an experience functioning without the therapist and in relation to each other from the outset. That was not how you started. If in the future you start new groups and structure it this way in advance, I think you will have an advantage.

Irv: One thing Al, there is one technical question I have, and it probably comes up lots and lots of times with you, namely, your idea that you have to get away from the hierarchical vector in order to work through the problem. Now isn't traditional analysis based upon the fact that you work through the transference distortion in the hierarchical vector and that it is possible to work through these authority problems that way.

Al: But it is much easier for the patient to work out the hierarchical vector transferred onto peers. It is much easier for them to tackle the authority in another patient, unless you've got a very domineering patient. Even then, the patient's authority is neutralized to some extent in the actuality of his exposing himself as a peer. The therapist is generally the last person with whom the patient works out vertical problems. Patients are constantly working with the hierarchical vector and more easily in one another. This does not mean that they shouldn't be involved with the therapist. They all are, but it just makes it easier for them. For example, take Nicky: Her mother doesn't really want to let her go. I don't think Nicky has thought of this, and it would be very important for you not only to let her go, but to encourage her in getting away to some extent from you as the parental figure as part of her working through. She has anxiety about this, but she should be supported because in part she also wants to get away, even though she has tremendous conflict about it. Is it you, Gerry, who has had the alternate meeting?

Gerry: They haven't had it yet, Al, but they are having it on Sunday afternoon.

Al: They haven't actually met yet?

Gerry: No, and in fact, I just thought about it. They made it Sunday afternoon, a nice, controlled day, you know.

Al: By the way, when they come back from that alternate, instead of reviewing what happened there, unless some of them do it spontaneously, ask them for any reactions to it so that they have the experience that you are not going to explore every last detail of what happened there, because this may be very limiting to them.

Gerry: Just let them deal with it spontaneously, or with how they felt about the meeting.

Al: Well, yes. Ask, "Are there any reactions to your first alternate session? You don't have to review it, but are there any afterthoughts about it?"

Mannie: In other words, it would be wrong to ask the question, "What happened?" You don't want to ask what happened. You are not trying to snoop like mother asking what happened.

Gerry: Did you have an interesting meeting, did you have a good time . . . or, but not in those words, how did you feel about it?

Mannie: No, don't ask that now.

Irv: Well, wouldn't it come up anyway? It is bound to come up.

Mannie: That's the point. It will come up if there's any frustration or acting out. I think you had a wonderful way of introducing the alternate meetings, Irv, asking members how they would feel if you, the therapist, were not there. Some said they would feel freer, some would be more frightened. Point out that they have different feelings, thoughts, associations, and probably activity in your absence than in your presence. Of course this would help clarify their transference reactions. Then the question might come up, Why do they have to secrete certain aspects of themselves from you because you are only an "as if" parent, they are acting "as if" they can't behave or think or feel in one way when you are there and can in another. Now in regard to the dream, I had some . . . Are you with us, Irv?

Irv: I sure am.

Al: I think maybe we ought to talk about how we are servicing you, and if this may have to do with your anxiety about our leaving you high and dry. We're throwing you into the—

Mannie: We're far away even though we're in New York.

Al: Go ahead, have the alternate meetings, we're not going to be around to repair the damage.

Irv: Well, you know, I think that my frustration really isn't the alternate meetings so much. Actually, I think it's—

Mannie: It's his analyst.

Irv: Yes, but I think it is more, and I think it is all in the oedipal vector. I think what I want out of your servicing, and I was a little frustrated about this last time, is that I would like the opportunity for not only presenting cases, but to get more didactic work. I think I am frustrated and I feel that in one hour, how can we accomplish what I want, which is in effect to get—

Gerry: You want training.

Irv: Yes, I want more training.

Gerry: Which brings up this thought we talked about at lunch back in New York with you, that I have been fantasying about since. Remember, I said, we ought to try this phone out, but I wonder why we couldn't set up a research grant, get a closed-circuit TV. Currently we're experimenting with the telephone.

Al: Perhaps educate the community in Seattle by allowing other members of the therapeutic profession to sit in on this.

Gerry: Well, this is what I was thinking about, that eventually as Irv and I work out more of our feelings and develop more of our skill that we might think about this as an idea for training people that are in remote areas, not just Seattle.

Irv: I think that is important. I feel the need of . . . maybe we could structure our sessions, so maybe we need more time. If you would be willing to do it so that we could, along the line, get more specific training in techniques and theory. . . .

Gerry: Well, my idea is that we do this first and—

Irv: Like, I know I'm getting way far afield, but I was reading Arlene Wolberg's article[48] in that journal, the one where you had your article on group mystique. I was quite impressed with the kind of conceptualization she had regarding ego development. A lot of my feelings revolve around my conflict about orthodox analysis, instinct theory, and libido as contrasted with a view of pathology as based primarily upon disturbances in interpersonal relations. I think my feelings about the alternate session relate to my conceptualization of how pathology develops, as well as to anxieties based upon oedipal conflicts.

Mannie: No matter how much theory we try to teach you, no matter how much didactic material we present, it will be meaningless in the therapeutic situation unless you are aware of the feelings, problems, transferences, and countertransference responses you have. You can read all the books in the world and we can give you all the lectures to no avail. It would be very simple for us to sit here and pontificate, but it will never really penetrate, never get translated into any kind of therapeutic action as analysts in your practice. This is my conviction. The reason I am convinced is that if you have an oedipal problem, it will make no difference how much technique you know, it is only going to be used in the service of the oedipal problem. You will continue to build your head and think you are building your penis, but it will not work, because you cannot solve the basic emotional problem by the accumulation of knowledge, degrees, or theoretical information. Your understanding will have to be derived from personal awareness. I am committed as an analyst to the idea that we are continuously struggling with repressive maneuvers to avoid consciousness of what is really going on. One of the functions of the good analytic teacher is to help you become conscious of this. Let's take Irv's problem about orthodoxy versus nonorthodoxy. You are quite right, Irv, when you say your anxieties are related to both theoretical issues and personal ones. However, you will learn more about the theoretical issues as you explore and clarify your fears, anxieties and fantasies concerning the alternate session. This is especially so because it is the most unorthodox analytic practice you could utilize.

Irv: I agree with you. I see that the alternate sessions focus on the basic problems, both theoretical and personal.

Mannie: Exactly! And you will learn techniques and theory much more directly if you work on the problem of your own involvement and emotional conflict with regard to the essential issues. You can teach a high school student with a good memory and an IQ of 120 all there is to know about techniques, but this won't make him a psychoanalyst. Psychoanalysis has to do with human experience and human interaction, not only with technique. A technique is something we use to objectify the process so that we have guidelines for our functioning within this commitment. We are trying to give patients a new kind of emotional experience, to enable them to fulfill their potential.

Gerry: I think I know what you are saying. What we are trying to do in treatment is to have the person experience the actual relationship that you are the therapist and he is the patient, more as it actually is rather than in its transferential character. Is that what you mean?

Mannie: We hope to accomplish awareness of the distortion of the real experience through transferences. This is what I am trying to accomplish here with you. Al and I are committed to the idea that if you can be aware of your counter-transference feelings, you are going to be free to apply technique and methodology and even develop your own technique, your own theory.

Irv: Let me interrupt, Mannie. What Al said before in his association to my dream was correct then. My fear is that you two might leave us high and dry. Will you service us as you feel we need the servicing? We are embarking on an adventure that will expose us to new kinds of problems, and my fear is whether we will be helped so that we can function as good therapists in a group.

Mannie: But this is manifest content. Behind this lies the struggle that is revealed in Irv's dream . . . a choice between one authority and another. This is the core of what is happening here. We are involved now in a series of distortions of the real situation based upon transference needs.

Al: I think Irv's dream has to do with the alternate meeting and peer and vertical vectors. Who is meeting whose needs and whose demands? is a question that enters my mind and coupled with it the question, Who is misusing whom?

You feel you are not being serviced adequately by those who are some distance from you. This expresses the feeling of last week. Now there is some concern, both that your patients will be exploited and that you will as well be. It is unclear whether it is by us or by the community. Also, I think there is a tendency to submit to the projectively hostile father. The husband of the woman who might act out sexually in the group is going to be a threat like the hostile fathers in the community. I think there is a question in the dream of who is helping and who is being helped. There is this question with regard to you in relation to your patients in the groups and with regard to them. Can they help one another? Can peers help one another; can one get help in the horizontal vector or does one only get help and security in the vertical vector?

Gerry: I just had a thought about that, too, something that is different about Irv and me which may account for why I introduced the alternate and he hesitated. I come from a large family. Irv is an only child. I also thought about the bus and the taxi, public transportation and paying a special fee to get where you want to go. What's the price you're going to have to pay?

Irv: Well, maybe the bus would be group and taxi would be individual analysis.

Al: One question that has to be worked through is what is the nature of human exchange and human transactions? There is anxiety about a human transaction in the horizontal vector. When people have transactions in the peer vector, there tends to be anxiety on the patient's part, that he is likely to act out. If he is likely to act out, the next patient is likely to do so as well. The therapist too is threatened. In his anxiety he may become too controlling and seek more *control* analysis from his supervisors.

Mannie: There is bound to be more activity in the alternate meeting. Some of this will be healthy activity and some of it is likely to be acting out. So what? In a sense they are acting out as a group when they as patients question their own resources without the therapist. This is a kind of acting out of an infantile position, that they are absolutely unable to have any rational resources or controls of their own when they are away from you. I would regard that as a kind of acting out in defense of infantilization, that they cannot function without the therapist.

Gerry: That is saying then, isn't it, that I can't function without parents, so how can they?

Mannie: Yes, that may be fair.

Gerry: I can't function without your help—how can they?

Mannie: Al, have you anything more to add about the alternate session? Let's use what time we have left for you to deal with some of the technical problems they are asking about, some of the problems that come up: management of acting out, combined therapy. What may happen in terms of the relationship of the alternate session, the individual session, the group session? Let's talk about this.

4

Socialization, Activity, and the Alternate Meeting

One of the principal questions with regard to group therapy is the extent to which the presence and activity of others abrogate or attenuate the traditional conditions considered essential for analytic reconstruction to take place.

Many beginning group therapists have had extensive training in the individual psychotherapeutic or psychoanalytic model. Often concerns about group therapy will be proportional to the extent to which background and training have been classical and orthodox.

The heightened activity, the increased interaction, the potential for socialization, the stimulation and provocation by patients and their fantasies, require the beginning group therapist to reformulate his conceptualization of how pathology and health will express itself in the group therapeutic matrix, and how appropriate interventions can be undertaken.

The training experience involves repetition. As the reader proceeds from session to session in this teaching and learning experience, he will notice this repetitive process. In a sense the repetition in the learning process parallels the working-through process in psychotherapy, although these processes are of a different order of magnitude and quality.

Irv: I'd like to follow through with some of the material that
we were discussing last week. I thought quite a bit about
the alternate session following our last meeting. I was convinced about introducing alternate sessions after thinking
of the advantages and the disadvantages. However, my
feeling—and I know that if you ask me to associate, I have
a lot of emotional reactions to it—my feeling is that I would
rather have an alternate session in my own office at a time
when I am not physically present. I've thought in terms of
how it affects me and also I think about the theoretical
aspects.

Mannie: Give us some of the feelings.

Irv: I think some of my anxiety has to do with the idea of
socialization. It would be more stimulating to the patient,
both sexually and aggressively, in contrast to what I am
familiar with in traditional psychotherapy. I know group
psychotherapy is not the same as traditional analysis. The
fact that patients have therapeutic experience with each
other in interaction makes a tremendous difference. This is
one of the good things about group psychotherapy. But you
add so much grist to the mill that your mill may not be
good enough or there just may be too much grist to deal
with all the kinds of extra material that come up. At this
point I don't see the value of socialization outside of the
therapeutic framework.

   If you have patients seeing each other interacting in a
variety of situations, and seeing husband and wife interacting for example, certainly all sorts of material will be
stimulated. However, this may attenuate transference and
make it more difficult to see what is transference and what
is not. It would be getting patients involved in a type of
social interaction which from my frame of reference I can't
see how it is going to be that beneficial. It is going to make
things more complicated, even though it stimulates more
material. In a traditional analytic setting, the material usually comes from the patient himself with little provocation
by the analyst. In a group setting you have this forced
interaction you talk about, and there is lots of cross-stimula-
tion by patients. If in addition you get patients interacting

in each other's homes, there is even more material to be dealt with. But I'm just wondering when does the material reach the point where it attenuates the kinds of projection which they can build up?

The other thought I have about the alternate meeting is that it gets patients too involved in each others' lives. In other words, it makes therapy too much a part of their life circumstances. A patient socializes during the week anyway, or if he does not, then that is one of the problems that should be worked out in therapy.

Mannie: This is Gerry, isn't it?

Irv: No, this is Irv, still Irv.

Mannie: I thought I heard a change of voice.

Irv: I can see that alternate meetings in each others' homes is going to be more spontaneous. A lot more material will be stimulated, but it begins to take on the character of social life and it begins to break down the distinction between the patient's life in therapy, so to speak, and his life outside of therapy. I'm sure you've heard all of these things before, but this is the way I think about alternate sessions.

Al: I'd like to hear Gerry's reaction to this. Have you got any, Gerry?

Gerry: Yes! I've thought about it and to me the issue is this: I think that there must be a different therapeutic model that we use in group therapy as contrasted to the traditional model; and if there is, there must be different constructs against which we try to project patient behavior or patient production in order to bring out the neurotic aspect of it, or to focus on the essential aspect of it. I know I have a lot of personal feeling about alternate meetings. I think these are less significant right now than are the theoretical conceptualizations of how you deal with the material that is presented. I am willing to go along with the alternate session as producing material. Group therapy is not orthodox analysis in a traditional setting and as soon as it stops being that, then you've got to have some different framework, a different way of looking at patient productions. In a group or alternate meeting, we have to contrast it with some other standard in order to recognize how much

is current reality experience and how much of it is transferential experience.

Al: You would say, then, that there is both latent and manifest
content to your feelings concerning the alternate session.
Now, Gerry, do you want to tell us what you think is the
latent meaning of Irv's communication with regard to his
feeling that at this point he would rather keep the patients
in the office at an alternate meeting?

Gerry: We've talked about this several times during the week, and
we clarified what our feelings are. I think Irv's wish to hold
the alternate session in the office represents his attempt to
push what is happening in treatment in a group into the
framework of orthodox analysis of the person on the couch,
where everything comes from inside the patient. I think he
tries to do this because he wants to do conventional analysis.
I think that he probably also wants control. The problem
seems to be: Where does the alternate session stop being
therapy because he stops having direct control over what's
going on?

Al: Do you think he might want this control because he's inse-
cure except with the model that he has?

Gerry: I think that this can be, although I think he is open to . . .

Al: Sounds like Nicky's mother.

Gerry: Well, maybe that's true: It is probably the same kind of
thing. Nonetheless, I don't think Irv or Nicky's mother can
give this up unless they understand their own emotional
relationship to it. Before you give up one model that you
understand intellectually, you've got to have another set
of parameters that you can understand.

Mannie: Irv, I want to say this before Al continues. If you've got
the space to do it in your own office, I'm for your experimenting under any kind of conditions as long as you're
willing to take the chance. I'm going on record as saying
that right now.

Irv: What chance do you have in mind? Do you think that
this is going to encourage some rebellious acting out?

Mannie: Well, no, I'm not concerned about that. All I'm saying is
that I'm for your doing it no matter under what conditions.
Letting the group meet without you is a great idea. We

think that there are certain positives and negatives in having alternate meetings in your office. But do it in your office, if that's the place you're going to be most comfortable in doing it at this moment. All right?

Al: I go along with that. I think we can settle for your doing it in the office until you have more of a sense of security or the feeling that it is constructive.

Irv: I know that a lot of this is my own personal feeling and stems from the fact that at this point I cannot even intellectually defend the idea of socialization and the problems therein. If I can get more help along that direction, then I might be able to see the thing in another perspective.

Al: One of the questions I think we ought to explore is why you view socialization pretty largely as a manifestation of pathology. That is, I think socialization, like any other activity, is both healthy and pathological; that it is resistive and positive; that it may be acting out but it may also be new behavior. It is not just one thing. To the extent that it is resistive, acting out, and pathological, you will hear about it and you can work with it. To the extent that it is reality-oriented, you can encourage it. Why would you regard members of a therapy group having any kind of socializing experience as necessarily dangerous or something to be feared? What is there in the socialization that gives you concern? There is no doubt that there is greater interaction, greater activity, both healthy and pathological, away from the analyst. So there will be a little less activity and freedom in your office than there might be outside. This may be a good way to start; see how it goes; perhaps you should exercise this control in your office and then see what they do. I think that you have anxiety and concern about their becoming sexual and violent, or, as Gerry suggests, that they'll get away from you.

Irv: These may be problems in a sense, but I don't think these are major problems for me. Patients might meet each other afterwards anyway, and socialize or even be promiscuous.

Al: Yes, but that is no reflection on you and your competence as an analyst.

Irv: Well, if I am actually making it part of my treatment struc-
          ture that they meet in each other's homes, then I'm more
          directly involved in setting up potential circumstances for
          acting out.

Al: Exactly, and you were talking about being secure with your
          own orthodox view of individual therapy as well as group
          therapy.

Irv: But I think I could deal with my own reluctance if I could
          better understand the framework with which we're dealing.
          I am most familiar with the analytic conception of placing
          a patient in a setting where you facilitate regression so that
          the origins of his neurosis can unfold, a transference neurosis
          develops and can be analyzed.

Mannie: All right, let's talk about psychoanalytic theory. You say
          you want to approach this as a problem of information in
          order to get the security that you want.

Irv: Perhaps if I had more information that I could think about
          then I'd be in a better position to see the reality or unreality
          of my own anxiety.

Mannie: I would like to offer this for your consideration: In some
          way you are saying that if you were convinced that you
          could help patients become healthier mentally rather than
          to go crazy with each other as they might if they ran out
          of control, you would then be willing to take this chance
          more freely. I think you are really asking, What are the
          chances that this will help them become mentally healthier
          rather than to become more mentally excited, more frag-
          mented and disturbed?

Gerry: I feel there is also this personal aspect.

Irv: I agree with you.

Al: Fine. Gerry, go ahead.

Gerry: I believe that it is quite different trying to understand a
          patient's production in terms of the test tube experience,
          that is, individual analysis, and in terms of the smorgasbords
          we have created with group therapy and alternate meetings
          in the homes. How do we see clearly the pathologic aspect
          of the patient's behavior and the part that may be healthy?
          How do we separate these out for ourselves and for the
          patient to make it a therapy experience rather than just
          an experience?

Mannie: All right, you fellows are disagreeing with me this morning, so I'm going to give you one more thing to disagree with. I have a hunch that your model of individual psychoanalysis is distorted. You may get very defensive with me, but I'm going to go way out on a limb nevertheless. I think that you haven't thoroughly explored the nature of the psycho-analytic model as it is currently understood. I think that you haven't really gone into this. For instance, somewhere you've got a notion apparently that the patient lives all by himself in the analytic situation, that the model of psychoanalysis is total social inactivity of the patient, of his continuous preoccupation with intrapsychic processes until his psy-chology involves only his relationship to himself, a regres-sion back to that period in life, his first year when he had no awareness of his relatedness to another person. You seem to think this is what is therapeutic in analysis. I should like to challenge this concept and ask for an exploration of it because it is a mistaken notion. You are at a stage of development in your view of psychoanalysis similar to the field's very earliest beginnings. Psychoanalysis today is in a phase in which we recognize the patient is not alone in the analytic chamber and that he exists in relation to the analyst and to the rest of reality. The old idea, which was a misconception, that the analyst and the analytic situation are merely mirroring what goes on inside the patient's head and that we are interested only in intrapsy-chic experiences and not the interpersonal or the social, is an idea that most practitioners have given up as a dis-tortion a long time ago. It is a distortion which Freud never let determine his technique, and he never wrote this way. Some disciples then misperceived the nature of analysis. You might want to read about Freud's one-day analysis of Gustav Mahler, the great musical composer. He did the analysis while walking through the park. Then they stopped and had their lunch. I know that there is a great deal of resistance to such an idea on the part of analysts of all dimensions, of all schools, and of all commitments as well on the part of patients. Again and again I come into contact with patients who resist the concept that it is not going to make it more difficult for them to be analyzed because they have a real-life experience or relationship with me, for example my students. They would like to immobilize me; they would like to make me their mirror. They believe it is in their interest not to have me move. They would like to have me so immobile that they could then control whether or not they will move, whether or not they will change. You cannot extract your patient from a real world in which he lives, and all the analysis of his intrapsychic processes will never become operationally useful unless he sees himself functioning in the real world and understands his inner and outer experiences within that world. This is a commitment on my part, and I'd like to hear your reactions to what I have just said.

Gerry: Well, I don't disagree with what you're saying at all. I only say that I myself don't know how to formulate in my own mind how we are going to use the information in group or in an alternate session, how to utilize it analytically. How does one intervene and say—

Mannie: Do you know how to do analysis? Are you asking how do you do analysis? Because you do analysis, whether you are in the individual or the group setting, in the same way. If I understood your question, at this moment you're asking how do you do analytic work with whatever material comes in. If this is what you want to talk about, we can.

Gerry: Well, no, it's certainly different, maybe this outmoded, traditional concept we've presented—

Irv: No, that's your presumption of my views, because I think you are misunderstanding because I don't subscribe to that model as you outlined it, Mannie.

Mannie: Well, what do you hold about socialization? Do you believe that socialization attenuates transference? Even if it does, it provides us with a lot more material about transference to analyze. Do you think that you are going to do better work if you regress the patient further? There comes a point where further regression leads into the position that some analysts have taken, that the patient must have a therapeutic psychosis. This is a theoretical position. Some, like Ferenczi and John Rosen, say that we should enter into the psychosis with the patient, but we had better know our way out. The theoretical commitment is to psychoanalytic psychology and not to socialization or against socialization. You need to ask yourself what is analytic psychology? For me, it is fundamentally the idea that the patient is not really perceiving and acting in conformity with reality because he does not see the reality. We must help him see reality as it is, so that he may be freer. This is what I think Freud meant when he said, "Where the id is, let the ego be." We must offer the patient experiences which help him better to understand the nature of reality, inner and outer reality, reality within the therapeutic situation and reality outside. And every time we can help him become conscious of what he does with this reality, positively as well as negatively, we are analyzing. Now we do this by a commitment to analytic psychology which says this can only occur in an attitude or in a climate of freedom. We must not be judgmental, we must not be directive, we must not be punitive. As we provide and support an environment of freedom, he will become freer to experience alternatives to his repetitive patterns of perceiving and behaving.

Gerry: To his repetitive distortions?

Mannie: Distorted as well as correct perceptions. He uses his old patterns repeatedly. This is a repetition compulsion and we want him to be able freely to explore what he perceives and what he distorts, what he does and what he does not do, so that he can then have the freedom to make new choices. The group setting does not preclude the possibility of doing analytic work. There was a period during which some early analysts said that for a patient to be sexual, to have sex, while he was undergoing analysis was antitherapeutic. The patient had to be dead before you could analyze him. Even if Irv says I'm projecting and I have set up a straw man, I feel this represents the direction of his position. He's saying the patient should not have living experiences if he is in analysis, because if he has too many experiences, we are not going to be able to analyze him, we shall lose control.

Irv: No, he shouldn't have living experiences with the analyst outside of the analytic session.

Mannie: Why not? If you question what kind of living experiences, I would go along with that. There are certain kinds of living experiences I would not want him to have, but why should he have no experience with the analyst except that the analyst sit silent behind him? I know a candidate in one of the training institutions who has not seen his analyst's face for years. He walks in, lies down on the couch, has a session, and the analyst gets up, walks behind the door, and the candidate walks out. He could never recognize his analyst *visually* any more than you could recognize us except for our voices. He knows his analyst's voice very well. This is the position you are taking regarding the nature of the relationship between the patient and the analyst. Why shouldn't the patient have some kinds of contact with the analyst?

Irv: Well, I'm thinking of social contact.

Mannie: I'm talking about social contact, such as a chance meeting at a lecture. I know an analytic candidate who felt deeply hurt by his analyst, who was giving a public lecture. He walked up to the platform after the lecture to tell him how great it was. He offered his hand and wanted to shake hands with him, and his analyst refused. Later he said he did this out of therapeutic necessity. I say, rubbish!

Irv: Well, I think you're right, Mannie, that I'm in the direction of analytic neutrality or sterility, isolation, or whatever you want to call it.

Al: I see the alternate meeting as part of the therapeutic process. I see the alternate meeting as offering the patient something that will help him to work through. I see it as providing an additional therapeutic intervention in the sense that it is an encouragement to patients to act on their own resources without the continuous, sometimes overprotective and controlling power of the therapist in the vertical vector. I see it as an opportunity for the patient to get away from the parental figure and see how he can function on his own. This does not mean the therapist will not be available if the patient needs him, but that he is constantly being encouraged, right from the outset, to test his own resources. Of course there may be some patients who cannot do this right at the outset. Perhaps their entry into the alternate meetings should be delayed. For the most patients, the alternating absence of the therapist is a very positive experience. They learn thereby that the therapist has appropriate confidence in them. While it is true that we want to bring out the problems of patients in the vertical vector, which you seem to feel the alternate meetings might dilute, working through really requires at the same time an encouragement to experience others, ultimately and increasingly, including even the therapist, as peers. This is part of the patient's problem. If we want to keep him always related to the therapist, always in the therapist's office, in a sense we are limiting not only his privilege, but the necessity for him to work through toward a peer relationship. When therapists say, "There's something about a group that is therapeutic, but I don't know what it is," I think one of these therapeutic elements is constructive provision of peer experience. Patients don't get well, many of them, because they are so infantilized by the experience with the therapist in the vertical vector. It is this, then, that I'm trying to emphasize. The value of the alternate meeting is as a working through to peer experience, not only as socialization.

Irv: Could you talk a little bit about the concept of regressing the patient so that a full-blown transference neurosis develops and using that to deal with the primary pathology as some individual analysts are doing, or at least the analysts that I know, as compared with the type of framework that you work with and the type of encounters you think are important in group therapy.

Mannie: I think that you cannot do analytic work without analyzing transference.

Irv: Yes, but there's a difference.

Mannie: Whenever you have a persistent transferential relationship, you are dealing with transference neurosis. It is not possible to have an ongoing, persistent relationship with anybody with whom you are in transference, where the nature of the relationship, the role positions, the statuses, support the illusion that you do not develop a transference neurosis, whether this is in a classroom with your teacher, in the family with your wife, or at work with your boss.

Irv: You mean the repetitive rather than a spontaneous—

Mannie: A transference neurosis is a kind of ongoing relationship
          in which the transference becomes one of the primary
          elements of that relationship. As an analogy, we might say
          that husbands and wives who persistently do not see each
          other realistically are suffering a "transference neurosis"
          with regard to each other. The difference between a hus-
          band and wife in transference neurosis and an analyst and
          his analysand is the analyst does not provoke this reaction
          by virtue of his own counterneeds and therefore is free to
          demand the exploration of that transference neurosis in
          reality. There is some mistaken notion here that a trans-
          ference neurosis has something to do with some magical
          relationship only with the analyst. A transference neurosis,
          like any neurosis, only means that the neurosis is one way
          and the analyst, by virtue of the nature of his experience,
          has remained as objective and as nonprovocative as he can.
          However, this does not exist in reality because the person-
          ality of the analyst in some ways plays a part provocatively
          to encourage or discourage certain kinds of transference
          reactions. That is one reason why we say you cannot under-
          stand what goes on in an analysis unless you also know the
          transference and countertransference responses of the ana-
          lyst. Keep in mind that when you talk about transference
          neurosis as being the matrix of analytic work, you are right,
          but you are also saying that it exists only in a test tube
          called the dyadic relationship with a so-called nonreal,
          neutral, sterile person. Let us explore more fully what a
          transference neurosis is. By definition a neurosis has a
          repetitive core in which one's feeling, thinking, and acting
          repeatedly are controlled or governed out of conflictual
          necessity in which the realities are distorted and certain
          mental mechanisms take over in order to protect the indi-
          vidual from being overwhelmed by the anxieties based upon
          a distorted view of the nature of the current reality.

Gerry: Do you want a good example of this?

Mannie: Go ahead.

Gerry: I just came to check our machinery and I see that Irv in
          getting it set up managed to knock off the recorder for
          the first thirty-five minutes of our conversation.

Mannie: That's cute, but, Irv, how about this definition of the transference neurosis?

Irv: Well, I usually define a transference neurosis as occurring within an analytic setting and referred to other types of behavior as displacements, but—

Mannie: What do you mean by displacement? It's a mental mechanism.

Irv: Yes, but what I mean is that it depends upon how you define it. Some people limit the concept of transference to that which occurs within the analytic relationship, and others include the same kind of phenomena that occur outside of the analytic relationship or when a person is—

Mannie: That's a distortion.

Irv: Yes, that's a distortion or displacement. I don't care what you call it; it's all the same anyway.

Mannie: But these distortions obviously occur in every moment of the patient's life.

Irv: That's right.

Mannie: These are distortions of the reality of the situation to which you are privy by report, as an analyst, when a patient talks about his relationship to his wife, for example. The story once again is screened through the distortions of the patient. You have no feedback, no check on it. Whereas one of the advantages of the group is that the other person involved is also present when he gives you his report of his perception of his misperceived behavior. As analysts, when a patient talks about the nature of his relationship to his wife, we do not know how his wife saw it. We do not know whether he is not redistorting the already distorted relationship. We have no outside checkpoint except our own relationship to him and his relationship to us. In the group, having the participants in experience before us, we have both parties to the distortion involved. We think this is good because we believe distortion is not a one-way process, including the transference of the patient to the analyst.

Gerry: May I interrupt while I switch reels so we don't lose this? All right, and now I think we'll get this part of it. And I hope it's as good as the first part that we missed. [As the recorder was working, this was a misconception that was undoubtedly related to personal needs at the moment.]

Al: Let me give you an illustration about this question of the transference neurosis. I have a patient in therapy, herself a therapist. She is nearing fifty. She has been in analysis ever since she was a late adolescent. Her first analyst, "in order to break through her sexual inhibitions," had a sexual relationship with her. Her succeeding analyst apparently kept pointing out her pathology, kept trying to get her to regress, so that she began actually to lead a more and more infantilized life. She appealed to me, saying, "Don't kill me, don't analyze me anymore. Help me, help me to grow up." My approach to her has been to emphasize her positive resources, and she has matured under this regime. She tells me that I'm the first friendly therapist she has had in an analyst. In a sense, it's because I've been treating her as a peer and wanting her to be a peer and not focusing on her transference neurosis or trying to develop it. Apparently, there was some conception on the part of some of her therapists that the way to help her was to get her to re-experience her old attitudes, but such an approach actually was infantilizing.

Mannie: On the basis of my clinical and supervisory experience, I am convinced that a transference neurosis will develop whatever you do. If you don't do anything but sit there, it will develop. If you open your mouth or don't open your mouth, a transference neurosis will develop. Transference neuroses are always present whenever two people have a persistent relationship in which neurotic needs prevail. When Irv says "Let's limit the concept of transference to the analytic situation," I am with him on that, because this is the traditional view. Transference is a distortion attributed to patients of analysis. But I want to add one point to our earlier discussion. Irv, I have the feeling that Al was saying earlier that you are giving additional control to the patient's life by including the alternate session without the immediate surveillance of the analyst. You are putting a piece of the social life, which he will have anyway, within the context of the experience in therapy. By putting a frame around it we will better be able to understand the social living of the patient outside the presence of the analyst. We are, in fact, adding a new control rather than diminishing the control.

[period of silence]

Mannie: What did we do, talk you down?

Irv: Oh, no. I'm just trying to think of what you were saying. I know that whatever you're doing, you're introducing something and you seem to understand what you are doing. I know that in what I am doing, I am limiting their socialization and controlling it, if you want to look at it from that point of view. I'm willing to wait two or three weeks and try to work on this before I actually introduce the alternate meeting. My groups are getting ready to move into an alternate session now. They are talking at this point about where they are going to meet, and I can steer it. I'm going to wait a couple of weeks and discuss it further.

Mannie: You don't really have to. You can let them hold it in the office because I don't think that is central. The very fact that you are considering the value of an alternate meeting means that you are saying that you believe that human beings carry on a life, an important part of their life, outside of the analytic office without the continuous surveillance of the analyst. Many of the orthodox analysts not only infantilize their patients, but make them addicted to analysis so that for some their total life is nothing but the analytic experience. It becomes the most significant of life's activity. Somehow you must help bridge the patient back into life. This has always been a problem of working through. Even the most classical analysts struggle around the problem of termination. The early analysts used to ask the question, How do I shift the transference from me to others? But this is not a solution; if you just substitute transference for transference, you're done. What we must try to do is shift from the analytic relationship to experiences in life which can be equally healthy. You might start this bridge early enough to be able to let it build as the patient grows stronger. Ultimately, the patient must be restored to life if you are doing decent analytic work. We cannot remain in the analytic situation forever and ever. One of the functions of a good analysis is to "damn the analysis," to abolish its necessity.

Irv: But you can say that having the patients meet at each other's homes is actually bringing the therapy into life, and that for many patients, they'll begin to make this their total social experience. Of course, you can analyze it and—

Al: Right, you can analyze. If they start making their relationship to group members the center of their lives and they neglect their own families or neglect their other responsibilities and interests, that can be worked with.

Mannie: There is hidden in our discussion a point for later exploration; namely, the feeling that all of the sureties, all of the reparative, all of the healthy resources lie in the analyst. If we take this position we are doomed. Very often when I do intensive analytic work, I hope and pray, I sit and wait for some break to occur in the real life situation of this patient so that we can move further. I insist, in my own mind, always to be aware of the fact that this person lives and must live with others, and not only and exclusively with me, and that I must not allow the patient to utilize the experience with me as if it were the totality of his life experiences. Does that make any sense?

Irv: It sure does and I think that this is probably important for Gerry and me. It is going to need some working through because I think it is something that we are not going to be able to understand or settle easily.

Mannie: I want to return to the earlier part of this session today. What happens to most analysts, what scares most of them away from getting into a group, and what makes you hesitate to promote the alternate session, is like what happened to the analysts around 1910 or 1920. We feel too much is going on, we get anxious because there is too much in the lives of the patients and we would like to try to limit what goes on so that we can do our work. Yet this is a very negative view. It is like the anxiety the mother has when the child begins to move, when the child begins to crawl, or start to walk. By the way, you might read the article by Mittelman[28] in *The Psychoanalytic Study of the Child*, in which he says it is not true that difficulties between mother and child first begin around feeding, that anxiety starts at this period because there is conflict around feeding issues. The child wants to be fed upon demand, the mother refuses, and the child is frustrated. Mittelman feels that the moment of conflict begins when the child develops motility, that when the child begins to move it makes the mother anxious. I think that most analysts are tremendously concerned about the wealth of activity that a patient may be experiencing in life which they can't control, that it's getting out of hand. There's just too much going on. The analyst would like to be able to stop the passage of time long enough to be able to get a bead on what is really going on.

Gerry: That when the kid is running around, crawling around on the floor, getting into everything is when the problems start.

Mannie: Exactly. I am always much happier working with a patient if he lives an active, interactive life outside of therapy, a productive, creative life, socially, vocationally, emotionally, artistically, with leisure time and so on, than if he is so depressed, so withdrawn, so involved only with himself or with one other, that there is no field for doing analytic work, like exploring alternative choices. The patient needs other kinds of experiences: vitality, investments, commitments; he needs objects to work with.

Gerry: In order to have something to compare.

Mannie: Exactly! Something to work with, something to compare, something to provide the chance that the patient may have a successful experience somewhere in his life. I need that in order to help a patient grow. He needs it in order to grow.

Gerry: Just a passing thought before time is up. The group had an alternate meeting last Sunday and Nicky didn't show up. I had given her the address, but she didn't get there.

Mannie: She's the girl with the mother?

Gerry: Yes, she's the girl with the mother. The group talked about it and they brought up some of their thoughts. I didn't ask them about the session at all, in view of what I had read and what you had said about not asking for a verbatim account and thereby cutting off the productivity of an alternate session. They did bring it up, however, and talked about their feelings about the session, and they talked to Nicky. They were very disappointed that she was not there, and angry, too. I brought up the other thing that Al suggested last week, that maybe it would be better than for me or her mother to be sure that she got there, that the group be sure and try to enable her to get there. So during the session the most remote and isolated unsocial patient in the group wrote out the address. He happened to be the one who was going to have the alternate session at his house. He gave her the address and the time. Then two of the other members offered to pick her up and get her there. They went out of the office with her afterwards. She didn't say anything, and they talked to her on the way out of the building trying to settle how she was going to get there, and she said that she could get there herself. I had pointed out in the group that I thought it best if she could get there herself; secondly, if the group enabled her to get there; and that as the least valuable experience, if her mother had to get her there.

Al: Here is the value of socialization. It would be very interesting to see if Nicky can get there on her own. It would be good if she could do it, but if she couldn't and some member picked her up, if this member could report, if he could see it, what transpires as he views it between Nicky and her mother as Nicky is trying to get out on her own. Think of how useful it might be for a group member to get a relatively undistorted, detached, and rational view of the relationship between Nicky and her mother as she is trying to leave her mother, so that Nicky's view of the mother can be explored.

Gerry: One of the fellows that offered to pick her up described Nicky's mother. He saw her out here during the week bring Nicky to the group session, and he said, "Boy, she's a huge woman. She's strong, she's just like my father and she won't let go of Nicky." So he was already relating this kind of thing, and the group is afraid to talk to the mother. Another member of the group got on just as Nicky's mother was getting off the elevator, having deposited her up here. Nicky's mother smiled and said "Hello" and the person wanted to talk to her but was just completely immobilized. In the group he said, "Maybe she isn't so bad; she seemed kind of friendly." The other guy said, "The hell she is, she looks like a wrestler."

Al: This is one of the values of the alternate meeting, seeing the patient's wife, or husband, or the patient's mother or father. Members get very valuable reactions to the significant figures which help the patient to deal, Nicky in this instance, to deal with her relationship to her mother.

Mannie: And socialization in the elevator.

Gerry: I noticed that during a session this week in the group, Nicky spent a great period of time physically interacting while she didn't say a word. She watched a person who was talking and kept taking this in, listening to what was going on and focusing on it. The group didn't know this and when I pointed it out, of course, she stopped.

Al: I'd like to make a prediction about Nicky, that she will make her best improvement as she moves into the alternate meetings, out of the hierarchical vector. She may have anxiety about it, she may have difficulty doing it, but if she can be induced to join the alternate meetings, she will be getting away from this mother figure.

Mannie: I'd like to talk about some of the contact I have had with my patients outside of my analytic office. In training, supervision, and in my social life, I am often involved in contact with patients, and we must get to the point where we can let ourselves be seen. We must be able to show ourselves and not be afraid to show ourselves, not be afraid of our patients' seeing us. The very fact that we are willing to sit in the group and let many pairs of eyes consensually confirm their view of us means that we are letting ourselves be seen. We need to get away from the idea that we have to hide out and not be seen by the patient. We may even visit in a patient's home, under certain conditions. We have to ask ourselves under what conditions we would and would not have outside contacts. I question the idea that the anonymous analyst is the one who is successful,

who can successfully treat patients. Anonymity is not going
to solve the problem. We have enough problems of anonymity in our patients. The question is, what do they feel about
us? This becomes the crucial element, and of course it
places a tremendous demand upon the analyst. It complicates his life considerably, but I think that if it is done
discriminately and judiciously, with therapeutic awareness,
with analytic insight, it can be useful, again, discriminately
useful. For some patients it can be disturbing and perhaps
even harmful. On the other hand, I see no reason why
analysts cannot visit the patient in the patient's home if
the patient cannot come to the office. The idea is to treat
the patient. You don't have to make a couch call, but you
can make a house call. This may be the only way to help
some people.

Irv: Or in the hospital, for instance.

Mannie: In the hospital, or in the home if the patient is sick, or
even in the social community. This is part of our not always
being in obscurity and anonymity, and in the darkness of
our analytic chambers. We have to get some light and some
air on ourselves as well as on the whole experience. This
is my feeling about it and I wanted to say it. I want you
to see me. I am willing to expose myself and let you see me.
If I make errors, I'll work at trying to correct them.

Gerry: We do need that closed-circuit TV. That's all there is to it.

5

Models, Roles, and
Individuation of the Patient

The ultimate goal of any psychotherapeutic intervention is to help the patient achieve growth, maturity and individuation. Whatever the theoretical model, whatever the clinical technique, whether the treatment be carried on in a dyadic mode or in the group, the objective is the same. We are responsible to and for the individual, the individual in interaction, whether we see him in individual treatment or in the group.

Though most therapists would agree that this is true, often the therapist attempts to force the patient to fit the theory rather than to use the theory to understand the patient and to modify it in the light of what is learned in the clinical transaction. In this chapter we discuss analytic neutrality, regression, transference, patient selection, and the choice of the therapeutic modality in terms of patient necessities as contrasted to rigid adherence to a theoretical model or technique.

Irv: I want to say one thing about our discussion last week. You said that our model of psychoanalysis was antiquated. I think that this is a semantic problem. I would like to define what my model is and then see what our differences are. The model that I have in mind is the one which Karl Menninger talks about in his 1958 book.[27] The model you have in mind may involve a different concept as far as the extent of interaction in which the analyst engages in the individual analytic setting. But it seems to me that my model is one that is currently used by most orthodox analysts.

Mannie: It was not Al last week who said that.

Irv: No, I know that was you Mannie; I was just saying hello to Al and you.

Mannie: It was I who stuck my neck out on that one.

Irv: Yes, I know.

Mannie: All right, Irv, I'm not sure that I am for Menninger's model either.

Irv: Oh, I'm not saying that the model is a good one.

Mannie: I have read Menninger's book on technique. Let's remember what he says. He is convinced that theoretically it is possible to conduct an entire analysis without the analyst at any time saying a single word. Menninger makes this unambiguous statement.

Irv: He makes this statement, but I do not think he makes it as forcefully as that.

Mannie: Probably I'm more forceful than he is. He actually says that it is theoretically possible from his position to conduct an entire analysis in which the analyst does not say a single word. He knows that it is not practically or operationally possible, but this is his model. Of necessity such a model must be rejected the moment you accept the possibility of doing analytic work of any kind in a group setting. The moment you are committed to working in a group, you have to give up this model because the anonymity of the analyst is immediately lost. You are immediately showing yourself. What I meant by saying that you are no longer in the current stream is because even orthodox analysts in practice recognize that you must show yourself. The literature today is continuously focusing on countertransference rather than on transference. Today the emphasis is upon what is the role, what is the function, what are the activities of the analyst? The function of analysis, no matter what your model, is a commitment to making unconscious processes conscious. This is our commitment as analysts; this is central. As such it is not limited to a technique, whether couch or no couch.

Gerry: Well, Mannie, I think that you stated it clearly. I have read over last week's session and we covered these issues pretty closely. I did not feel so strongly when you said it was a cockeyed model, but Irv did! This may be because of the way you said it rather than the concept. I think you pointed out that there are people who tend toward this notion of an analysis without saying a word. You also pointed out that there is a lot of thinking which is contrary to this. I do not know whether we can gain anything by hashing it all over.

Mannie: I agree with you, Gerry. I want to say this to Irv. You have your model. See what adaptations you have to make in terms of the real necessities of patients. Remember that the orthodox model is based upon the orthodox position, that only healthy patients can be analyzed. That is, if a person is more quantitatively and qualitatively ill, more sick than neurotic, you should not do analysis with him. This is still the orthodox position. Most of the patients that I see here at our clinics are sicker than the kinds of neurotics for whom the orthodox analysts believe psycho-analysis in the classical sense is appropriate.

Gerry: I wonder, Mannie, does this have something to do with Szasz's recent article?[43]

Mannie: Yes sir.

Gerry: Just in the last issue of the *American Psychologist* he said that the training analysts were setting up even more rigid criteria than they had before for training candidates. They would rule out those applicants who have overt pathology, whatever that would be.

Irv: There is just one other issue which I think we should discuss. I don't know if it is worthwhile to spend the time on it today. It is the point that some analysts say that regression is essential in an analysis. You must regress the patient. Now I know that working from the model of group analysis you do things that are different than what you would do in classical individual analysis. These other procedures may be even more therapeutic for many patients. However, I think that the idea that an individual must re-experience in relationship to the analyst the actual early conflicts and that the analysis of this is what is essentially therapeutic is the keystone of analytic theory.

Mannie: All right, let's do it now. Regression is necessary and always occurs. Regression exists the moment you establish a transference relationship. Remember that transference is a term, a concept, that applies to the analytic situation in which the patient relates to the analyst in an as-if way. This as-if is by definition regressive. In whatever we have written we have said that in the group more activity occurs than in the individual situation; that is, there is more activity of every kind, more material of every kind, regressed and pathological as well as more positive and healthy material. The issue is: To what extent must the patient regress in order to benefit from the therapeutic experience? This is the central issue, and I should like to formulate this general hypothesis for myself as follows: It will depend upon the necessity, the pathology and the positive potentials of each individual patient, as to the extent to which he must regress. There are those who are committed to the idea that a therapeutic psychosis is necessary if reconstructive work is to be done. Such concepts start with Melanie Klein, who believes that the adult patient must go through the paranoid and depressive phases of child development. It goes along with the Sullivanian concept that you have to break through the self system; that is, the ego boundaries must be destroyed in order for the patient to regress sufficiently to be reconstructed and reborn. In principle these practitioners have not demonstrated their ideas. Theoretically and clinically I would reject this for patients whose ego boundaries have already broken down. If you are dealing with a very well-supported and defended neurotic with lots of ego strength, you may permit a deeper regression in terms of the transference relationship. If you work with a person who is regressed, whose self system is already destroyed, whose ego boundaries are so fluid that he has no sense of personal integrity or stability, then to use this model routinely, rigidly, and mechanically and to apply it to him is not to serve the patient well. The classical model of treating a schizophrenic analytically as described by Kurt Eissler in his 1951 article in the *International Journal of Psychoanalysis* is that before you can analyze a schizophrenic, you must first build the ego and its defenses, repress the psychosis, and then analyze for an understanding of and a coping with the nature of that psychotic experience. You cannot analyze a person who is in psychosis, according to the orthodox analytic position. So let us be very cautious about saying that all patients must be regressed to the same level. Every patient regresses the moment he accepts the authority and the transference position of the analyst. The question is to what extent do we encourage it. Every time you ask for a patient's dream, you are supporting and encouraging the regression and the transference. One of the best ways technically of deepening the transference is to ask for dreams and to work with dreams because you encourage the illusory, the nonreal, the unconscious material. The way in which you de-emphasize, attenuate, the transference and the regression is to talk about the intercurrent realities, to deal with current life situations on an ego level. A good analysis for me is to find that happy mixture of emphasis upon ego and unconscious material which is appropriate for this particular patient, but which may or may not be an appropriate admixture for any other patient.

Irv: You mentioned that you do a lot of individual analysis, and at our first meeting the question was raised, Which patient is a poor candidate for a group? For which patient is a group a poor setting in which to work, and for which is it the best setting?

Al: I think you can put a psychotic patient in a group. For example, I had one psychotic patient in a group who insisted on telling dreams exclusively. I took the position with him that I did not want to hear his dreams, at least not exclusively. I would let him tell a dream occasionally, but later in the course of treatment, I told him, "I don't want to hear any more about your dream," but I would ask someone else for a dream. I think you must take a differentiated position with patients in a group. Some need to be confronted with reality more appropriately and should not be encouraged to get into a regressed state; whereas with others, such as neurotic patients, who as Mannie says have a stronger ego, you may ask for dreams. It depends upon what the person needs. Generally you can work with any kind of a patient in the group.

Irv: So group could be the mode of treatment for whomever you are treating, generally speaking?

Mannie: Every treatment mode is uniquely individual in my estimation. There are no mechanical rules. I think such would be a misconception of psychoanalytic treatment. Read Freud's case studies. He never treated any two patients alike. He analyzed Gustav Mahler in one day walking through the forest. Where is the couch there? Where is the model there? Where is the anonymity? Where is the regression?

Irv: But that would not be considered analysis, would it?

Mannie: Freud considered it analysis and wrote it up as such. Freud performed analyses lasting only three to six months. Now some analyses last eighteen and twenty years, and even more for analysts.

Gerry: Stop it!! In other words, you feel that one must be discriminating. You cannot treat each patient alike even in individual analysis.

Irv: Yes, but now the question is, Why individual analysis at all then, if the group is such a successful medium? When should you recommend individual therapy for a patient and when group therapy? Can you deal with an obsessive compulsive and work through this type of character structure? Can you work through with a phobic patient? If you can do all of this in a group, then why undertake individual analyses?

Mannie: A good question.

Al: I have trained a nonmedical analyst to do analysis in groups. She has confronted me with what she says is a reality; namely, you can treat any patient in a group better than you can treat him individually. Now I think this is a somewhat nondiscriminative position. I have apparently so convinced her of the merits of group that she says it is a countertransference problem which prevents me from putting everybody in a group. Now I think there are certain people who require longer preparation before entering group therapy.

Irv: That is a good point. In other words, at what point do you introduce a person into a group? Can you put a person right into a group, or does it depend upon the individual? How much preparation is necessary?

Al: Usually I put patients in after one consultation. A great many of them are people who have had individual analysis.

Irv: What if they have not had any previous psychotherapy?

Al: I would say if they have not had any previous psychotherapy, this should be explored with them. The whole question of how they feel about group should be explored with them. For example, I have a patient whom I have been treating for three years. She is a very isolated person and I would like to put her into a group. I have not been able to help her work through her panic yet about being with people. While she is much more secure with me now, she still resists entering a group. I feel she will come around to the point where I can introduce her into a group.

Gerry: Say, this presents a question, Al, that has come up with me. I have one group which has not had an alternate session yet. In this group is one girl who, when I talked about the idea, became very fearful of the idea of meeting without me. She calls it being alone. She is dependent and close to a few people in the group. She has been in the group for almost three years, but she is very panicky about the introduction of the alternate session. I have been proceeding on the basis that she has the strength to take part in the alternate session. I think she can and I think that this is a resistive measure on her part, but I wonder, when you say this, whether I am being tough.

Al: In one way I believe if I could get this woman into group, she would be pleased. But I can't get her to take that step. There is another woman I have who is herself a therapist who had a very traumatic experience in a group with another group therapist. She has been considering returning to a group, and I think she should at some point and will, but first she should have a more positive experience in individual analysis, a more positive experience with me and feel much more secure with me before she starts group.

Irv: Well, from a theoretical point of view I was wondering whether it is not advisable for a new patient who has not had any psychotherapy at all to at least develop some kind of a positive relationship with the therapist first or whether the therapist should not explore history before he introduces the patient into a group.

Al: Yes, I would say that is probably so. I, for one, would like to introduce patients into a group when there is both a realistic, relatively secure rapport between the patient and the therapist as well as a positive transference. It would of necessity be negative too, but the prevailing feeling toward me should be positive. There would be some attachment, some security with the therapist. In practice I do not always find myself able to do this because of time problems or of finances. The patients cannot always afford the kind of preparation I would like to give them.

6

Interaction as
Associational Flow

Group therapists are faced with the problem of formulating a model of the group therapeutic process from which will flow the direction of their therapeutic intervention.

A group may be treated as a whole with interpretations to the total group in the model of some of the English group therapists, such as Bion,[6] Foulkes,[14] and Ezriel.[11] One may engage in individual therapy in the group, taking one person at a time, with the others serving as onlookers—a technique similar to the position of Perls and Moreno. It is possible to attempt to treat the individual through the group process as do Whitaker and Lieberman[47] in their model of "Focal Conflict Group Therapy." One may use selectively with each patient the multilateral interactions of the members of the group as one would use the associative flow in individual analysis, in accord with the position of Wolf and Schwartz.[51]

This latter conceptualization is committed to the idea that the reparative influence in psychoanalysis in groups stems not only from the therapist's interventions, but from the transactions with the co-patients as well.

Any theoretical model and technique of intervention may be

used in the service of some unconscious dynamic need. Unresolved symbiotic needs in the therapist may determine his homogenization of the group and treatment of the group as a whole, as if the group were one person. This same determinant could lead to the analysis of each patient separately, while others look on, as the major focus of therapeutic activity.

Some group therapists worry about contamination of the intrapsychic productions of one patient by another patient's interaction. The unconscious dynamic determinant of such a concern might be related to unresolved primal scene conflicts, unresolved compulsive compartmentalization conflicts, or unresolved conflicts about impregnation fantasies, among others.

The interactive flow may be focused on in a way that differentiates and individuates the patients in the group or, on the contrary, that loses sight of the individual and treats everyone the same.

Mannie: Okay, fire away.

Gerry: First, we ought to gratify you guys a little bit. Nicky got to the alternate meeting. She started talking. They did not report what she said. One of the girls said in the regular meeting that they felt they would like to hear her talk in the regular meeting and say some of the things that she felt about me that apparently were expressed in the alternate. She talked previously in response to some urging by me in individual sessions; but now that she does not have any individual sessions, I don't know what this change will mean.

Al: What impact is the alternate meeting having on the others in the group and on yourself?

Gerry: For me I find that it is a good idea. I am enthused. The other members of the group seem exhilarated. They come in and they are giddy. When they come into the regular session they seem to be giddy, to be interacting with one another and not as afraid of me or ignoring me a little bit more in the regular session. And they are saying to each other, "How come you're so different in here?" and "How come you're such a bossy guy at the alternate session?"or "You don't like to hear anything; you're always bitching." They asked Harry, "Why do you go to sleep in the regular session when you are a pretty nice host?" He is the man who is having the meetings at his house. But we have not gone too far on it. They have not said a lot and I have not tried to cross-examine them on their feelings about this because I felt it was extremely important from the point of view of Nicky that she feel that this was outside my purview, that I was not going to request a report.

Mannie: Good, wonderful.

Gerry: Now the members of the other group, when the idea of introducing the alternate was suggested, have all kinds of anxieties about it. They have fantasies of having some kind of an orgy outside of my sphere. They think that this will be the outcome of socializing and getting out together. They are all very much afraid at the same time. So I think I can see what you mean; the controls will be there anyway.

Al: It sounds very exciting. Of course, at some later date—

Gerry: Are you guys speaking into your microphone? You're very quiet.

Al: How's that?

Gerry: Much better.

Irv: Wonderful.

Al: At some point, maybe guided as much by Nicky's reticence as anybody else's, you can begin to—not ask what happened—but have some curiosity about the differences.

Gerry: Well, I did. I asked them for afterthoughts. I remembered you said something about that and I said, "I don't want a report, but I wonder if anybody had any afterthoughts." Ethel, the acting-out girl, was the one who said "Yes." She had some thoughts about it. She wanted to know how come Nicky would not talk in the regular session. She felt she ought to talk about some of these feelings that she has about me. I said to Ethel, "Well, maybe you have some feelings that aren't being expressed here. How do you feel? What is it that you feel you want Nicky to talk about?"

Mannie: Wonderful, wonderful.

Irv: Could you ask a question something like this: "Would the group go around on the difference you noticed in your feelings in the two settings?"

Al: Give them a chance to enjoy it.

Gerry: But what I tried to do with Ethel was focus on why she
wanted Nicky to express feelings, whatever they were,
about me. I interpreted that this was asking Nicky to
carry the ball. And so we went on on that basis. I think it
was good for Nicky because she laughed, she watched and
she responded in a nonverbal way and responded with a
yes or no to a few questions in the regular session. Oh,
another thing, my secretary noticed that Nicky came into
the waiting room after the first alternate session and smiled
and said hello to the secretary. She has never done this in
all the time she has been coming in. Usually she would
just walk in and sit down like a mummy on the couch and
stare at the floor of the waiting room.

Mannie: That's just wonderful.

Gerry: My secretary also noticed that Nicky was talking with the
other group members outside when they were waiting to
come in for their regular session. So apparently it is loosen-
ing her up, but there is a long way to go.

Mannie: Of course! Don't be impatient. Gerry, take a minute to tell
us about what happened in that individual session that
took place after the alternate. You said you asked questions
and she answered you. . . . What were the kinds of responses? What kinds of things did she respond to?

Gerry: This is important. I said to her, "I'm wondering whether
you were able to get to the alternate meeting on your own
or whether it was necessary for your mother to enable you
to get there. She said no, she had to go with her mother,
but then she responded—The spontaneous part was that
they had sat down and planned out the route and found
the place without any difficulty.

Mannie: Wait a minute. That sounds like the preceding week when
you had been planning with her as to whether one of the
other members of the group could pick her up. Remember?
Well, it sounds like she is talking about . . . doing her own
planning following your example of the week before.

Gerry: Yes, and then I noticed that she would respond. She has
never answered a question, even a direct question, before.
She seemed to be able to speak three, four, and five sentences. So I went on with other questions, trying generally

to see if she had any afterthoughts and feelings, and she would not answer. Every time I asked her a question about direct activity, she would talk. I said, "Well, have you been doing anything around the house? What have you been doing at home?" She didn't say anything; that was too broad. So I said, "Well, have you been doing any house-work?" And she said yes, she had done some ironing. Then she went on to say a few more things. So I found out that what she was responding to was action, without any thoughts about it. We went on in that vein for the whole hour. What I think came out of it, the most important thing, was this comment that her mother had to go with her to get her there, but she took part in planning how they would get there and she sometimes drives, but not all the time.

Mannie: Nicky sometimes drives?

Gerry: That's right.

Mannie: Very good, very good.

Al: Nicky will be a very interesting patient to study as a person who will have gotten the impetus to get well through the alternate meetings, through an experience alternatively without the presence of the authority figure. I would say that indications so far are that the alternate meetings are critically necessary for her and she is enjoying an immediate result. It works for her because of the way her mother is, because you believe she has the ability to rely on her own resources.

Gerry: You mean to focus on this aspect of it.

Al: The alternate meeting is a necessity for her. It is critical.

Gerry: I really feel that it is making a hundred per cent difference. I think I can work with her now where I was terribly frustrated before because there was no movement. She was like a wooden Indian.

Mannie: Yes, I think this is Al's meaning. Al says that this is a wonderful research example, a wonderful clinical piece of evidence of the value of the alternate session for certain patients. It is the difference between therapy and no therapy. That is what he means by a critical quality. Whether you say it to her or not is beside the point. You should be aware of the fact that the dynamics here represent some investment of confidence in her, some statement on the part of the authority figure, "Yes, you can have a life without me, outside of my orbit of influence; of course not too far outside."

Gerry: That's right, yes.

Mannie: But it is beginning to move in that direction, which means the possibility for her opening up and growing and being an independent human being.

Al: In the formation of a therapeutic group in the first place the therapist is saying to each patient, "You don't have to live and communicate only with authority, along the vertical vector. You can relate to other people as well, peers in the horizontal vector."

Gerry: And that can be healthy.

Al: And that, itself, is a movement toward health. But a further extension of this movement is if the patient works without the therapist in a growth-promoting situation; and that is the alternate meeting.

Gerry: Yes, I see. . . .

Irv: I would like to get to an issue that we have raised a number of times. Many group therapists are doing primarily individual therapy with a group looking on. They involve themselves with single patients, analyzing each patient independent of the group. They are not really dealing with the repetitive, interactional processes. They are not involving the other members. I know that this has been brought up by you a number of times and yet I think it is something that I tend to fall into doing. I feel sometimes that in trying to activate the group I am acting like a master of ceremonies. "How you you feel about this?" and "How do you feel about that?" I know that it was mentioned a few meetings ago that the group has to be educated to use certain therapeutic devices, like going around. I know that if you ask a patient's association to something he might say, "Well, my mind is a blank; nothing comes to my mind." If you were seeing him in an individual session, he might say, "My mind is blank," but then you would have a flow of associations from him for the rest of the hour. In the group you don't have that unless you then look at what happens in interaction or what the patients bring up later or how they feel later in the group. The thing I am concerned with is doing analysis in a group setting without doing individual therapy. Also, there is a subproblem, namely, what is the effect on the other patients, the contaminatory effect of one patient working through an oedipal problem; let's say working through a desire to kill me, working through an impulse to kill me as the oedipal parent?

Mannie: You don't have any such patients like that, do you, Irv?

Irv: What's that?

Mannie: Do you mean you have a patient who wants to kill you?

Irv: Who wants to kill me in terms of repetitions of his fantasies, in terms of killing his dad.

Mannie: That was meant to be facetious. But your anxiety indicates that maybe that is the problem with the group. I wanted to tell you an experience of mine in regard to what may be going on.

Irv: Okay.

Mannie: Maybe what you do in the individual situation is say to the patient, "What have you got on your mind?" And he says, "Nothing." Then you sit back and remain quiet until he talks, because you are convinced that something will occur and something does occur. He has to struggle with this resistance. He must come forward and produce. Perhaps in the group you get too anxious to be able to be silent. You say, "Have you got any associations?" and he says, "None," and then you have to do something with it instead of sitting back and waiting. If you can sit back and wait, then something would be done with it. Maybe somebody else might respond. In fact, rather than ask a particular one whether he has any association, you might think of saying, "Are there any associations?" and leave it for anybody to associate, even to his dream, for example. Are you experiencing more anxiety in terms of your own activity or inactivity in the group as contrasted with the individual situation?

Irv: In the individual situation I feel that I am not as active. I don't feel as much of a need to be as active in order to get patients to interact. This is going to be lessened after the groups have met in alternate sessions, I think, because they are going to have to be functioning and interacting. My need to get involved as much as I do will be lessened.

Al: I think there are a number of factors that go into our tendency to work with patients individually in the group. Perhaps there is a need on the part of the analyst to homogenize the group. It is a little easier to deal with one patient at a time, but if the analyst does this, he instructs the group in a way of working. He says to them, "You are my co-therapists or my assistants." In effect he tells them always to analyze and understand and work through with each patient, one at a time. Now this is a way of working and it is based partly, I think, on our training. We are trained to work with individual patients. Of course there might also be a countertransference problem. That is, once we are in a triangular situation ourselves, the person we are working with may, for us, be a symbolic father or mother. Let's say we are working with the projected father. If our relationship with this patient, who is a projected father, is one of anxiety or if we fear castration ourselves, we may go into a homosexual defense. We may then look for some attitude on the part of the rest of the group as the homogenized mother, or if we are dealing with the projected mother in a patient, we may, depending on our history, be dealing with this patient in a somewhat inappropriate way, as we try to cope with our own triangular anxieties. I think that for one thing, it is important to try to be aware of this possibility. Second, if a patient presents anything, before the therapist interprets, ask the other group members for their subjective reactions. You can also ask for their analytical reactions, but generally those are forthcoming. There are plenty of analysts around in any group. When somebody is being analyzed individually, I ask the rest of the group for their subjective reactions and generally I don't reward people for being analysts. It is true you can analyze only one person at a time. You cannot, even when there are two, or three or four people interacting, analyze these two, three, or four at the same time. You still have to take them one at a time. That is a concession to individual attention which we have to make.

As soon as you have worked this way, they will work this way following your example. If your example is not to reward the individual by giving him your total attention, the group will do likewise. Always turn and ask for an interaction, a subjective response. This provides multilateral experience in their working with each other. They will begin working this way and be very grateful because you are encouraging their interaction in a multilateral dimension.

Irv: This sounds very good and I wonder if you could exemplify it a little bit.

Al: Let's take the thing that is most personal, that is, hardest to deal with in a multilateral way; namely, the presentation of a dream. Usually when somebody offers a dream, we ask for associations. Often the group tries to interpret or analyze it. I would interfere at that point. I would ask them to give their subjective associations. Otherwise one patient presents a dream, the group analyzes it, the therapist adds his contribution, somebody else presents a dream, and the group analyzes it, and so on. Soon it becomes individual treatment with a group of analysts. In other words, dreams are the most individual and personal things that appear in a group. When people free associate to other people's dreams, they bring in their own problems and we see something that reflects their own psychodynamics.

Mannie: Let me elaborate on this. Irv, you were aware you used the word "contaminate," with reference to the effect of working through with one patient, thereby contaminating other patients.

Irv: What I meant was—

Mannie: I did not care what you meant; but I wanted to call it to your attention because I think it represents the kind of prejudice, the kind of necessity within yourself which is really behind the problem that you raised. That is, there is some view on your part that you must work individually lest you contaminate the other patients. That is, if you work with this person alone in secret in the individual situation, you can do anything with him. Nobody else is going to get hurt by it because you will analyze it. Now I think this view, that if you and I are talking about oedipal material and Al listens to our oedipal discussion he is going

Irv: to be hurt by it, contaminated with it, is the view that
           continues to perpetuate in you the necessity to work indi-
           vidually. This is one of the elements in your difficulty.

Irv: Well, I am wondering if it will intellectualize the patient
           who is not involved.

Mannie: Al has already pointed out that apparently you can intel-
           lectualize. But if you will deal with his subjectivity, his
           inner feelings, his own free associations, you will avoid this.
           However, if he is going to be intellectual, why worry about
           it being contaminating? He is not going to hurt the other
           patients if he is intellectual. The real problem comes when
           he's going to have a big emotional reaction to a working
           through of the oedipal situation or the association to
           oedipal material in someone else, which triggers off his
           anxiety with regard to the triangular situation. It is not the
           intellectual problem that you really are concerned about,
           so I think that you don't want to double talk yourself out
           of this situation here, Irv, but try to understand it. What
           you seem concerned about and I think rightfully, and it's
           the concern of everybody working in groups, is how far,
           by allowing multilateral interaction, do you disturb the
           equilibrium, the security, the stability, the homeostasis of
           other patients who vicariously participate in the inter-
           action?

Gerry: You said that when a patient tells a dream, this is really
           the most individual and private exposure. If someone tells
           a dream and then associates to it, I will ask the group,
           "Who has some associations to this, or does anyone have
           any associations to this?" as Al suggested earlier. Some-
           times they throw in some analytic comments, but very
           often they give subjective associations. Usually if one tells
           a dream, then they all look for this attention by telling
           their dreams, even though you may attempt to have the
           group give their subjective reactions. They avoid both their
           reactions and analytic interpretations in favor of telling
           their own dream.

Al: That is all right. There is a place for dreams in group
           analysis just as important as in individual analysis. All I am
           saying is that we should try as much as possible to get
           people to react subjectively to others' dreams.

Mannie: The fact that they look for attention is something that you will expect in terms of the competitive nature of their relationship to you. You will discover that if you are not working with an individual patient to the exclusion of the others in the group, they will not have the sense of deprivation and the need to be so competitive for your attention. They will feel that they are getting something out of the working through of one person's dream since they have all participated with their feelings. Incidentally, in that connection I believe—and this is quite different from Irv's feelings and maybe even yours, Gerry—that I am much more active and much more interactive in the individual situation than I am in the group situation. I believe that patients are much more interactive in the group than in the individual situation. I tend to pull back and let the group members interact among themselves, and the members take over more of the activity. I am the only stimulus, the only outside experience in the individual setting, whereas all the other members of the group tend to provide stimulation and provocation among themselves in the group.

Gerry: I think that's right, Mannie. I think I, myself, do not say as much in group as in individual sessions. I have another question and that's getting back to the technical—

Mannie: Wait a minute. Didn't Irv say that he seemed to find that he needed to be more active?

Irv: I think it varies. Let me say this, that I think I have gone through several phases in the way in which I have interacted in the group. Previously I let the group develop their resources, but now I think I may have been too inactive. I was operating on the group dynamic principle—let the group evolve, let the group do this, let the group do that; and not realizing that the therapist really is there to analyze and deal with the resistances and transferences, that he has an active role and that he is doing something other than group dynamics. I'm not running a group dynamic group, so that led me into a more active kind of phase.

Mannie: Right! Very good!

Irv: But now that I have the alternate sessions coming up, I think their interaction and dependence on their own resources will increase. My role is going to be different.

I can sit back and look for the repetitive factors that are occurring and try to deal with these. I think that the group will develop its own way of working through, but I agree that they will, of necessity, follow the example I set. That is what I wanted to explore this morning—a little bit more of what way one works with a group of patients without getting into the problem of doing individual therapy. For example, telling dreams. When a patient tells a dream, very often before the patient himself gives his own associations, someone else in the group is giving his thoughts and feelings about it.

Al: I would try to establish a way of operating. I think the dreamer should have the first opportunity to free associate to his dream.

Irv: And people should wait until he is finished.

Al: I don't know whether it needs to be that rigid, but that would be a general principle that I would try to adhere to because other members' associations are likely to interfere with his.

Irv: So we must get the dreamer's associations first. We must get his association first, free from the influence of the associations of the others.

Al: I think he deserves this freedom first. You asked for another illustration of how this operates. I have a group of analysts-in-training, in their third year. At the meeting before last I asked Jim to go around because I said he had been somewhat removed and remote after the first three sessions. He was terribly involved in the first three sessions, and about three weeks ago he raised his eyebrows when I said analysis was as effective in a group as it was individually. He asked, "Do you really believe that?" And I said, "Yes." Then I thought, "This man has retired after the first three sessions where he was very involved and very anxious; he worked something through." I think he worked it through largely in individual analysis. So I said to him that I thought he was talking in his individual analysis and not in the group and would he go around. We all reacted to the controlled way in which he spoke, very deliberately, very thoughtfully, with no spontaneity to it, very reasonably. Now, three people in the group attacked this behavior very hard. One said he was a phony, that he had a tremendous amount of hostility, that he was quite anxious about it and was afraid to demonstrate it. Another felt he was contemptuous. Still another felt he was self-righteous. Now Jim got very defensive, said he was honest, and so on and so on. There were things he said he could tell his individual analyst that he could not tell us. The three people who attacked him were able to explore their transferences to him, and even to struggle and explore possibilities and ways of their working through in the group. All this time Jim kept saying, "See, it's all your problem; it's all your problem." Now this got him angry again and I kept going back to him, telling him that I thought it could not all be their problems and even his insisting on this was somewhat an expression of a problem of his. By persisting in this attitude what we came to was . . . he started associating. He began to recount when he was five years old—from about five to the time he went to high school, he went to a boarding school. He felt very abandoned and there was a very sadistic schoolmaster who, if you did not know the answers and were not always the best student in the class, you got whipped. Now he managed to be very anxious but always the best in the class and had to be very competitive with his classmates because if any of them were better than he was, he was liable to get whipped, so he had compulsively to show his thoughtfulness and reasonableness there in group and demonstrate to me as the sadistic schoolmaster that he was beyond criticism and beyond reproach. He acts this out all the time in any group situation. But we got to this with a hell of a lot of struggle. I think what I am trying to demonstrate here, in this going around, is that several people were exploring their transferences. The member who was going around himself was acting something out that we finally got him to look at. Now I think if you work this way, you're not working individually.

Gerry: Yes, I think I see your point.

7

Autonomy
Versus Ritual

In the course of the learning experience students frequently bypass their peers and focus exclusively on the authority. In so doing they deny their own as well as peer resources and over-idealize the authority.

In this session the participants explore their feelings about conformity, traditions, rituals, and community acceptance. The trainees reveal their emotional necessity to cling to tradition in spite of the teachers' exhortation to be innovative and let the structure be determined by the current realities and inventive response to necessities.

Irv: Another thing that we were wondering about was the possibility of formalizing our study program a bit more.

Mannie: After we hung up last weekend, Al and I began to talk about what was going on. We should talk about how we are doing and where we are going. One of the things I said to Al was that we talk about the importance of letting patients do whatever they can do with one another and for the therapist to remain out of the situation except insofar as he enters in with his expertness. He should let them interact, and there is a need to hold back and be more passive because of the group situation tending to demand greater activity of the therapist. I then told Al that the impression that I get is that we do not encourage you two to interact. What we do is talk to each one of you separately as you present and never give you two a chance to interact. What do you think of that?

Gerry: Well, I have looked over the notes and noticed that there are only a few places where there is an interchange between Irv and me.

Mannie: Yes. In fact, if you noticed, I tended to say, "Hi Irv; hi Gerry." What do you think of that?

Irv: Yes, in other words, we have been more or less talking in a singular dimension.

Mannie: Right. I think we ought to examine this. I have a hunch that there is a similarity to what happens in group therapy in what was happening here, though of a different order. I said to Al, "I believe that what they do is talk to each other in the alternate sessions!" That is, during the week you have meetings and you talk about your concerns about learning, but while we are around you don't interact with one another; you relate exclusively and individually with us.

Irv: I think we are depending upon you two as the authority figures. We are not trying to work things out between ourselves. I suppose that our working between ourselves does come during the week.

Mannie: That is what I thought. Certainly I think we ought to try to get you two to interact with each other instead of our trying to be so expert and answer every one of your questions immediately upon demand. In the long run you have to utilize yourselves during the week without intervention.

Irv: Of course! We have before we met with you fellows and we have to anyway, naturally. But the thing is—I guess we have been relying upon you two very heavily.

Mannie: This is the basis of all good supervision, to keep focusing on your interaction, your own involvement and basically the countertransference problems. I wonder whether the plea this morning, "Let's structure this more," is not a way to try to escape from that focus. This is not a lecture system although there is no reason why we cannot incorporate lectures. But the beauty and the value of supervision is that it is a control analysis; that is, the analyst becomes familiar with his own functioning vis-à-vis a patient or a group of patients.

Gerry: Irv's question reflects the feeling I have too. One thing we do want is supervision, but we would like something more than this.

Irv: We have two problems. What you say is quite correct but we do not have anything around here that can offer us the type of formal structured course work that you have in New York City.

Gerry: When you are supervising someone, he may be also in some formal training.

Irv: Or at least you presuppose some formal training prior to supervision.

Mannie: Yes, I suppose so, but you know formal training came after analysis and control analysis. I wonder whether you really are not continuing, at least emotionally, the attitude that reading is not sufficient. If I were to tell you, if I were to read it to you, if I were to say to you what we and others say in articles and books, this would be more structured.

Irv: Well, I do not necessarily need lectures if we can organize along certain readings. The question is, Why do you formalize a three-year training program? Why do you have a course on dream interpretation, a course on psychoanalytic thinking, and a course on the borderline patient, etc?

Mannie: We do this perhaps because we are victims of conformity and of ritual. I have a hunch that we do not know and we may never know what is the best way to make an analyst. We really don't know. In fact, I have raised this again and again as a director of training and have said, "How do we know that the best way to make an analyst is to follow this traditional curriculum?" I have just done a survey with the aid of one of my assistants of methods of training in this field. There is not a new idea that has come up in the last fifty years. The one new experimental idea was that someone decided that perhaps a course in nonsense syllables was needed, that is, to expose an analyst-to-be to streams of nonsense language where he would have to respond to the emotions behind the communication so that he would be encouraged to think about the latent aspect rather than to respond to the manifest content. It is a problem of all analysts-to-be. This is the only bright, new idea in teaching; the curriculum itself has never been questioned. You teach a course in dreams, you teach a course in technique, you teach a course in psychopathology, psychodynamics, and so on. You asked me a question. I gave you the only answer I can.

Irv: Let me get at the latent meaning of it then, which is more apropos. I think what we are really asking is, Can you help us and train us to be analysts?

Mannie: This is what we have been doing. I think that when you ask for more structure, it reflects some anxiety. I think we ought to talk about the anxiety because we accepted this contract to teach you, a social contract mutually agreed upon. At least from my understanding this is what we are doing.

Irv: To train us to be analysts then?

Mannie: Obviously. We would not train you to be engineers or geologists. What have we been doing these last few weeks?

Gerry: Mannie, I think that the anxiety that Irv states and I feel is the one that we have spoken about a lot of times before. It is this. It would be nice if in accord with our long list of credentials and getting this kind of supervision and training, we could have some nice, formal program with a nice union card.

Mannie: Yes. You are still worried about your community's attitude toward you.

Gerry: Well, yes, I think it is the community . . .

Mannie: I wish you two would take a trip into New York in the next couple of months to see a new show that opened on Broadway.

Irv: I heard about it; my wife was telling me about it.

Mannie: It is called *The Far Country*. It is a good play, the story of Dora. It is Freud's struggle against tremendous odds, against the rejection of not only the community, but his mother, his wife and his best friend because of his daring to explore the human mind. There were great odds against him. It is well done, with dignity and feeling. You see that this is still the necessity even though it is seventy-five years later. All of us who are committed to psychoanalysis continuously are faced with rejection by the community anyway. It is in part because of the nature of man's resistance to being aware of his own inner mechanisms. This is why we do analysis: so that people know why they are anxious. In this instance you know it has something to do with some latent feeling of insecurity in yourself which gets latched onto the reality. Yet you still respond to the anxiety with the question, Can we instruct you? Can we solve it by changing the world? You have to face the fact that we are pioneering in this activity, supervising and training you over the telephone. We really do not know what the outcome will be.

Gerry: This may be the way in which we can look at a different kind of training. We brought up the questions, How do you train an analyst anyway? and, Is the formalized program at the Institute the one and only way? Our experience here is certainly an innovation as much as is the idea of using nonsense syllables.

Mannie: Of course. And like all other new ideas they follow necessities. You had a need and we said, "What can we do to meet your need?"

Irv: And that seems to be the way in which inventions work anyway. There is a need and you try to meet the need in some way or other. I had the feeling that the alternate session was something devised on that basis as well.

Mannie: I think you are right. I have always thought that Al originated the alternate session because he recognized that if he was going to treat a lot of people in a limited amount of time, he would have to give them something else, something additional.

Irv: Yes, that is my feeling about how it originally came about, and then it was worked out in terms of its theoretical and clinical implications.

Mannie: Maybe. You know, he is very honest. When he sees our transcript of this, he will tell us if it came out of his necessity or out of the necessities of the patients. Probably it came in part of his necessities and some of his anxieties about how much he was giving to them. I have talked about these kinds of things with Al for years, that out of our own necessities we do things with patients. We see this in the training of young therapists who think up a new gimmick to reach a patient because they are terribly anxious about not doing enough for the patient. We had a trainee many years ago. I thought this student was disturbed. I thought she knew little about formal psychology or psychotherapy. But she was magnificent with schizophrenic patients. She was available to them twenty-four hours a day. She loved them, she supported them, she was concerned about them, she protected them, she was always available. And these very seriously sick schizophrenic patients improved! Now, I do not know whether this was analytic; I do not know whether this was "good therapy"; but nevertheless she helped these people and nobody could deny it!

Irv: I am just trying to figure out why you brought in that example.

Mannie: Because I think that she had some need to do something extra because she realized her limited skills as an analyst. She had to give them something of herself and so she made herself available twenty-four hours a day. I think all of us are in part masochistic. We have to have some masochism in us to be able continuously to take the abuse that gets handed out by patients daily in the normal course of work and not retaliate, and make no personal demands on the patient. We have no right to make demands except that we be paid for our time and skill. The needs of the patient are central. It is the basis of the contractual arrangement. Now the question is, How far can you go? Do you have the stomach to take feces rubbed in your hair, the way Frieda Fromm-Reichmann did? I have not the stomach for it. Yet obviously her necessity, her capacity or personal being in which she could take this, made a contribution in terms of a new movement in understanding how to work with a schizophrenic patient.

Irv: What you are pointing out is that the pathology of the therapist is a crucial determinant of what type of work he undertakes with patients.

Mannie: Let me put it this way, his pathology *and* his strength. I do not think it is only the pathology which determines it.

Irv: Well, you have to have strength as well.

Mannie: Exactly. Also your resources or potentialities. I think it is the person of the therapist that very often determines how he will practice, with whom he will practice, under what kind of conditions and so on. Even if the social necessities call for one thing, he may or may not be able to meet it. He may have to change and create some new necessities.

Irv: You have given us a lot of things to think about here today. Gerry and I have had anxieties which are related to feelings about formal training. I suppose we could spend the hour on it, but now I would like to talk a little bit about a case I have that I am seeing in individual therapy and speculate about what could be done in group therapy. Let's take a look at it from what is happening in individual therapy and see if this patient could really be handled in group therapy. It is a case of a twenty-year-old boy who was referred to me by his minister. He attends the university. He came in because he was upset by sexual impulses. He had a collection of pornographic literature and he thought that this was not in conformity with his plan to be a minister. Since the age of four he has had a masturbation fantasy. He imagines, while lying naked on the bed and masturbating, that he is a woman. He imagines he is ruler of the universe and he rules everybody in a very sadistic and controlling manner. His mother died of multiple sclerosis when he was about six or seven. He had considerable difficulty with his stepmother and more particularly his father, who is an agnostic. He himself is religious. His father is always tearing down the son's religious ideas. I will not get into too much of the history here except to try to focus on an hour that I had with him.

Mannie: Good, go ahead.

Irv: Characterologically he shows a severe obsessive-compulsive character structure with considerable hostility seeping through. He is rigid, very isolated, very bright, an intellectualizing sort of chap. Now—

Mannie: Irv, before you get into the case, how many times a week do you see him?

Irv: I see him twice a week.

Mannie: How long have you seen him?

Irv: I have seen him since December.

Mannie: I see. You have seen him about five months and that means you have seen him about ten times a month, about fifty sessions.

Irv: Yes, something like that.

Mannie: All right, let's stop a minute. Gerry, are you with us?

Gerry: I am here. I am with you.

Mannie: All right now, Gerry, what do you think treating a patient like this is like? Give us your fantasy about it. What do you think the treatment process is going to look like? How do you think he is going to relate to Irv?

Gerry: I find myself stumped. I think that someone like this is probably going to be very unspontaneous in his hours. I do not know what he is like, but I feel that he would need to be cranked up. He would have to be pushed and I wonder if, in working with him in individual sessions, this is what sessions are like: him squeezing out a few pieces of information and sitting and waiting and maybe having to crank him up, crank him up, and crank him up to get him to talk in order to learn about what is going on. I do not know. Maybe on the other hand he does talk a lot. I would see him as someone who in a group might be withdrawn. I don't know. You have not had him in a group though.

Mannie: Say, Gerry, do you think he will make any homosexual passes at Irv?

Gerry: Sure, I think he will. I do not know how, what way.

Mannie: Irv, what do you think of Gerry's responses?

Irv: I think they are kind of rigid and rather stereotyped. I don't know why he has that image of what an obsessive-compulsive would be like. It must be related to the type of patients he has worked with and maybe how he sees himself. I don't know. Of course, I feel a little hostility towards Gerry today anyway, so I—

Mannie: Oh, is that right? Why?

Irv: What?

Mannie: Do you want to talk about it?

Irv: No, I would rather not talk about it.

Mannie: Do you want to tell us what happened with this patient? Go ahead. What did happen? How did he function?

Irv: Well, let me tell you about his functioning in the past five months. He originally desired treatment when he came in. Shortly thereafter he felt he had no problem at all and that he was really healthy. He completely avoided going into his history or talking about his early fantasies or any of his sexual problems. He focused upon minor difficulties at home. He was anxiety stricken by the arousal of his homosexual feelings about me, and he immediately became infatuated with a girlfriend at school. This was the first time he had ever dated a girl. The first three months of therapy he was involved with the girl and that obscured practically everything. I was able to point out the defensive nature of what he was doing in his attempt to escape from therapy.

Mannie: Just one minute. You recognize the definition of flight into health in your case there, don't you? The flight into health is not only a defense against his homosexual interest in you, but his defense against exposing his pathology, his feelings, to the analyst. He is, in other words, defending himself against treatment by taking a flight from his illness into an assertion of what is health, in terms of what he feels is his illness.

Irv: Right.

Mannie: And this is a characteristic way of resisting the very acceptance of treatment. This is not unusual; it is quite characteristic. It may not be as dramatic as this in other instances, but you will find a piece of this in practically every patient entering analysis. They will do something in the beginning to maneuver the situation in such a way as to assert the denial of their illness. Do you get the point?

Irv: Right, right.

Mannie: All right, go on.

Irv: In the past month he has really begun to work. He has begun to wonder about his masculinity. In a denial form he says, "Well, good gosh, I don't think I have any latent homosexual problems." And his concern about himself and whether he regards himself as masculine or not has come up. The concern was voiced originally in a displaced kind of way, worrying about some of the problems of some of the ministers whom he has met who were somewhat effeminate. Then later he spoke of his own concern with respect to his own masculinity. During this period he transferred to me as father and I have become the person who is going to criticize him, beat him, laugh at his religion. Anybody with education is going to laugh at the fact that he is religious. Until recently he in no way connected his fantasy of being a woman, which he has had for a long time, with feelings of being feminine. In his last hour he presented two dreams. One dream had to do with two ministers dressed up in special garments who were taking part in a special kind of liturgy. He had spoken of receiving the sacrament of holy communion. He spoke of it in a rather hungry way. He felt that the trouble with his religion is that they do not serve the sacrament often enough and he wanted to get the sacrament. In this particular dream when he associated to what came into mind when he saw the ministers dressed in their liturgical garb, his jaw dropped and he appeared quite shocked. Then he said, "Well, they are dressed something like women. But that would not be my reason for being interested in liturgy; that's fantastic." Then he spoke a little bit about the possibility that maybe his interest in liturgy may be related to feminine fantasies. Then he spoke during the remainder of the hour of the sacrament of communion, of wanting to be an Episcopalian, of wanting to get the sacrament served to him. He said he was always interested in more orthodox forms of worship. Finally he said, "I've always respected authority." When he said that I raised my eyebrows and asked, "You have?" He looked at me and said, "What do you mean?" I said, "Well, you certainly do not seem to have gotten along well with the authority of your father." This, it seemed to me, provided the essential link in his associations and he began to relate his feelings toward his father and his feelings toward the church and the nonconformist position which he has. I suspected as he was talking about this that this whole religious commitment of his was his peculiar way of trying to work out his oedipal conflict with his father by trying to oust father by his religious involvement and at the same time satisfy his homosexual, feminine wishes. He associated to the church being his adopted family, and he spoke about how he is even more conservative than his church. He is working out his father rebellion even in his church. Much later, after being placed in a treatment group, it became evident that his longing for the orthodoxy was a religious derivative of his longing for his "true" mother, who had died when he was a youngster, and a rejection of the stepmother. The liturgical interest and demand for liturgical (feminine) attire were also derivatives of the desire for fusion with mother. Then he said, "But I can't tell you all that stuff; I feel that you just don't know anything about it." Then I related it to his father and said, "Well, if you were talking to your father, would you feel the same way?" He said yes, he wouldn't know anything about that; I would have to explain it to him too. In talking about the communion and feeling that he wanted to be an Episcopalian because he could not get enough of the communion, I said, "Well, what is it you want?" He said, "I want the presence of the Lord through the bread and the wine." I asked him further about this and he said he wanted the "symbolic presence of the Lord" and then later he said, "I really want the real, objective presence. I feel I don't apprehend the Lord." At some point I asked, "Well, if you really felt His presence, where would you feel it?" He answered, "Physiologically. I mean with my feelings." I asked, "What do you mean?" He said, "Right in the pit of my stomach I suppose." I said, "In your stomach?" And he said, "Good God, you don't think I have any cannibalistic fantasies or desires?"

Mannie: He had two dreams, did I understand that?

Irv: He had two dreams, one—

Mannie: That was one of them?

Irv: I forget what the other one is.

Mannie: It was presented at the same session, reported in the same session, but you don't recall it?

Irv: I don't recall it.

Mannie: Interesting!

Irv: I don't know why I do not recall it.

Mannie: That is interesting. Okay, let's get Gerry's reactions to all of this.

Gerry: I am back where Irv said he is hostile to me today and he does not want to say why. I do not get this, but at any rate I feel like—I don't have any comments on this.

Irv: The point I was raising is this. Here we are seeing that this patient's particular religious interests are in rebellion against his father. Most of what is coming up now is on the basis of his fantasy. It is an intrapsychic kind of exploration. Of course, it is manifested by the kind of rebellion he has at home with his father and their difficulties. The question is, in group therapy how would you be able to deal with—

Gerry: Well, you would not know unless he was in the group and could see how he activates this material. You were just starting the dream when I went and changed the tape.

Irv: In this hour all of this very personalized material, the dream, the associations to religion, to what it means to him, all unfolded so to speak. Now the point is, in a group it would not unfold that way; it would not come up that way. I am sure in a group someone probably would say to him, "Why are you interested in this anyway?" And he would probably talk about his interest in liturgy in some way and I am sure we would understand it. But the pathology would express itself in a different kind of way.

Mannie: Perhaps in the same way! For instance, he has a strong piece of resistance in the fact that you are a Jew and not an Episcopalian. He knows this, Irv. This is reality. He also says you are a man and therefore you do not understand this any more than his father. He knows this and this is a reality. But in a heterogeneous group, where there are some women, he might turn to a woman and say, "Of course *you* would not understand this," or to somebody who is an Episcopalian or a Methodist he might say the same. There might be somebody in the group who would not be as agnostic as you might be. He does not really know whether you are agnostic or not. He has made you symbolically the father who is agnostic. But obviously there might be somebody in the group who is a believer, someone who is more accepting and supportive of his position. You cannot have a problem with men without having a problem with women. In other words, all of us have problems with both men and women, to the extent that we have problems at all. You get the point? Gerry, are you with us?

Gerry: Yes, very frustratedly so.

Mannie: Go ahead, take a moment.

Gerry: I don't know; I am pouting. I cannot say anything.

Mannie: Looks like you two guys need to clear up your hostility before you can interact with one another.

Gerry: I felt in regard to this patient that you seem not to look at what other ramifications these ceremonies and all these things had. For instance, he had these two women creating communion.

Mannie: Remember, these are men dressed as women. These are not women, but men dressed as women. He is hiding the masculine problem he is hiding.

Gerry: Well, what I was getting at was that they were giving him some kind of food and that was . . .

Irv: . . . ceremony; I don't think it was the communion though.

Mannie: That was an association he got to in the course of his speculations, isn't that right, Irv?

Irv: Yes. Then he started to talk about communion and wanting to retain his religion and to be a crypto-Episcopalian so he could get more communion.

Mannie: And he is going to be a Catholic before you get through with him.

Gerry: Well, the point is he wanted to get fed though. He wanted to get fed in a mysterious way by a man who is dressed like a woman who makes food.

Mannie: Isn't that really what the homosexual maneuver is?

Gerry: Yes. But I do not know enough about what this patient, what these things mean to this man, all of these various things; whether you, whether your preconception—

Mannie: Gerry, don't get defensive yourself. Everyone of the patients in your group would probably say this when you ask for associations to the dream. One is entitled to have a fantasy and to be stimulated to have one's own fantasies and free associations even if one does not know, so long as one recognizes that this is fantasy and not fact. Patients will say to you, "You know I cannot associate to the presentation of a dream of another patient because I do not know enough about him." There is still room for you to take a flyer. I do not know any more than you do—

Gerry: Well, I can't ever see anything in a blank card.

Mannie: I don't know any more about Irv's patient than you do, yet I am willing to associate to it.

Gerry: As I say, that is my problem. I cannot associate to a blank card. I want more information.

Irv: Well, I can . . .

Mannie: You are being defensive about something. Okay, have your fun. Why don't you have an alternate session, and struggle with it.

Irv: Listen, I think one of the problems is that in order for us all to interact an hour is not really enough time.

Mannie: Oh, an hour is a lot of time. Stop complaining. You are putting the problem outside of ourselves. If you have five minutes, you can still enjoy it. Enjoy five minutes! You do not have to have four hours. Have whatever the reality offers and enjoy it. If you are free to enjoy it, to make the most of it, do it; but do not put the problem outside of ourselves.

Irv: Well, I think that in terms of myself, I have been more eager to get the experts to tell me things than just to take a flyer like you did and just talk and discuss some of these things.

Mannie: One of these days you two have to be experts too. You cannot always have us as experts. You know, this is part of your growing up.

Irv: I think there has to be some reality too. For example, there should be some reading we should be doing or something . . .

Mannie: I would like to make a recommendation. Read as much Freud as you can read.

Irv: Just *The Collected Papers*,[16] you mean?

Mannie: Anywhere. Read as much Freud as you can read. I think there is no substitute for reading Freud, if you are going to be analysts.

Irv: What about Fenichel?[12]

Mannie: You can read Fenichel too, but I think Fenichel is too well organized already. He has deprived the material of some of its human quality. I would much rather that you read Freud. Read his cases in *The Collected Papers*. I think you have to get the feeling for it. I think you have to be exposed to the human quality that comes out in the cases. Fenichel is a magnificent source book. I think Ruth Munroe's book *Schools of Psychoanalytic Thought*[29] is a fine integrative source and reference book. But I think that they are more useful when you need references and quick resources. For growth, vitamins are important to us as adults; but if you give kids vitamins and not mother's milk, you will be depriving them of contact with the breast.

Irv: Right.

Mannie: And I think a baby needs contact with the breast. All right?

8

Violence and Sex

Group therapists are anxious about the possibility of violent or sexual acting out on the part of patients in groups they are treating. In fact, many conservative individual analysts use this argument as a reason for refraining from utilizing the group modality. For the same reason some group therapists will see only sexually homogeneous groups. Of course with adolescents there may be some justification for such a procedure, but even with them, heterogeneous groupings can be successfully employed if the therapist is not too anxious.

In some instances a therapist's concerns can be nonverbally transmitted to the membership of the group in such a way that patients may act out sexually or violently for or against him. This is similar to the formulation of Johnson[23] or A. R. Wolberg[48] about children acting out parental impulses that are repressed but communicated via super-ego lacunae. If the therapist is uncommitted to the group model and has such underlying anxieties, he may unconsciously provoke the group to behave with violence or sexuality to bolster his conscious argument against the group process itself.

Many patients hesitate to enter a group because of their anxiety about possible sex or violence. This can be a projection of their own latent hostile and/or sexual impulses onto the other members of the group. We would also point out that initial anxieties and questions about trust of other members may reveal underlying mistrust of self. As in individual analysis we can look upon fantasies about the therapist as containing projections about the self, so in the group, fantasies and expectations about co-patients contain projections in regard to the self. Other patients may seek to join therapeutic groups in order to act out their sexual and aggressive fantasies.

These issues become of particular importance when we consider, for example, concurrent treatment of a husband and a wife in different groups. Such a situation allows for triangulation, not only within their own group but across groups in terms of the spouse's group. It also stimulates questions about privacy of communication in groups. A patient may fear that a co-patient will reveal information to his spouse who is in a group with the spouse of the first patient.

All of these anxieties relate to significant reality issues in terms of diagnosis and evaluation of the patient's ego capacity to manage impulses in an outpatient setting. It is essential to determine the patient's ability to exercise control of impulse as a first step in determination of the suitability of the patient for group treatment.

Gerry: We have a lot of things to talk about.

Irv: We have a lot of problems today.

Mannie: Go ahead.

Irv: One of the problems with interaction is that we may not be able to get it all down for transcription because our girl had some difficulty last week when we all started to interact together. So we may have to forego that for the pleasure of seeing the transcript when we are through.

Mannie: Well, do the best you can with it. Any delayed reactions to last week?

Irv: I have some. Do you want to start out, Gerry?

Gerry: I was just going to say that when you told me you were angry with me for some reason, I could not do anything, I could not associate. I thought, "Well, if you do not like me, I will not produce." That was one reaction I had. Mannie, you asked in the session last week what my associations were to Irv's patient. I had all kinds, but I could not think of anything when you called upon me and I think it was related to this. I was just holding out. You were holding out on me and I was going to hold out on you.

Irv: I think my reaction to the whole session is to feel a little freer. I enjoyed your statement, "Take a flyer!" I thought, "Well, I should be able to run as well as anybody else!"

Gerry: Is that why you went out and took golf lessons last week?

Irv: I don't know.

Mannie: I think that you will discover that if you take sufficient flyers, you won't have to run so fast.

Gerry: Well, that brings up my anxieties. I took a flyer. I had a couple come to me a few weeks back about going into group therapy. I had never worked concurrently with both a husband and wife. But I said, "Well, I will! Irv does this sometimes. A lot of people will do it; I will do it." He is a very paranoid person and she is too. She provokes him. He has a delusion that she is out being promiscuous, which is his projection in this case. Last night she went to the alternate meeting, and about one o'clock in the morning I got a call from her mother. The wife was all upset because he had pounded the table and hollered at her, threatened her, and threw a beer bottle in the house or out in the street. She went racing down the street screaming and the neighbors picked her up and took her to her mother's. Her mother wants to know whether to take out a complaint and have the husband committed and what they are going to do to protect her. She is pregnant. Once before she had called the police. She did not file a warrant but threatened to do so. Since then he has not hit her or done anything except pound the table beside her and threaten her and tell her if she opens her mouth he will belt her and things like that. But this presents a problem because they are both in groups. The groups meet one following the other. The other night his group had met and he had not shown up. Her group met and as the group was leaving, he was waiting for her out in the hall and he said as a couple of the men came out, "Is that the one that is giving it to you? Is that the one?" They heard this and were very disturbed. At the next meeting some of them brought this up and said, "Gee, this guy is too damned crazy; you should not have him in a group." Which of course brings up my anxiety. This is one of the problems with having an alternate meeting away from the office. What are we going to do with a person like this? They are afraid.

Mannie: Do they have fears of a similar kind of person who is not a husband or a wife of a co-patient? Why don't you explore why they are afraid, why they are anxious because this man is a rugged character. You see, I would not respond to this kind of reaction of a patient in terms of the reality situation. You do not get anywhere that way. This man, from what you say, is no different from any other man in the community. He is just a little more so. You tell me he is not really dangerous.

Gerry: This was the way I was responding to it, the way you are talking about it. Well, I cannot deal with the reality, I have to deal with what is going on beneath this. But I have this anxiety. Sometimes a person in the community who is not in treatment takes a gun and goes chasing after someone he thinks is fooling around with his wife. I have a responsibility to my patients. Am I doing something foolish? I feel that maybe I am doing something foolish in seeing this man in the group.

Mannie: What is the chance you are taking? Let's look at it. For a patient that is one thing, but you are the analyst.

Irv: I think what Gerry is afraid of is the possibility that this man is going to get violent with his wife's co-patients as a result of his delusion and his poor controls and he is likely to conjure up something and strike somebody in the group.

Mannie: I think you have to answer that question, Gerry. I think Irv is right that that is where it is. Gerry, you have to answer the question on the basis of your best knowledge. If you think that he really can be that violent, then maybe you had better start seeing him individually and try to support him, try to relieve some of his tension. Perhaps see him and his wife in a combined session if you really feel this way. From what you have said so far, I do not have a feeling that you think a change is necessary. Now anybody can go off the handle and anybody can get violent, but you can only take a risk in terms of the probabilities. If you believe that the probabilities, the chances, are that this man can be violent and can hurt somebody else, he does not belong in treatment as an outpatient.

Gerry: That is right.

Mannie: He should be treated in a hospital, in an institution.

Gerry: Yes.

Mannie: Now we always make that kind of decision consciously. Once we have made the decision, then we have done the best we can.

Gerry: Well, that is where my question resides. Is this man treatable as an outpatient or does he need to be in the hospital?

Mannie: Let's talk about that problem because that is not a problem of group or individual or anything else. It is a problem of outpatient versus inpatient.

Gerry: I brought this question up to him after the group. He had come to the office and waited for his wife. He had raised a ruckus at the last regular meeting. Then he waited for his wife. They went out and he talked to her outside. I was still here closing up the office. They came back in and asked if they could talk to me for a minute. She was hysterical and crying because he was accusing her of fooling around with these other men. He said he was "angry" but this was his delusion (he did not use the word delusion), this was "his problem" and he "hated women anyway." By then I was questioning in my own mind whether this man has the inner control to keep this at the level of his fantasies, his feelings, or is there a danger here of raw hostility breaking out? Should he be in a hospital?

Mannie: The answer to that question in my estimation must be based on history. You want to talk about this man because I think you see you cannot get that answer in terms of the moment. You cannot judge their history on the basis of what she is reacting to now. You have to make an evaluation of the man in terms of his personal life history.

Irv: I think there is another problem and it is that Gerry is involved in a triangle because he is actually seeing the husband and wife. I think we have to look at the provocative behavior of the wife as well. It depends on what they are trying to do with Gerry.

Mannie: Yes, provided you can continue to treat them. But he is making a more crucial decision. He has to make the decision of whether he is going to continue to treat the two of them, whether they are still going to remain in treatment. You cannot really work on the problems until you decide that this person is in treatment with you.

Gerry: That is right.

Mannie: I feel Gerry is saying he does not know whether he ought to continue to treat this man.

Gerry: That is exactly the question I have in mind. I verbalized it to you that way this morning, Irv, when we had a cup of coffee ahead of time. Should I really be seeing these people in treatment or should I discontinue treatment with them? I have that question. I think that you can only look at it in terms of the whole overview, the long history of the man, but I do not know enough about this.

Mannie: How long have you seen him, Gerry?

Gerry: I have only seen him for two or three individual appointments. Two with him and two with his wife. Then I put them in the group, and they have been in the group about two weeks.

Mannie: What happened in those sessions that you had with him? Does he seem to be the one that you think is dangerous?

Gerry: You are asking what happened in the individual session?

Mannie: What did he talk about, what did he present, what were the facts that you got, what is your impression of those two sessions before you put him into the group? And what has happened in the group?

Gerry: In those two sessions it was a presentation of the problems he felt were there. I did a few tests with him to get some appraisal. I got the impression that he was denying his own promiscuous feelings and desires and projecting them onto his wife. I got the impression he is a very fragile character. I did not get any long history. It was not presented at the time. I did not directly take a long and involved history. I let him present things as they came and tried to make some appraisal on this basis.

Mannie: That raises the question about whether you should not think of trying to get a better basis for appraisal by taking some kind of overview of a person's life before you put him into a group. This is a legitimate question to be explored. If the plan is to put somebody into a group, you ought to have some kind of structured view of that. Maybe Al would answer this differently if he were here. But it seems to me if I were not going to see this person over the long range individually, if I were not going to do analysis in a more classical individual sense, and perhaps even then, I am not sure I would just let him float around. I think in my first session with every patient I tend to do some evaluation of ego strength and the extent of pathology, a tentative dynamic diagnosis.

Gerry: I do have some indication of this. Apparently his hostility is not just toward his wife. He apparently had a fight with a man at work that was of the same kind and he belted the man. Apparently there was no serious injury, but there was a fight and he described how the man had been asking for it and how everybody else where he worked has this same impression and they thought he was right in hitting this person. He had a very pleased, gleeful, and sadistic look on this face when he told me this. I confronted him by saying, "You seem to get a pretty big bang out of the idea that you beat up this man," and he immediately put on his defenses. I do not really know about other incidents in the history and it is a question. If I knew myself, if I had seen this man individually over a long time and had a good understanding of the history and how he had acted, I would know better how to arrive at a judgment whether I could see him on an outpatient basis.

Mannie: Why don't you get that information? I don't think you ought to come to this kind of decision, a decision not to treat him or to hospitalize him on the basis of insufficient information. Find out the facts before you make a decision to drop a patient and not give him a break in life, not give him an opportunity to work out his problem, because there must be something good in that he is even willing to come to see you. I think you ought to call him in and explore this very directly. You can tell him that you are concerned about his violence; that he will get into trouble with the law; that he may hurt himself and others; that he will be incarcerated; you may be compelled to hospitalize him; and you want to explore this with him. What has his life history been like with regard to violence? Does he feel he has sufficient controls?—not whether he is justified in belting somebody or not. The question is why he has to belt somebody in order to solve a problem, and to what extent he has to. Because if it is just a matter of his being somewhat violent, if he is going to belt somebody, throw a beer bottle or something like that, this is a problem which must be worked out. It is not a reason to incarcerate a man, it is not a sufficient reason to institutionalize him. This is something to work with and to treat and to struggle with and to help him with and to make this the focus of your work together. If at the end of your interview or two interviews you come to a decision that he can be worked with on an outpatient basis, you might even say, "Look, I know you are angry; the reason you get violent is because you are angry. Maybe there is some other way you can find to express it; maybe you can control this. I would like you to try not to punch or to hit or to use your hands on your wife or anybody else and see if you can control this until we can work it out. I am sure I can help you express your anger in another way." You have to support the ego in this kind of situation.

Irv: In other words, you do not think Gerry can work this out in group with him? You do not think that he could deal with this problem, that this would not come up in the group and he could try to explore it with the group?

Mannie: Yes, I think he can. I would not pull him out of the group as long as you already have him there. I would still let him continue in the group, but I think, Gerry, you need some assurance. I think you are anxious about it and I—

Gerry: I know I am.

Mannie: There is no reason for you to remain anxious about this. It seems to me that for you to be able to act in his interests you need to be less anxious. There is no reason why you cannot call him in for an individual session in an emergency situation. There are other kinds of emergencies where it is legitimate and appropriate for you to have a couple of individual sessions simultaneously without pulling a patient out of the group. Surely you ought to work on this in the group. One of the things I would work on in the group is why he did not come last session, and explore his resistance to working on the problem, because you will get the support of the group.

Irv: What if he says, "I don't know," and drops it.

Mannie: I would ask the group to respond; I would hold back and see. You can goose him with your silence. You know what you are really doing when you say, "Suppose he says, 'I don't know.'" You might as well close your practice. There must be ways of dealing with the "I don't know" response. This is resistance. Our entire effort can be expressed as the successive overcoming of the resistances. Of course, he is going to be resistant, and the patient that does not know, does not want to talk, is not really a patient because our work involves a talking method.

Gerry: I think we can move on from this now because I have at least a better feeling about it myself, some assurance within myself and less anxiety about it. His group has an alternate tomorrow. If he gets to it, I may hear more about this at the next regular session.

Mannie: And I wouldn't be so frightened by the fact that the wife and the husband have been fighting. Apparently they have been fighting for a long time and he has not murdered her yet; there is no reason to assume that he is going to murder her now; and the fact they are going to hit one another . . . they have been doing this for a long time.

Irv: What about this man, whose controls are pretty weak? What about the placement of his wife in a mixed group with other men? Doesn't this just add more fuel to the fire? He would think his wife is promiscuous anyway, even if she just walks down the street. Would placing the wife in a mixed group be overprovocative in such a situation? This is an added threat.

Mannie: Right. And maybe you had better say that to him if you believe it. Maybe you had better get them to talk about this and why it is an added threat. You see now you begin to have controlled situations. Now you can confront them with the fact that obviously it is a therapeutic relationship with these other men; it is not a session for sexual relations.

Irv: Well, I have some sexual acting out going on in my group. This is the first time.

Mannie: Do you want to talk about this sexual acting out?

Irv: I would like to talk about it. On Wednesday, Leo, the fellow who feels homosexual impulses toward me, started off the meeting by saying, "It has finally happened; I slept with Sally all night last night."

Mannie: He slept, huh?

Irv: Well, yes . . . Leo was extremely mad when I dropped the regular individual session with him. He was just boiling and he pouted for three or four sessions in the group. He was angry. He had a dream a couple of weeks ago in which he was home with his mother and his Uncle Louis, who was drunk. His Uncle Louis cut the tail off his pet cat. He got so mad he beat the hell out of his Uncle Louis and then he got some glue and tried to glue the tail back on the cat. His association to it was that he felt that the umbilical cord had been cut, though he originally responded to it in terms of castration symbolism. Sally is a girl who denies a great deal, has a lot of physical complaints. She is the one whose history has been that of acting out. She goes out, gets drunk, and picks up somebody and sleeps with them. When she is very lonely, she cannot stand to be alone. She is extremely anxious; she always has to be feeding herself in one way or another, either drinking or food or bowling or promiscuity. Her husband is impotent and she has had relations with him only about six times in the past two and a half years. She has been through several marriages. I gave you a brief history on her. Anyway when Leo said to the group, "I slept with Sally," Flora's immediate response was "How nice," as if a couple of lovers had gotten together. She then said, "Now why did I respond that way?" Sid was mad. Tears welled up in his eyes and he really got mad. He did not like it. He felt he had been left out. It reawakened memories of his parents sleeping together while he was left in the other room. Leo was anxious but trying to play it cool. Sally was very defensive, very resistant to exploring the situation in terms of what it meant. Leo's associations finally were that he was mad at me. He did it to spite me. He did not like the way I sat around in the group in a seductive way, lifting my legs up and smoking a cigarette. He did not like the fact that I was the big cheese in the group. It bothered him and he felt that my movements were seductive. He was really mad at me. The way the thing occurred was Sally got drunk and called Leo on the phone. Leo was seduced by Sally. Sally really did not explore the episode except to say she felt anxious. She wanted company and she did not know whether it had anything to do with her feelings toward me or not. She was reluctant to explore the matter. The group talked about it in terms of their feelings and Leo finally projected his fantasy onto me and two of the other people in the group. The fantasy was that we were going to cut him up, rip him to bits, beat him up; he was going to be thrown out of the group for this deed. Sally had the feeling that she was going to be thrown out of the group too. In some ways she associated Leo with her father. She used the expression, saying maybe this was her desire to get her "phantom father." They had been in the group for a long time and had been making overtures to each other. They both had had fantasies about inviting each other out, but they had not done it. Now the group has had about three alternate sessions, and I stopped seeing them both individually about three or four weeks ago. They both reacted strongly to it. I am sure that this is in some way a reaction to me, to the cessation of the individual session, and I suspect the freedom that they gain from the alternate sessions.

Gerry: Well, I have been thinking about it. My reaction is that Sally did seduce him and he was projecting this seduction onto you. He also expected retaliation. I think that when you brought it up the other day, I had a feeling that you were much more anxious. Today you seem to present it in a way that is just a matter of fact. It is like any other incident you might be reporting in the group and yet when you brought it up the other day, you were very anxious.

Mannie: I would like to say this; that maybe the most wonderful thing that can happen to both of these people is the fact that they could have been sexual with one another and not be destroyed by the group. Maybe the most positive thing that can happen to both of them as well as to the group is for these two, Leo and Sally, to have had sexual intercourse and to come back into the group expecting to be thrown out of the symbolic family because of their incestuous activity, both of them expecting to be torn apart, he expecting to be castrated and destroyed for it, and for them to come to recognize that this is not what happens in reality. Even though this was based on a very negative motivation, it can still be a very positive experience if used properly. They may yet learn that it is possible for them to have sex without being destroyed. It can be a very rewarding experience: you can use this very constructively in treatment. Now you have anxiety about their continuing to do this. Obviously they may continue to do this for a time. Ultimately, if they continue, it will be in resistance to working out the problem. You have to confront them with this resistance. Why do you feel that you have a necessity at this moment to guarantee that they will never do it again?

Irv: My own anxiety.

Mannie: Right. Now this is your anxiety, but it may not necessarily be therapeutically in their interest to act on your discomfort.

Irv: Right. I think I can check it and understand it and work with the situation.

9

History Is
Tradition-Forming

A knowledge of the literature and an awareness of the experience and thinking of capable and competent predecessors are important in approaching the treatment process. Though much can be learned from one's own experience in listening, and so it must be, it is foolhardy not to avail oneself of the wisdom of one's forebears. At the same time it is hidebound to impose a rigid, frozen frame of reference on the unique features that individuate one person from another and that differentiate the treatment process for each.

A focus only on pathology is rigid; healthy patterns are also important. Behavior is multidetermined, and analysis implies an understanding of the multiplicity of determinants in any piece of behavior. One needs to explicate the conscious and the unconscious, the current and the historical, the positive and negative implications of patient activity, and use each in an exquisitely discriminating fashion, as is appropriate.

A therapy group has a history and has traditions, but it is important from the perspective of analytic psychology that the therapist not be caught up in the denial of individual differences by overemphasis on group dynamics or on homogenization of the members into some anthropomorphic entity called The Group.

All of us have conflict about breaking from the security of tradition. The balanced therapist respects what has gone before, but is innovative and not bound by tradition. He is rather freed not to have to repeat as he knows and masters it.

Growth or learning as a therapist is in some ways similar to growth and development of the human being. As we grow in a family, both the traditions of the others (the family) and the originality of the person combine to help him make his own niche in the family circle.

Irv: Say, I had some difference with you last week, and it probably reflects an underlying rigidity on my part. When we were talking about adolescent groups, I got the impression that you supported the idea of plunging into the group and keeping your eyes and ears open and just see where you go; see what happens. Certainly you have to do that anyway when you do therapy. However, I have the feeling that there is a body of literature, a body of understanding, about adolescents and about working with adolescents. Other people have worked with adolescents in group and they are experienced. One should have some idea of what the nature of the adolescent's ego defenses are. One should have some awareness of how others have worked with adolescents, what their goals are. To my understanding, when you work with an adolescent, you are working primarily on the ego level. Of course, sometimes you might want to go back farther, but primarily you are dealing with their intercurrent difficulties.

Mannie: I do not have any argument with you. I remember talking about your young patient last week. You wanted to know whether you ought to introduce him into a group or not. In that instance the indications were positive. In all cases you cannot know too much before you start. I am not a know-nothing. I am not pro-irrationality. You need training, knowledge, and discipline. The more you know, the richer your experience, then the better the experience for the patient. You cannot start with knowledge outside and superimpose it upon every patient-therapist situation. You have to let the patient teach you how to treat him. Each patient has a quality of uniqueness, even though we find generalities in the literature. If we treat every father that comes in like the father of "Little Hans" or if you treat every woman that comes in like "Dora," you will very soon be treating nobody. There is a uniqueness about the course of therapy which cannot be predicted in advance no matter how much you know and no matter how experienced you are. It is a very human, growing, developing situation which creates its own history. One of the problems, I think, that makes for difficulty in doing research in psychoanalytic work is that not only does the patient have a history and the therapist have a history, but the analysis has a history and makes history as it moves along. This is a very complicating factor. You cannot predetermine how the course of any analysis is going to go. I know that there are some colleagues who would disagree with me, but I think their position reflects a rigidity and it is a denial of the patient's centrality.

Gerry: I think I understand what you mean; that you have a certain set of ideas, a certain kind of understanding of people and what you can and cannot do in the group. But if you start with a frozen frame of reference, you certainly cannot hear what is going on and you cannot adapt yourself to the multiple membership of the group. . . .

Mannie: Even in individual analysis this is so. A group becomes ever so much more complicated because it is natural to fall into group dynamics. It is difficult to attend to the diversity of individual patients. In individual analysis, if you start on the assumption that first you analyze the horizontal vector or what is the intercurrent, or, on the other hand, the vertical or what is the history, and then you go to sexual, then to the aggressive, then to the libidinal, and finally you work down to the birth trauma; or first you start with the genital, then you move to the phallic, and go into the anal, then back to the oral, such a plan reflects rigidity on the part of the analyst and probably never occurs so fixedly. But if you start with such a conception, you tend to dehumanize the nature of the relationship, and it will never be therapeutic. Patients will terminate analyzed but they will come out an analyzed machine, not a human being. I urge you not to be know-nothings, not to deny your knowledge, not to deny science and discipline and understanding of human beings and the techniques and mechanics of doing analysis. I also suggest that probably one of the most important characteristics of a good analyst is the capacity to listen, to be open to material from within and without. Patients will teach you how to treat them if you can really listen to them with "evenly hovering attention." You do not have to superimpose a straight jacket upon them. If you have made a mistake, they will let you know, if you are sensitive to them. Our problem and my problem still is that occasionally with certain kinds of patients I will get so defensive that I do not, I cannot even respond when they tell me I am making a mistake and I hear it and know they are right.

Irv: Yes, I think it is a real good point, and I think I saw just one side of the thing. In other words, I think my feeling was well, there *is* some literature, there *is* some knowledge.

Mannie: And, by the way, the adolescent is the most neglected age group. If you work with adolescents, you cannot do an analysis in the classical sense. The adolescent is developmentally not suited at the moment for a deep analytic experience. Be supportive, be ego-oriented, be current-reality-oriented. Through the biological upheaval of adolescence, a group of adolescents will encourage one another's anxiety and one another's acting-out capacity. You have to set limits. You have to be much more active with some groups of adolescents, that is, theoretically and generally, than with other groups of adolescents.

Irv: Well, I think I am a little concerned about this acting out with adolescents more than I am with adults because—

Mannie: Are you concerned about the adolescents or their parents?

Irv: Well, I suppose in reality it is the hostile society, fathers and all that.

Mannie: Let's talk about what we are really anxious about.

Irv: But there has to be some reality too, even if I have some unrealistic anxiety, because you are dealing with a group of patients who are underage. For example, when I thought of bringing that nineteen-year-old into my group, Al's comment was, "Well, is it a male or female?" If it was a male, it was okay, but introducing a nineteen-year-old female into an adult group was questionable. He gave me the impression that he felt that would be letting yourself in for trouble.

Mannie: I think that is Al's reaction, but we ought to ask him to speak for himself when he returns next week. My reaction is that the determining factor is whether or not you think the person can tolerate the experience. If you recall, we talked about that last week; about your couple that was acting out, the sexy married couple who were beginning to murder each other. You have to take some calculated risks. Every time you put a patient in the group, every time you put a patient on the couch, every time you open your mouth and make an interpretation, you are taking a calculated risk. If you have not the courage to act with probabilities, you really should not be in this business. You are going to have to become stronger and you will become stronger and more secure as you have more experience and more certainty. For example, in the instance of the adolescent, I think you are quite right. As you say, you do have a responsibility also to the parents, because the patients are underage. Besides, the parents are going to pay the bill. Many child therapists run afoul because they become antagonistic to the parents and refuse to relate legitimately and realistically to the parents.

Irv: Yes, I think this brings in some other questions. I noticed that we are just relating here in the vertical vector. Gerry, I do not know why we are not—

Gerry: I cannot seem to interrupt you two. I feel that in terms of this adolescent group setting, that the concern here that you, Irv, had is that I am doing something which is dangerous or that I may not know what I am doing. I know I do not know all about working with them; I do not certainly know enough about it. I think what Mannie was saying last week, when he said it was a good idea, is that he liked the idea of trying it with a mixed group or not having an alternate. I think you can still work with a group like this. I do not see what real danger it presents unless you communicate the expectation that there is going to be acting out. Somehow I think you might communicate that to them. If you go in with the expectation that there will be no acting out, that does not mean there will be none, but at least you are not communicating that idea to them.

Irv: Well, very often adolescents come to the attention of the courts because of sexual acting out. I do not know if in your group you have many kids who are in difficulty because the girls are sleeping with some of the fellows. Now if you take them on, and place them in a mixed group, and they have this kind of problem, being very impulsive, and have additional problems with their impulses because of adolescent change and biological upheaval, I wonder whether or not in a situation like this you are giving them more stimulation than they can handle. That is my question.

Mannie: That is a legitimate question.

Irv: Yes, I am just questioning this. I think even if the root of some of my anxiety might be some underlying fear that someone is going to get after me or something like that, nevertheless, when you are working with adolescents. . . .

Mannie: There is reality to that kind of a formulation.

Irv: Yes, and that is the thing I wanted to explore! That is all!

Mannie: All right. Let me react to what you have been saying. Adolescents are very difficult and we all apparently have some fear of our own adolescent tendencies. Most of us have a great deal more amnesia for our adolescent period than for our infancy. This anxiety, of course, must be recognized, must be respected; that is, the anxiety of the therapist, not only the anxiety of the patient. Maybe if you are going to start working with adolescents you might ask yourself, what kind of adolescents, and in what kind of a group? You gimmick our discussion considerably when you say these are court cases.

Gerry: I did not say they were. Irv did.

Irv: I am just assuming. I am just assuming one kind—

Mannie: You gimmick the problem considerably when you deal with court cases. I do not know whether I would like to treat a group of adolescents who are court cases, as a group. I think I would not mind taking a couple of adolescent court cases and putting them in a group where the others are not that kind of sociopath, or who have a history of difficulty with the law.

Irv: In other words, you would have some real neurotic adolescents.

Mannie: I would.

Irv: That makes sense to me because it seems that if you have a group of character disordered patients, you have really got a problem.

Mannie: Your first adolescent group ought not be a group of sociopaths. Most of the young people who come into treatment, most of the adolescents that come into outpatient treatment in private practice, are not the kind that get before the courts in New York. Those who come before the courts are the kind that get treatment usually in clinics, outpatient or inpatient treatment settings, but rarely in private practice. Private practice demands a certain kind of economic, educational, and social background which tends largely to inhibit the acting out process. Where an adolescent does act out, you still have sufficient resources to support the ego of that adolescent or he would never get to your office in the first place. So you have different kinds of adolescents; and I would be hesitant to take on in private practice a group composed only of eight or ten sociopathic juvenile delinquents who have hit the courts.

Gerry: I do not think I would want to.

Irv: I think that clarifies my thinking. You got to the crux of the matter. With any kind of group, you have to consider the people that compose the group. There are some who are a lot more attractive than others. In a group they are the ones that draw the attention and draw the interest. Maybe there are one or two females that are getting all the attention and the bad looking girls are being left out, and this is structured in part by the actual situation.

Mannie: But isn't the reality structured by the same differences, and don't these people face these same differences outside of therapy? If they daily face these same differences, shouldn't they work their problems with regard to them through? Don't you see, you do not really help the person by saying that because this person is lame or blind or has a long nose or crinkly hair or whatever it is, because this person is an unattractive person, therefore he is not available for group therapy. Or because the other one is a shining beauty, therefore she is the only kind of person that will benefit from group therapy.

Irv: No, I was not saying that. I was just trying to look at some of the external forces that shape group movements.

Gerry: I was thinking, Irv, this depends upon you too. I think that Mannie's point is well taken. If you respond to this as a problem and protect them from it, then you are certainly not going to be able to help them in the group. But if you give a girl who is not so pretty a chance to experience a new reality in the group and help her work it through, then this is treatment. As long as you think about this reality as if the person needs to be protected from confronting it, it is anti-therapeutic.

Irv: No, I was not saying—

Gerry: Well, you are talking about acting-out adolescents. You are concerned about this and about the parents. It seems to me that there is through all of this—this is my feeling, I do not have any defense for it, it is just a feeling—some element of your needing to protect, to control so you can protect. I think it was the same when we talked a few weeks back about the alternate session. I think that this same need on your part pervades our discussion here, which is the way you are looking at it. I do not think that there is any argument with what you say. The ideas you are talking about are perfectly understandable and I think I agree with them. I am sure Mannie does. You are protesting so that it sounds like it is again a protection on your part.

Irv: No, no! What you say is true to a degree. I may tend to be a hovering mother. But I think in this situation what I was concerned about was some comparisons between individual and group therapy. In individual therapy a very unattractive person comes in and she has a therapeutic experience with you, but the fact of her unattractiveness never really comes up in the situation.

Gerry: The hell it doesn't!

Mannie: It should! It is a reality!

Irv: No, but I mean what do you say to her, "You are unattractive!"? I mean it comes up in terms of what—

Mannie: Doesn't she know she is?

Irv: Yes, I mean she will tell it to you, but she does not have the same kind of experience that she does in a group situation where the other girls are being responded to. . . .

Mannie: I have an association I would like to share with you two. I feel the way Gerry does, that behind this is some fear of the overwhelming amount of pathology that you anticipate will exist in the group. This is what Gerry is talking about when he refers to your need to protect. One of the most instructive experiences I ever had with Al was when he was supervising me. We were talking about the dreams of a patient that I was controlling with him and he said, "Well, can't you find anything positive in this dream?" It was a very moving experience and I have learned a great deal from Al in that very experience. Because one person is less attractive, because another is lame, or still another is not a kind of outgoing person, your task I think, and the task of the co-patients, will have to be directed toward the question, Isn't there anything positive in this human being? Can't we relate to any human being also in terms of what is positive? Do we have to see only the pathology? Is this all that we can find in a person? Are we responding always only to the apparencies? Is there some recognition that there are differences and there are positives and negatives in all of us and that no matter how beautiful a face one may have, the other may have a beautiful soul? I think you have to look for the positives and not respond only to the pathology in your patients. This was true of our acting out couple last week, for example. I think this is true of adolescents. I think this is how we encourage group monopolizers, as Irv said, because they happen to be handsome, intelligent, or have attractive personalities we let them steal center stage. You have to find positives in the others who are not Marilyn Monroes or Clark Gables.

Irv: This brings in another factor. You are talking then about something other than analyzing what is behind what is going on. What you are talking about here is the fact that you have to encourage positive things.

Gerry: No, I do not think so, Irv. I think he is saying that when you analyze what is going on, you can only bring out the reality. The reality is that there are differences, there are positive and negative aspects to each of these people. That is what analysis is going to bring out.

Mannie: Right, Gerry, I subscribe to that fully. That was what I tried to say. What is the matter, Irv?

Irv: I am thinking.

Mannie: I think you did not get the point and I think Gerry did. I think he restated it perfectly. You seem to reject analysis as having anything to do with the positive potentials. You think that analysis has only to do with ferreting out pathology, Irv, and this is what scares you a little bit because you misheard what I said. You did not get the point and Gerry did. I think you have to come to grips with this, that doing good analysis and working therapeutically with a patient is not just analyzing the negative; it is also coming to grips with the recognition of what is positive in each person; for if there is no positive, there is no success.

Gerry: Well, there could be no therapy because there is no person.

Mannie: I once criticized group therapy. I think it was legitimate and I wish Al were here to interact with me on it. I used to be critical about group therapy because I thought it encouraged only the hostile feelings and I asked, Why isn't loving feeling encouraged? Why doesn't the analyst say sometimes to the group, "Here you have spent these last six months, these last three weeks, these last six hours or last six minutes expressing only hostile feelings toward one another and toward your friends, mates, children, and so forth. Doesn't anybody here have any loving feelings?" Now I think this is just as good analysis as saying, "Doesn't anybody here feel hostile?"

Gerry: I think what you are saying is that in treatment or in analysis, you have to face the fact that there are a variety of feelings and if you are only seeing one of them or only concerned with one kind, then you are going to miss the point of the person that is there because there has to be at least two feelings or he hasn't any conflict.

Mannie: Exactly.

Irv: Very often people interact hostilely in a group to ward off close feelings.

Mannie: Very often they have friendly feelings to ward off their hostile feelings. There are facades of healthy and positive feelings, like the feeling for the Marilyn Monroe in the group that we were fantasizing, or that I was fantasizing. So you have to go to what is behind this; you have to see the positives and the negatives. That is, if you go to what is behind the facade, you will discover behind the facade that we all have both strengths and weaknesses, limitations and powers, and we have partial powers, partipotencies rather than omnipotence or impotence.

Irv: Yes.

Mannie: We are back in our old argument again. If you see all the power in the hands of the analyst and all the pathology and the impotence in the hands of the patient, we are caught in the vertical vector, and we will never resolve it.

Irv: In line with that, Hulse[22] said that you cannot work with a patient in a group unless the content of his material can be communalized. He was saying that if people are having intercurrent difficulty, or problems which are very subjective, you cannot work with them in a group. I do not really understand the point of view because it seems to me that you really could not work with anybody in a group if you could not work with people who have specific individual kinds of problems. It seems to me that everybody's problem, no matter what, has some relationship to other people because we are all people.

Mannie: However, there is a problem with the communalization idea that Hulse had and that most of the group dynamics people have. You ought to be able to relate to a person and it is pretty hard if you do not speak the same language or if you do not have similar kinds of life experiences. The group itself becomes a shared experience and develops part of the history of the person as well as of the group. But what we are concerned about, I think, is not that the group creates its own traditions and its own history and so on, but about the denial of the individual differences and the uniquenesses that get caught up in the homogenization process. But it does not mean that this does not occur. We are only concerned that analysis of a group trend or a communalization will not lead the individual to the resolution of his conflict and his ambivalence, but he certainly must communalize if he is going to be able to be part of the group.

Gerry: I have been changing the machine and I have not had time to think about all of this, but something you said struck me. Certainly it is worthwhile to look at how the individual utilizes a group dynamic or responds to the group dynamics, but that is not going to analyze why he does that.

Mannie: Exactly why he uses it the way he does.

Gerry: Yes.

Mannie: Everyone of us grew up in a family, and a family has group dynamics. It has family dynamics. The conflicts that I develop in my family are quite different from the conflicts my brother develops. His relationship to the rest of the family is different from mine by virtue of the fact that he was older and I was younger. If you want to understand me, understanding the family dynamics is not going to be sufficient. You also have to understand what I did with the family dynamics. This means analyzing the family to a fare-thee-well is not going to help me overcome my anxieties and my conflicts and my ambivalence. You are going to have to analyze what I did and how I felt and how I reacted to the very same situation or conditions that my brother had.

Gerry: Well, they were not the very same.

Mannie: The group dynamics were the same, that is the point. It was the same family, it had the same name, the same traditions, the same parents, the same group identity, the same rules and regulations, and we in the family lived in the same way. You see, this is the manifest content. You remember in our paper on the mystique of group dynamics we suggested that the group dynamics were the manifest content and that the psychodynamics were the latent content. We are interested in the transferences and the distortions that make up the latent content, the personal, the individual.

Gerry: Yes. but don't you think the personal and individual responses continually change the group dynamics?

Mannie: I do not think so. I think it contributes to them and it probably has an influence, but I think the group dynamics are very resistant to an individual action and influence.

Gerry: I do not mean an individual one. But when an individual responds to other individuals in the group, in the family say, when the child responds to the family and the way the family is set up and its dynamics, depending on how he responds, it either intensifies some dynamic or causes anxiety in other individuals and some modifications and changes. I mean, there is a change going on.

Mannie: There is continuous interaction and continuous change. I wish Al were here to discuss this from his point of view, but from my point of view this is what happens in any group situation. Let's take a family. Obviously when a third member or a fourth member or a fifth child is born and is added to the family, the family changes some way, does it not? The reality situation changes and yet every time you add another individual to the family, what you do is to make it more difficult for the next individual to alter the nature of the traditions and the processes and the structures that have historically developed, because it adds more history. History tends to be conserving. History tends to be tradition-forming. Roles become more fixed and places assigned to newcomers.

Gerry: So the newest child in a sense has got a harder job in the family group and with regard to the group dynamics of the family because—

Mannie: I do not know if it is a harder job, but he meets a more rigid structure.

Irv: Yes, in other words, he is not as much a part of creating the family culture.

Mannie: I would guess that in a family of six, the sixth member, that is, the fourth child, probably has less effect in changing the family culture than the third child or the second child or even the first child. That is, that last child may change the structure some. He may rebel against the family culture, maybe get out of the family culture. However, his capacity to make significant change is less, comparatively less, is relatively less than any of the other children.

Gerry: The same is true of working with people in groups. When you begin, the people who are in the group at the start form it with you, and new people coming in have to adapt in a way. I have a good example of this. When we started our sessions here, I made a change and took people from two different groups and made two new groups. They did not really know what the "family culture" or what the group was. For several weeks before they formulated their own set of ways of going about things or their new operations, there was a fluctuation between one group appropriating it in terms of their past history and the way they did things, and then the other group's way. And they verbalized this. The first night I think three new people came in, three from one old group went in with five from another and they felt that they were going to have to adapt to the way the five did it. Then the second night they took over because they happen to be healthier and stronger, longer in treatment. The others said, "Hell, no, we think it is your group." Then the third night the group said, "No, we think it is your group," and it went back and forth until they stopped talking about whose group it was and now it is the group's group.

Mannie: One of these days it will be our group.

Gerry: That is what I say; I think it is now.

Mannie: You are having a struggle coming to grips with the frame of reference within which you are going to be able to do therapy, but the emphasis of the analysis is not on this kind of interaction. This is great small-group dynamics and has much value for social groups, but it is only after they get through this phase that they can begin to work on the psychodynamics and interaction with one another within the setting and you can analyze their unconscious feelings and projections, their dreams, their distortions, and work through their resistances and their conflicts. Unless you do that, you will not be making a significant contribution to the cure for which they are there.

Gerry: Well, they brought this in and we never really focused on this switch back and forth as such, but only in terms of individuals and how they felt about this and what they were doing with it.

Irv: Here is how I think it can come up in terms of working with it. For example, in a group that I had, every time I introduced a new member, one of the men would talk about his seniority in the group and his longevity. He would be very angry at the new member. He would always bring up in a session or two how the new member did not know much, really was not part of the group, why should we have him anyway. And the group got wise to this.

Mannie: Was this his younger brother?

Irv: Yes.

Mannie: Did you analyze it as his younger brother?

Irv: I think, yes, it was his younger brother.

Mannie: Good.

Irv: But the group caught on to this and the group said, "Gee, how come?" and they called him the Seniority Kid. They had a label for him.

Mannie: How cute.

Irv: It happened so many times over the history of the group. Maybe we had six or seven new members and practically everybody in the group had an opportunity to see him at work with his brother and we worked on it until we worked the thing through. But the group caught on right away.

Mannie: The group's catching on confronts him with his manifest behavior. Then the analysis of this relationship to his own family experiences, where a younger brother takes over the family or he fears he will take over the family, becomes the analysis of the repressed material, of the unconscious material, which has motivated and determined his behavior toward patient after patient that was introduced into the group. It probably affects his work relations with other personnel, his school relations, and his family relations.

Irv: You once said that when we had time it would be good to talk about the treatment of the only child. It seems to me that placing an only child in a group is a wonderful type of new experience for someone to have a family experience that he never had before, to learn how to share and to get along on a deeper level than he ever had an opportunity to before.

Mannie: It is probably the preferred mode of treatment for the only child; that is, the group is the preferred mode of treatment. It is probably extremely difficult, maybe impossible, to resolve the problem of the only child in an individual analytic relationship. I would like to see a research study done on that, and my prediction is that there are more failures with only children in individual analysis than with any other kind of treatment.

Irv: Would that be because the individual analysis just reinforces the only child's pathology and you never can really get to analyze it because the person wants an infantile, mothering kind of relationship, and gets it really?

Mannie: This is the characteristic relationship of the individual treatment situation. The only child tends, that is, if the only child is as often happens, an isolated child, tends to perpetuate that isolation in adulthood so that he has very few horizontal or peer relationships.

Gerry: Can I throw in something here? Irv said that the only child wants the infantile relationship and gets it. I think, too, that the only child wants to get out from under this kind of oppression, being the only focus of the parent.

Mannie: Excellent, excellent.

Irv: I agree with you, Gerry. In other words, I think that he wants to get away and yet he wants to stay. I think that is the conflict.

Mannie: That is the ambivalence.

Gerry: I know, but you were just saying—

Irv: And I think this is the conflict in any kind of neurosis, in any kind of disturbance; the patient wants the type of infantile gratification that he is getting in his neurosis and at the same time he wants to free himself. I think this is what you have to work with all the time.

Mannie: There is another aspect to this. It is the nature of classical psychoanalysis in an individual setting to encourage, to foster, the transference to the analyst as mother. This is the nature of first roles. The first transference relationship generally is the nurturing person.

Irv: And usually it is the last thing to really be analyzed in an analytic situation.

Mannie: Sometimes it is never analyzed and unfortunately this is what happens in many analyses . . .

Gerry: You are making me feel good.

Mannie: . . . is that this is never really worked out. You take a man in his relationship to his analyst. He works out the competitive feelings, the oedipal struggle, and that is the end of his analysis. He may never really work out the basic relationship to the mother starting with the oral phase.

Irv: Yes, but actually this is what real analysis should be, it seems to me, to really—

Mannie: There is a difference between what it should be and what it really is. We are talking about day and night very often. We are talking about the fact that we deal with all kinds of pressures for shortening the analysis, for getting through with it, and for the limitations, by the way, of individual analysts who have theoretical differences, for example, who tend to reject the importance or validity of the siblings. See, we are back at the question we started with because most analysts tend not to spend as much time in working through the sibling relationship as they do the authority relationship.

Irv: Very often it is difficult to do in an individual setting.

Mannie: Exactly.

Irv: You just cannot see it.

Mannie: This is one of the beauties of the group situation.

Gerry: I was just wondering whether in the group you have a structure against which you can see this sibling pathology and help, but in the individual session, you do not have it. But why can't it come up? If it does, I guess it just depends upon the individual patient. There really is nothing there to focus it.

Mannie: It means that the analyst has to be conscious of sibling relationships. You see, Gerry, the analyst has to be conscious of it and willing to pursue it. He gets it only in secondhand report. He cannot use it very often unless there are some circumstances that are very strange. For example, I had an older brother by the name of Irving and my analyst's first name was Irving so that some of my problems with my older brother came out in the transference. In addition, we had a real life encounter in which we could work out some of these problems. But suppose my analyst's name was Joe or something else instead of Irving. This may never have come out; he may never have pursued it because there is no provocative situation in which you can work out this kind of thing.

Gerry: Well, that was my point, Mannie, that in the individual analysis it is like a motion picture being projected into the air; there is nothing against which to look at it and see whether this is or is not reality.

Mannie: There is little real experience that you can work out. You have to work on secondhand experiences. The group will provide you an experience in depth, a real experience for everybody to undergo within the therapeutic frame. This is a great advantage.

Gerry: What am I getting at is this. The patient knows that the transference problems regarding siblings or the pathology regarding siblings is there, but the therapist does not know it. In the group the therapist can know it, where in individual sessions he cannot know it unless there is some accidental reality which allows it to be seen.

Mannie: Or unless he pursues it.

Gerry: He cannot pursue what cannot be seen.

Mannie: He may still ask for it since he knows the family constellation.

Irv: I had an experience like this in the group the other night. One of the men who was getting ready to terminate treatment in about four or five months. He has come along real nicely. He came into the group and he reported a dream in which he killed the general manager at work. He started associating to it, that he was getting me out of the way and wanting to take over and lead the group. He said to the group, "You are all weaklings, I am the only strong one here." Then he started to take off after one of the women in the group who is the domineering, controlling one and for whom the ability to dominate and control has positive aspects. She is the one in the group who asks other people to interact. She will say, "What is the matter with you, Joe? You are retired; you are not talking to us." Even in her domination there are some healthy aspects. She is the only one who really seeks people out. Well, anyway, he was trying to blast her and finally he said, "Where is your hat, that lousy hat you had on last week?" And as he started to talk, he realized that he was really re-experiencing his trouble with his sister, and this came out very dramatically.

Mannie: Wonderful.

Irv: But I have seen him in individual therapy for a long time and he has talked about his conflict with his sister. I never saw it in action, but here it was in action and, of course, I was involved as well, if I really look at the thing. It was an actual living out, re-experiencing, and he finally saw how irrational it was. Here he was trying to talk about her hat, which was of course a ridiculous kind of thing. He then began to realize something was screwy here, "I am doing something here."

Mannie: I want to underscore your point that you were involved in that reaction.

Irv: Yes, definitely. You can see it; in his dream, too.

Mannie: The problem of siblings and the only child is really a new dimension which group therapy has contributed to the consciousness of the individual analyst. The analyst has always been aware of the fact—

Gerry: Can you speak up a little?

Mannie: Yes. The analyst has always been aware of the fact that a family consists of parents and children, but I think there has been a tendency, especially in American psychoanalysis, really to neglect the sibling relationships.

Irv: When we speak of the factors in emotional development, or let us say, in personality development, we always talk about the individual as a unit unto himself and the family as another unit. I do not recall much literature about the influence of siblings.

Mannie: Take a look at Ackerman's book on family dynamics.[1] You
will see this worked out pretty well. But you will also find
it in several of Freud's papers. And you might also get that
very early paper on the only child by Brill[7] that appeared
in the Modern Library Edition.

Irv: Oh, that one was a long time ago.

Mannie: Yes. It is now out of print.

Irv: Doesn't Adler deal with this to a degree?

Mannie: Yes. And don't forget *The Psychoanalytic Study of the
Child*. In almost every volume, every year, there is some
material on the sibling aspects. The brother-sister problem
has been largely neglected. Incidentally, you remember
Robert Lindner? He wrote a very interesting paper that
appeared about 1953 or 1954 in *The Menninger Bulletin*
on the relationship between brother and sister, a very interesting paper in which he tried to demonstrate for generalization the way in which brother and sister relationships
can be so interlocked as to move them both in the direction
of the same kind of pathology, a *folie à deux*. There is a
great deal of complementarity that occurs merely on the
basis of the adaptation of one sibling to another. For
instance, I have often said this to mothers, that if the first
child is active with the hands and athletic, the second
child is the student, more scholarly. They adapt to one
another. The second child seems to select a field of operations in which he can succeed in which the earlier one
has not yet demonstrated competence. I am saying the
organism has to select some area within the field situation
in which it feels it has a chance to get love and acceptance
and to attain mastery. The older child has already usurped
one part of the field and therefore the possibility of mastery
there is more limited. It wants to adapt; it wants some life
space, too, some turf. Archimedes' principle probably operates here. No two bodies can occupy the same place at the
same time. So if the older child is already occupying some
domain of life experience, the other one will pick a different one, generally.

Gerry: Terrific.

Irv: That is a good thought.

Mannie: And we see this happen in the group by the way, day by day as the group grows. I think this is part of the study of sibling interaction. We have much to learn about it, but there is some validity to this general principle of complementarity as an adaptive aspect of the human organism. Well, it's time to sign off.

10

Oedipal and Pre-oedipal Derivatives

In different countries the analytic climate may influence emphasis upon one or another developmental phase in terms of the etiology of pathology or the focus for treatment. For instance, American psychoanalytic work has focused more on the oedipal competitive issues, whereas many English and South American analysts concern themselves more with early object relationships of a pre-oedipal nature.

The treatment modality used, whether it be individual or group, may have a bearing upon the ease with which oedipal or pre-oedipal material comes into focus for examination.

Some people feel that the primary relationship to the therapist is emotionally equivalent to the relationship to the pre-oedipal mother. It is necessary in analysis to clarify this pre-oedipal transference as well as the oedipal one. It is also essential that both oedipal and pre-oedipal transferences to the father as well as to the siblings be clarified.

In the analysis of any behavior including dreams one must pay attention to both oedipal and pre-oedipal components. Naturally, at one time or another in the course of an analysis or with one or

another patient the focus will discriminatingly be placed on one or
another set of developmental factors. This is timing.

Mannie: Are you with us, Irv?

Irv: Yes, I am with you. Gerry has not shown up yet. I don't
know what happened to him. He cannot blame me today.

Mannie: Do you think you two are resisting?

Irv: What do you mean, "you two"? Gerry, not me.

Mannie: You were late last week, weren't you?

Irv: I was not late.

Mannie: He was late last week.

Irv: He was late last week, but there was an overt reality reason
for it. Here he is now, he can speak for himself.

Mannie: I see.

Gerry: Good morning, good morning.

Irv: Are you resisting, Gerry?

Gerry: I must be. It is not "am I?" I find myself late two mornings
in a row.

Irv: Why is it? What is it all about?

Al: Very often, when I go on a vacation, there are one or two
persons in a group that either do not show up or come late
when I return. With many of them there is a wish to take
flight when I am gone. It gives them an opportunity to
escape, or they pay me back. If I go off when I please, they
are going to do the same.

Gerry: This is probably true. Just resistant to the world anyway,
because I have one heck of a time getting up on Saturday
morning, but that is—

Mannie: You don't work Saturday?

Al: Do you want to keep this time? We could make it later if
you like.

Gerry: I would rather keep this time as we already have it.

Mannie: You have it. It is all yours.

Irv: Say, you raised a very good point last time, and I am just
wondering about it. You said that in individual analysis
very often one deals with the competitive father struggle,
but you never really get to it or it is very difficult to get to
the pre-oedipal factors or to the early anaclitic ties to the

mother. I am just wondering about group, for example. Oedipal problems come up very markedly in the group, but what about dealing with the level of mother relationship that you were talking about in terms of group?

Mannie: Al, do you want to talk about it?

Al: I find it comes up. I think as soon as you are in an oedipal relationship, you are bound to produce the parent of the opposite sex.

Gerry: Al, you are awfully hard to hear this morning.

Al: I think the pre-oedipal material comes up if we are alert to the fact that it is part of the oedipal struggle to be aware of the parent of the same sex as the patient. As a matter of fact, I have had a patient in group who is so threatened by the mother figures in the group that she has been just paralyzed. I have had to take her out of the group. Of course, they still appear in the individual analysis, projectively speaking, but in the group she was just too threatened. She hopes to go back and I hope to put her back, but then the threatening mother enters our dyadic relationship.

Mannie: All right. Now I want to restructure what we were talking about last week and perhaps we can move forward from there. First of all, I think that even in individual analysis the primary symbolic relationship with the analyst is probably to a mother figure. I think the patient views the analyst, in individual analysis, as a mother. This is primary, regardless of any other distortions, any other projections which may occur. First, because when you come to a therapist, whether in the group or in the individual situation, you come for nurturance, succor, support, help. These are basic relationships to the mothering person so that no matter what kind of a manifest transference or other projections you see, you can be sure that the underlying and latent relationship between patient and analyst always carries with it, at the same time, a relationship to the mother figure. Are we clear on this item?

Gerry: I think so. And I do not see this problem that Irv brought up. I mean, I do not see it as a serious problem. I know in my groups that this is very frequently the material that comes up with many of them, a transference to me as mother, not in terms of an oedipal problem.

Mannie: We said last week that in American individual analysis there is a tendency to avoid two kinds of problems: the problem of the siblings and the working through of pre-oedipal material. What I was saying is that we tend too often to work out only the oedipal, and sometimes the phallic. This was an important contribution of Melanie Klein, but she was nondiscriminatory in that she said the oedipal was of no consequence, that only the pre-oedipal was of significance.

Irv: And didn't she postulate an oedipal struggle before there were even object relations?

Mannie: Exactly. In fact, she suggests that the ego comes with birth. And you know, Garma and Rascovsky in Argentina say that there is a prenatal ego, which is a mystical concept.

Irv: This is what I do not understand, the idea of talking about oedipal factors when there is no relationship. That really mystifies me.

Mannie: It depends upon whether you believe the assumption of Melanie Klein that human psychology is triangulated, the split object problem. To get a triangular relationship before you perceive others, other than yourself, seems to be pretty complicated. There is no developmental evidence for this, but Klein bases her theory on this assumption. By the way, we have a chapter in the book that Al and I are finishing on the nature of triangular psychology; that is, we try to differentiate monadic, dyadic, triangular, and a tetradic psychology. At least we struggle with the problem. I do not think we know enough about child development except reconstructively to be able to answer the questions very well. But I do know that you must try to explore with every patient, in the individual or in the group situation, relations with a father and with a mother, both oedipal and pre-oedipal, as well as oedipal and pre-oedipal relations with siblings. This is, in part, why the one-child family, the analysis of the only child, is complicated. Well, I have tried to summarize last week's discussion.

Gerry: I was wondering if Al had any reflections on the things that we have talked about in these weeks when . . . yes, I guess I did want him to be around here.

Al: Just let me say something about the pre-oedipal. As soon as you mentioned it I thought of two patients that I have had, both schizophrenics. One, a physician by the name of Sol, who would relate projectively to everybody in the group as if he or she were a mother, or he would homogenize the group into a mother and he would plead with us to be kind to him and to take care of him and soothe him, to look after him. If we did not play this role all the time, he would feel hurt or rejected and frustrated and angry. This was a constant acting out of the pre-oedipal. The other man, Bill, also was schizophrenic and would run to the alternate meetings and get there first and eat up all the food before anybody else would come, also viewing the group as a mother who must provide for him. Now in these cases, the pre-oedipal material was very obvious.

Irv: Yes, but in those cases, Al, these are men who are already functioning in a pretty regressed way, anyway. What about persons who regress as a result of the therapeutic situation?

Al: I think if we keep in mind that we are interested in the patient's relationship to the mother and start assuming, as Mannie has, that in a vertical relationship to the therapist and in its more diluted aspect to co-patients, that this exists on some level, that we are aware of it and begin interpreting this as a possibility, that patients become more alerted to it in one another, and that we will begin getting to the material.

Mannie: In every dream we have regression. It is in the nature of sleep and dreaming that we get regressed material. If you approach the dream only in terms of its manifest content, or only in terms of its oedipal material, you will not be using the opportunity, for example, to deal with pre-oedipal material that is in every dream. It is a matter of your attitude, not a matter of whether they give you the material. The material will come to you willy-nilly. The moment you begin to have them turn into themselves, begin to introspect, begin to free associate, you will get pre-oedipal as well as oedipal material.

Irv: It is a question of your frame of reference then.

Mannie: It is a question about you as the analyst in your orientation, what you are willing to pursue, what you are willing to accept, what your commitment or conviction is as to what you will work with. For example, I would like to stick my neck out in this context and say that if you told me I had only one problem to work out with every patient that comes into my office, but only one analytic problem and no other, what problem would I select as the most important single contribution I could make to any adult patient, I would say I would like to work out the oedipal problem. Here I have a commitment, a conviction, a theoretical and practical and technical devotion which colors all of my work. I do not exist, I do not work in that kind of a limited situation where I am permitted to work on only one problem, where there is no alternative. But if you force me against the wall and say what is it that I think would make the greatest contribution, I would say this. And I could give you any number of reasons for it, why I have come to this conviction. Others might say that if they were limited to one set of factors, they would want to work out the oral problems. Still others would opt for anal problems, or for family problems. Under such a forced choice I would want to attempt to help work through the oedipal problems. A good therapist does not get himself caught up in a theoretical or practical situation where this is the only problem he sees or works on.

Al: You also asked about any reactions I had to the previous material, and I had a lot of reactions, but I do not know whether it would be productive to go over the whole thing. In the material I got this week, Mannie and I were looking over parts of it, there was some question about an acting-out couple and the adolescent group, and you felt that I would hesitate about introducing a girl of nineteen. I thought about it. I have had little experience with adolescents in group, little direct experience. I have listened to other people report on this and I must admit that I would have some anxiety about working with a mixed group of adolescents despite the fact that a great deal here depends upon the therapist. This is what I would say, on the basis of clinical experience and supervision of group therapists who have worked with adolescents. Some of them have never gotten any kind of acting out and others get it pretty consistently. So I think it has largely to do with the therapist's attitude. If the patients feel the therapist is anxious, they may act out their resentment and punish him for being controlling about it or concerned about it. Some professionals will not mix the sexes in an adolescent group and they are concerned about such sexual acting out. I think that I would be quite discriminating about whom I put in a mixed adolescent group. There is a therapist I am now supervising who has a fifteen-year-old patient, a girl, who is quite promiscuous. Recently she became pregnant and her therapist had to notify her parents. A person that will act out this much, it would seem to me, either has to be in a group for a while where there are only girls or the therapist has to work individually with her to a point where she is not acting out in this kind of way. Otherwise it might have too destructive an effect on the group. On the other hand, there may be adolescents who are so rigid and unfree that it would be a marvelously liberating experience for them. It would give me anxiety if a group of adolescents were having sexual relations with the possibility that some of them might become pregnant. I know part of this is based on my concerns. A year or so ago a group therapist was being sued by the mother of a young girl who had become pregnant by a man in her group. One sees this kind of complication as a possibility arising in group therapy. We have to take a reasonable risk. It would be too threatening to me to have adolescents in group having sexual relations with the possibility hanging over my head that one of them might get pregnant.

Irv: What about the notion of introducing a nineteen-year-old female into a regular group?

Al: I would feel a little more secure if she were twenty-one, but I think I would put certain kinds of nineteen-year-old girls into an adult group.

Irv: What is the difference between nineteen and twenty-one? Why would—

Al: It is just a matter of law, you know. . . .

Irv: How do you mean?

Gerry: Statutory rape and nonstatutory rape.

Irv: You are talking as if you are the one that is sexually involved with her.

Mannie: Good for you, Irv.

Gerry: Well, maybe there is some of that in it, but I feel that we could be sued on legal grounds in that we brought the parties together.

Mannie: You mean sued for malpractice or nonprofessional practice or negligence. You have insurance, haven't you?

Irv: Yes, but we do not want to use it.

Mannie: Neither do I and neither does Al. But what I am saying is that obviously each one of us is going to have to make this kind of a decision in terms of our own anxieties, and our own comforts, and the percentage of risk that we are willing to take. For me, I prefer Al's earlier formulation that you have to be discriminating, that you make this decision in terms of the individual and the individual necessity; that to make the generalization that because it is a nineteen-year-old girl, a young woman, and therefore I will not put her into a group with adults, a heterosexual group of adults, as a mechanical safeguard, I would look upon as a rigidity perhaps reflecting a problem in the therapist. On the other hand, I think it would be equally rigid and would be equally reflective of a problem if I took the position that I would put every nineteen-year-old girl into a heterosexual group of adults, regardless. I think this decision has to be made very, very specifically and in terms of your knowledge of the individual patient, and the composition of the group. That is why I think you should not overlook Al's cautionary made earlier in our discussion, that you really ought to know something about the patient before you put the patient in a group, that you really ought to explore that patient a bit. You really ought to have a relationship with the patient. You really ought to know something about the psychodynamics, the pathology, the potential for acting out and so on. And it is on the basis of your knowledge of the patient that you make a certain decision at this time.

Gerry: Well, this threw me off track. I don't know. I got lost.

Irv: Maybe I was excluding Gerry. I was really sore when he came in late again today and I was wondering—I had a thought during the hour—wondered whether or not his coming in late had something to do with me or his feelings toward me.

Mannie: Have you two been having your alternate sessions?

Irv: Oh, yes. We have been having millions of them.

Mannie: How does it go in the alternate sessions? Is it any different in the alternate sessions from what it is here?

Irv: Yes, I think so.

Mannie: How is it different?

Irv: Well, we have the nurturing figures in the sessions with you two. We are trying to feed with you around, and in the alternate sessions we just hang onto each other. We feed each other in the alternate sessions and here we feed from you.

Mannie: I see. It is good that you express it. Gerry, what do you feel about that?

Gerry: Well, when he said this it sure made sense, because when I was coming down this morning I was thinking, "Oh, well, if I am a few minutes late, Irv can get the call in anyway, he'll be there." How does Irv get up in the mornings, anyway? I don't know—it is along that line.

Irv: Yes, I get here and I set up everything and then you waltz in, you know, and sit down.

Mannie: He walks in and says, "Good morning, fellas." Well, I think in this matter we will let you two fight it out.

Al: It sounds like the problem you were discussing before about the alternate meetings. Whose house is it going to be at? Who is going to assume the responsibility?

Irv: That is what I was thinking this morning.

Gerry: I thought about that, too. I thought, well, Irv can set up the machines. He is always there first anyway, and I dial the phone.

Irv: Listen! Good to have the family together again! See you next week!

Gerry: Righto, 'bye now.

11

A Psychotic Episode

Although our general routine is to treat the patient in the group
only, without private, individual sessions, circumstances can arise
that necessitate modifications of routine.

Mannie: Hi, how are you?
Gerry: Very good.
Mannie: Who is missing today?
Gerry: Nobody! Irv is starting the machine.
Al: How come you are so early today, Gerry?
Gerry: How come I'm so early? I guess my guilt is overcoming me.
Irv: Early, baloney! You just got here one minute ago!
Al: I see, I understand.
Irv: Something has come up on this general subject of acting
out, and I would like to talk about it. You remember Sally
and Leo that I spoke about? They acted out sexually with
one another.
Mannie: Yes.
Irv: There is so much here I don't know exactly where to begin,
but I'll start this way. Here is what happened. They slept

with each other. Sally called Leo one night, drunk, and they spent the night together. I feel all of this started when I stopped seeing these people individually and when we introduced the alternate session. Leo's reaction to loss of the individual sessions was one of intense anger and hostility, and he was almost going to leave treatment because of that. Sally's reaction was one of denial. She said, "Oh, boy, I'm glad to get rid of these individual sessions." But following that she started to go into feverish activity, getting involved in all sorts of things and behaving and thinking in a psychotic manner. Although I had made attempts in the past couple of weeks to try to get Leo and Sally to explore their feelings toward each other, they tried to steer away from it and they resisted in group dealing with the material. Also the group somehow tried to avoid it; the other patients didn't try to push it forward at all. I was quite anxious about them and I was thinking over in my own mind before the group meeting just how am I going to deal with this issue. My opinion was that their acting out is quite destructive to both of them, and they had to be confronted with it in the treatment situation. Sally came in about twenty minutes late at the last meeting. She was incoherent and flighty and talked in an over-symbolic way. It was apparent that she was having a psychotic episode. I waited a while hoping that Leo would say something or that Sally would begin to deal with her relationship to Leo. Sally did start off by saying something like, "Well, I've been tied to authority all my life and I'm really breaking down the authority now." The suspense built up in the group and Leo didn't say anything. He looked like a statue and Sally just looked at me. Someone in the group said, "Well, what's going on? Isn't someone going to tell us what happened?" Sally finally admitted that she had seen Leo, that she needed to see Leo, that she needed to talk to somebody, that she had so many things racing through her mind, and she was kind of defiant. Leo seemed to be quite defiant. He didn't want to talk about Sally and him. Then it began to appear to the group that Sally was having a real psychotic break. Flora began to cry, the tears rolled down her face because it immediately reminded her of when her sister had been hospitalized, and Flora said, "Oh, the group's going to be destroyed when something like this happens; we're not going to be able to work things through. This is terrible what is happening, and if we all can't work together, we're going to lose the group." Flora got awfully excited. Then Leo began to cry. The group talked a lot about what they thought the two were doing. Mary called Sally a black widow spider. Somebody saw Sally and Leo as a mother and son. Leo is much younger than Sally. Leo admitted that he terribly missed the individual sessions and he began to cry and said he missed me so much that if he gave up the acting out with Sally, he was going to be all alone again and he just couldn't stand it. He cried and was very upset. Some members in the group began to talk about how angry he was at me following the discontinuation of the individual sessions. They said that he was just trying to get at me through Sally, and some people speculated that Sally was trying to get at me by going out with Leo. The group went around on how they felt about this, but the important thing was that after the meeting I asked Sally to stay for a moment and I made an appointment to see her the next day because I was concerned about this psychotic-like behavior she was showing. She came in the next day and was very neatly attired. But again she was very flighty, talking in an over-symbolic way. She had had a dream about Leo in which she saw Leo's body broken and twisted into pieces and she was picking him up in her arms. Somebody in the group had accused her of castrating Leo. When she was out with Leo that night after she called him, she said to him while they were bowling, "Boy, I could really cut your balls off." But she forgot that. She also recalled having another dream where she was saying goodbye to somebody and she was crying, she woke up crying. She talked a lot about Christ during the hour and relating Jesus to her father in some way. Her father left her when she was about three or four years of age, and I had the feeling that what was happening here is a reactivation in the transference of what she must have experienced at the time that her father left, plus a combination of the feelings toward the mother and toward the father. In other words she identifies her father as Jesus in a way. She has a tremendous ambivalence about her father's leaving. On the one hand he rejected her and abandoned her, and on the other hand he was a great figure and the mother drove him out. What is happening here seems to be that she is reliving the intense emotions of her father's leaving and that this was triggered off by my not seeing her individually, although she had to deny her feelings and her great hostility. This psychotic-like episode represents a defense against her feelings of intense anger toward me which she couldn't handle. Now during this hour when we spoke, I said, "Well, what do you think your behavior is like, what do you think it has been like the past couple of days?" She said, "Well, I would say it's kind of schizophrenic, paranoid type."

Al: She said?

Irv: Yes, she said that. That it's kind of schizophrenic, paranoid type, and then she laughed and then immediately cried. I told you about the dream she had the other day where Leo was coming toward her and he was broken and bent and twisted. . . . So I am wondering how much of this represents a real psychotic episode and how much of it represents a reliving of feelings during the abandonment by her father and an attempt to manipulate and coerce me.

Al: Gerry, I wonder whether you would pursue the question that Irv asked. Irv asked the sixty-four-thousand-dollar question. He says, "I'm scared. Is this for real, is this woman for real, is she really going psycho?" I wondered whether you wouldn't try to be responsive to his question because he says he's scared.

Gerry: Oh, you mean do I think she's psycho?

Al: Irv, did I understand you right—

Irv: I think you read me quite well. I'm concerned about this.

Mannie: You said, "Is this for real?"

Irv: Yes. I'm not sure whether this is a real—

Al: Or whether she is acting this in some way, whether—

Irv: Acting out, whether this is a transferential acting out.

Gerry: Well, I don't know then what you mean by real. I think it is real and she is acting crazy, but is this something you are going to change the course of treatment about or are you going to use it as you would anything else. People act crazy in treatment.

Irv: Well, the thing is that everybody—she has really communicated to everybody around her—

Gerry: Have you ever thought of her as a person who has the weakness for potential psychotic episodes during treatment? I mean, you've worked with this woman in treatment for some time, you must have some—

Irv: She's an acting-out character who has very low frustration tolerance for feelings. She cannot handle feelings and when feelings get intense she runs. I have always felt that she uses denial. When she is overwhelmed by intense feelings she either somaticizes or she runs. I have never thought about her as one who was going to break down and have a—

Al: She is psychotic in my opinion, but you know, she's not a hundred per cent psychotic. Nobody is. If she can say she is schizophrenic, paranoid type, she has some reality-boundness.

Irv: Oh, she does, and she recognizes that she has been sick and she recognizes that she has been in and out. She says "I'm just going in and out."

Al: Irv, can you tell me what your subjective reaction is to this experience?

Irv: How I feel?

Al: Yes.

Irv: To the acting out or to the whole situation or just to her crumbling?

Gerry: Why not all three?

Al: Yes, let's get all of it.

Irv: All right. I think that initially when they acted out my question to myself was, What is going on here, and what are they doing, and why are they doing it? And I was hoping that by dealing with it in the group we could get to analyze what was going on.

Gerry: How did you feel about their having sexual relations?

Irv: I think I was scared by the implications of this. My feeling was, they are acting out with each other and it can lead to trouble. It can lead to trouble for me and it is complicating things. Let's try to analyze this thing and find out what is going on. I also saw in this a potentially healthy aspect for Leo in terms of the fact that he was making a heterosexual move despite all the hostility that was contained in it. What happened was that we could not deal with it in the group. When the group tried to deal with it, it seemed as if Sally and Leo were reluctant to associate to it. They were keeping mum on what was going on. Then Sally behaved psychotically. I doubted that she would decompensate that badly. I was skeptical about whether or not her manifest behavior was a true reflection of her state or whether it was some kind of manipulative attempt on her part. When I saw her individually I recognized that she was experiencing what seemed to me like a paranoid episode. Thoughts were racing around in her mind, and yet at the same time she was in good reality contact. She looked good although she said she had not been sleeping. She said it took her about forty minutes to write my check out. She gave indications that she was all right and there was reality contact. So that I just had a big question mark about the whole thing.

Al: Do you feel there was anything good about this?

Irv: Oh, I think this is a wonderful thing if we can work it out and analyze it, because I think what we are seeing here is an intense defensive avoidance of very basic feelings which she must have had at a very crucial time in her life, which is the core of her relationship to men and to her mother and to people and to her feelings.

Al: Are Sally and Leo and the members associating and examining the experience?

Irv: You mean this experience now?

Al: Yes, in the group.

Irv: It just came up in the last group session that Sally was so disturbed. Oh, and Leo called me up after the session. I asked to speak to Sally after the group meeting and she stayed behind for about five minutes so I could arrange for an individual session with her. Then I got a call from Leo about fifteen minutes later and he was very worried. He asked, "Do you think Sally is going to be all right?" and he was very upset.

Al: He didn't ask for an individual session?

Irv: He didn't ask for anything. He said, "I'm going to be all right, but I'm really concerned about Sally."

Al: I think there are positive aspects to Sally's and Leo's having this affair, positive aspects in the sense that she has had a relationship with a man who apparently was not impotent, is that true?

Irv: I assume that they were able to consummate the union.

Al: But it was Sally who developed an enormous amount of anxiety which she could not handle. If we take the position to deal with all the transferences involved in what happened, to all the possibilities of resistance, not only of Sally and Leo but of everybody's reaction to it, it can turn into a productive experience. And if the therapist can do this as well, not in the group necessarily, but you and Gerry can explore it and you can explore it with us. I think we can assume, to begin with, that Leo is hostile and destructive toward Sally and hostile and destructive toward you in some degree, but not altogether. I am not clear in my own mind whether you are the father and she is the mother to him or whether she is an extension of you or how much he is punishing you in this acting out, but these are aspects to be explored. Of course, if he is doing this he is also being destructive toward himself.

Irv: Yes, the group pointed that out last time. The group said, "Boy, you are really trying to get all the fathers after you, aren't you."

Al: The question is, from a practical point of view, whether this can be worked with in the group exclusively or whether certainly Sally, I think, should be seen individually as well. There is a question in my mind. Why were two people making such strong appeals to you to continue to see them individually as well? You cut them off from the individual sessions. While we have emphasized the importance of not providing combined therapy, it may be that a person like Sally, for example, that is, a pre-psychotic person, may need some kind of supervision, like the adolescent, some kind of vertical vector that does not let her escape into unconsciousness. It is a question even with Leo whether it was wise to just cut him off from individual sessions when he was pleading. I think you said he cried about losing you. I am not quite sure I understand what you felt in denying them in their appeal to you. My position generally is whenever a patient has to see me alone, I say yes, and then if I see it is a resistive thing or in some way destructive to the patient and will not facilitate the analysis, I try to work it out. I will work it through with them until they can return to the group and work exclusively in group. I feel I should not cut them off if they are making very strong appeals unless in some way I feel reasonably sure that this won't be experienced as a very destructive thing or actually be in some respects destructive.

Mannie: This raises another question. You can get caught on the horns of these dilemmas all the time. If you see her privately then she is forcing care. If you see her privately then you will provoke fantasies and wishes in her that she may be seduced, and also the fear of it. If you do not see her privately you are not going to give her the supporting vertical relationship that Al says she needs. You have a number of paradoxes here which cause, I think, some of the difficulty you have; there is a question as to what you ought to do. Gerry, what is your reaction to all of this?

Gerry: I have been thinking the last few minutes we have spent a lot of time on this and I don't know whether we have gotten anywhere. I don't—I'm uncomfortable.

Mannie: All right. Just so we don't think that we have spent time without getting anywhere, let me try to summarize some of the things that I think were said. First of all, Al was quite clear in the statement that he thinks she is psychotic at this point. Secondly, Al suggested that the positive use of this experience will come in the attempt to explore two aspects of the work, which are the two aspects which play a part in acting out with any patient; namely, the transference relationships and the resistance. Third, it was suggested that everybody in the group ought to be given a chance to explore their feelings about the actual breakdown of Sally and the incidents of their acting out, that all ought to explore their transference reactions as well as their realistic reactions to this. Al also pointed out that in a patient who is pleading for some kind of wish to be heard, we had better listen to the patient and evaluate before we say no from any rigid theoretical or technical position. It was also suggested that when a person becomes actively disturbed it might be important to give them a supporting relationship with an authority figure to stabilize the situation, even if we are committed to the idea that it might be possible to work it out in a group. Al also suggested as a practical generalization that in understanding this relationship we might recognize that we can do differential treatment for the two participants in an acting out interaction. That is, you might, for example, with Sally give her the individual session, but for Leo not give it. It is important also to understand and to explore the nature of the reaction to the differentiated treatment or the individuated treatment. Finally, we also made some generalizations about the nature of seeing the activity, whatever the activity is, not exclusively in its negative elements, and to deal with our own fantasies, associations, transference reactions, and anxieties in trying to come to grips with what is really going on, or what we might do.

Gerry: Yes, well Al, I mean Mannie, I think that those are all things we have talked about and I think those are things that Irv knows. But what I felt was we didn't really get to any resolution of the question so far as Irv is concerned. I know what Irv wanted out of this because I think he could have said each of those things and knows each of those things, but that isn't why he is anxious.

Mannie: Well, let's ask Irv.

Irv: Well, I think that I wanted the opportunity to talk about it in order to understand what is happening, what she is doing, why she is doing it, and what we can do to help work this thing out so it will be productive. I wondered whether it is wise to see her individually or not, whether by seeing her individually I am saying to her, "You are really in a desperate, dangerous situation and I have the feeling that you cannot make it alone and I don't have any confidence in your ability to make it."

Gerry: This is what I was getting at. . . . We've talked about all of
           these things and I know you wanted to talk about this and
           that you are very anxious about it, but I don't feel that I
           have understood what your anxiety is about.

Mannie: He has anxiety in front of us, you and both of us. He has
           some anxiety that he has taken a fairly rigid position com-
           mitted to the group situation and he is concerned about
           his present experience as to whether he is going to do right
           and whether we are going to approve of what he is doing.
           He is saying this again and again. I think you are not
           listening to him. I think you are trying to get him to say
           something you have in your own mind. What do you think
           he has been trying to avoid, Gerry?

Gerry: That is a good thought. I don't know.

Al: Well, look, Irv, if you have these doubts then you should
           for a week or longer explore and see if you can work it out
           in the group. If you feel it is going to make her feel you
           are very anxious about her and reinforce self-doubt and
           it does not give you an opportunity to test how far you can
           work therapeutically in the group, wait a while. Or you
           can ask her and Leo how they feel. Do they want to see
           you privately? You don't have to pull her out and do it.
           Maybe that would be provocative. Do they think there is
           any need for it? Get their associations to it. Maybe you
           will find that they themselves are trying to provoke you
           to give them private sessions, to force you to do it, and
           you can analyze the whole thing in the group. I think you
           ought to respect your doubts about the necessity for private
           sessions if you feel that you know them better than we do
           and it may well be that you can work this out in the group,
           but let's get their feelings and associations into it.

Gerry: Wait a minute now. Mannie asked what did I feel. Well, I
           think you said it somewhat earlier when we were presenting
           all this, that they are acting out for you. They are acting
           out about your feeling about the group having an alternate,
           which we have talked about before, and their socializing.
           We spent two or three Saturdays talking about socialization
           and your anxiety about the patients meeting and acting
           out sexually with one another and having alternate sessions
           outside of here. Now you are setting it up so their alternate

session would be in here. I think what you are saying is, "Look at how uncomfortable you have made me feel because look at what these people are doing."

Mannie: In other words you think he is trying to punish all of us by saying, "Look what we have done."

Gerry: Well, that's what I feel. I have felt for forty-five minutes that he is punishing us in some way.

Irv: You know, I don't feel that way at all. Maybe that is involved here, but I don't consciously feel it at all. I feel that something has really moved in the treatment of both of these people.

Mannie: You know, Irv, I have a feeling Gerry is saying that maybe you provoke this acting out in order to be able to tell us, "Look what you are doing to me and to these people. You know, these people get psychotic if you let them socialize." I think this is what you have been saying, Gerry, is that right?

Gerry: Yes.

Irv: Do you think so? Do you think this is a manipulation on my part?

Mannie: What do you think, Al?

Al: I don't really think so. How about you, can you say whether you are putting us on the spot?

Irv: I don't feel I am putting you on the spot. I feel that this is something that we have got a tremendous amount to learn from because if we can really work through with Sally what is happening here, I think this is going to be a major turning point in her treatment, and the same thing holds for Leo.

Mannie: Irv, you know we all believe in multidetermined behavior and each one of us knows that a dream might have fifty-seven different interpretations, each one of which may be equally appropriate on some level and in some context, and each one of us is going to use whatever interpretation of the dream we think is most appropriate and most useful to our necessities and the patient's necessities at the particular time.

Gerry: Exactly, Mannie, and that is what I am saying. I felt, Irv, we were talking about something very meaningful in terms of the patients and something which can be used and understood. In many ways I think that what we have summarized and talked about is very productive. But I don't think it dealt with the way you feel about this. You have been talking, but the way you are talking about it does not make it sound like you have reached any new intellectual knowledge or any new conceptualization of what is happening with these patients. You have said all of these things before.

Al: I get a funny feeling. I think if I were the therapist and this was the first experience I had of two patients getting together and having a sexual relationship and one of them began acting psychotic, I get a feeling I would be much more anxious. Now maybe that is my problem, but I feel that Irv. . . . I don't feel any anxiety from you . . . a lot of excitement, yes, but no anxiety. Now if the excitement is that in a sense certain defenses of Sally's have broken through and perhaps there is more certainty that she can recover more and more of her reality-boundness despite this—

Irv: Well, that is how I feel. I feel that I can work with her. In other words I don't feel that—

Al: Maybe it was my anxiety based on my putting myself in your shoes that made me say right away, "Let's get individual sessions."

Irv: I mean I'm anxious about the situation, but I feel that there is movement here and I can work with it. I think that what I was asking for today primarily was for a clarification of her psychotic-like behavior.

Mannie: The formulations sound great. We are talking about the feeling.

Irv: As far as my feeling about it, I was scared to realize that she was behaving psychotically, and I wanted to get help in bringing her back to reality.

Gerry: Yes, but throughout all of it you didn't say anything about these things that we have spent so much time clarifying and intellectualizing about in these previous sessions. How do you feel about this, having stated so strongly how you felt about socialization, about alternate meetings, about having the patients meet in their homes instead of here in the office? These are the things that I feel were left out and that determine in some part why you are spending the time on it.

Mannie: Gerry is very good, I should say, very astute.

Al: That is, Gerry, are you saying that with Irv's concern about socialization, he is demonstrating that socialization is dangerous?

Gerry: Yes, but he hasn't said that.

Irv: Because I don't feel that in this situation.

Gerry: Well, why don't you feel it? That is what I am asking. Why don't you feel it?

Irv: Wait a second, wait a second. Let's be a little reality-oriented here. I feel that these people were doing something and I am trying intellectually to understand what they were doing. Now on an emotional level, what has happened surely scares me. Surely it rouses anxieties within me. There is no question about it. However, I feel that my job right now is to try to work with this material, try to get Sally back to where she can—

Mannie: That's right! I think one of the early points Al made is that you can only work with this material if you understand your role and your transferences and your feelings in the situation as well as hers.

Irv: That's right.

Gerry: Well, that's what I was trying to say.

Irv: Now, what do you feel I am avoiding here, Gerry? Do you feel I am avoiding my . . . you felt that earlier I was trying to beat Al and Mannie over the head with this or something?

Gerry: All of it.

Irv: In what way? I was saying, look what socialization—

Gerry: You kept saying things that we have already talked about and they had already talked about. We had explained that the conceptualization of the problem wasn't new, so why do you have to keep talking about it, but not talking about it?

Irv: I could have said the same thing when you were talking about the patient you were discussing last week.

Gerry: Well, maybe you could have.

Irv: I mean you can say this about anything, anytime you try to bring up a case. I think you have some other beef here. I just wonder if you are trying to get back at me for what happened last week and this is what you, what really is going on because—

Mannie: You mean if he comes on time, you shouldn't try to take over the session?

Irv: I'm sure that is what he is reacting to.

Mannie: You guys need an alternate session.

Irv: I think this is ridiculous because I know I am anxious about the situation. There is no question about it, but I also feel that I want to work with it and I can work with it. I was just—this is the first time I have had a patient who has decompensated like this.

Al: Gerry, do you feel excluded from this experience today?

Irv: I am sure that is what he feels.

Gerry: Yes, I feel excluded, sure I do.

Irv: I think that is why you are taking all these shots at me.

Gerry: Well, maybe it is why I am taking shots at you, but nonetheless I still think there is an issue there. Whether I am using it to take a shot at you because I feel excluded is one thing, but nonetheless this is the way I see you acting on it.

Mannie: I think it is a great day, fellas. How is the weather out there? We have beautiful spring weather and the opportunity to go out and fight it out in the park. I think the two of you ought to go and have an alternate session, and let's go on with this next time.

12

Lateral Transferences
in This Training Group

Affective components of interaction have multiple determinants. History, expectations, and character patterns color current interpersonal activity. Genetic issues, life stages, and helper-helped dimensions may be aroused and woven into the fabric of conscious content. Competitions within one's profession, one's community, and among professionals are a part of the emotional content of the learning process. Though self-esteem is a private experience, publication allows social validation.

Mannie: Al, I think you put it well this morning saying that maybe we ought to have Gerry and Irv tell us about what kind of transferences they have been having to us and to each other. Some of this provocation seems to be between you and me. Maybe we are in some way playing roles that ought to be explored more consciously by the four of us. What do you think?

Irv: I think it would be good to explore that. I do not know what is going on between Gerry and me. Although he raised a good point last week, I think he is resentful when I monopolize the session. I had a big need last time and I think I feel some resentment if he talks a whole session, too. Gerry was late some mornings. Now I do not know what it is all about, Gerry. It could not be just to me then. It must be to the whole thing or our whole experience.

Gerry: Well, I think I hinted at the feeling, I did not consciously label it. I did call Mannie "Al" and felt that I did not like the idea that Al had a vacation and we were kind of working along without him. That may be why I've been coming late, but one thing we know is that we compete.

Irv: You and I.

Gerry: Yes, compete. Like yesterday afternoon when this patient—

Irv: Oh, that was no competition. A psychiatrist referred a patient to us, both of us—

Gerry: He did not. The patient came in and asked for me. What do you mean?

Irv: Somebody referred somebody to us and before I know it, Gerry has him in his office. That may influence what transpires between Gerry and me.

Gerry: This is part of my problem anyway, so I would think that I relate to Mannie and to Al much like I do to anyone else whom I put in an authority position. I say put because that is me.

Irv: Didn't you put them in an authority position?

Gerry: I do, you see, and that is why when Al goes out and takes his nice vacation I get mad and stay home because I have got to be one up all the time. I think this is what I am doing with both of them. I had a good fight going with Mannie last week about something.

Irv: I think Mannie was fighting with you though, too. I think Mannie was kind of provocative if you ask me.

Mannie: I generally am.

Irv: I think . . . it is hard for me to know what the transferences are here, I mean in terms of what I am doing.

Gerry: I have a feeling about this.

Irv: What do you think I am doing?

Gerry: Well, not about you, but about myself. I think I feel about Mannie more like I do about my older brother. He is about the same size, shape, but does not have the beard. I feel Al would be my father, very ascetic looking, very quiet. When he talks, you are supposed to listen, and this is the way I feel about it. I remember one session we had before Al was away, where I could not hear him and I had some fantasy of his sitting on the edge of the chair like we do here, really trying hard to get his voice into that microphone and listening to us very intently. And Mannie said, "Well, you know what he is doing; he is looking up at the ceiling."

Mannie: You are right! Exactly! A beautiful description of what goes on here!

Gerry: Then again, the way Mannie will often say, "Well what do you think about that, Al?" And I feel that Mannie slides right out of a question he does not want to answer and bounces it into Al's lap.

Mannie: Al said he did not get that last comment. Repeat it, will you, Gerry?

Gerry: I say I sometimes feel like we will ask a question or we will say something or you have an idea, Mannie, and instead of expressing it, you say, "How do you feel about that, Al?" And all of a sudden he has it sitting in his lap.

Al: Gerry, how did you feel about your father and brother? You described something about them but—

Gerry: My father I would describe as a person that if you differed with him you could never have the right answer. He was always right. Even if he pronounced a word wrong, you could show him a dictionary and he would still go on and tell you that you were stupid and so was Webster and tell you how to pronounce the word. I think my brother is more subservient to authority and I guess I think I must be feeling that way about Mannie.

Irv: You mean that he is subservient to Al?

Gerry: Yes, but only in the way that I am, which is not really at all. He is getting one up.

Irv: You mean Mannie is? Well, Mannie takes a lot of the time though, he is very directive and he sort of calls Al in. He says, "Come on in, Al, what do you think about this?"

Gerry: Yes, on the surface, or manifestly, I feel like he is saying, "Well, Al, you are the real authority here." But Al does not have a chance. He has him coming and going.

Mannie: That is wonderful.

Irv: How do you feel about this, Al?

Al: I do not feel this. I feel Mannie is always trying to draw
           me out and I have a tendency to sit back more. Mannie
           is much more openly reactive than I am.

Gerry: I know that is true, Al, but what I say is that this is the
           way I feel. I think that this is my transferential kind of
           feeling. Because I do not see you and I do not know you
           that well, it is not based on what really happens, but it is
           what I have to have happen.

Irv: I had this feeling when I was driving home in the car
           the other night, thinking about Al and Mannie. I was
           thinking that Mannie always seems to be the one that
           responds to us. In other words, he responds with warmth
           and is always in there relating very closely with us, direct-
           ing and interested. And Al seems to be more in the back-
           ground. I began to speculate and I wondered what is Al
           really like in his groups and what is he like with other
           people? He does not seem to relate in the same kind of
           way that Mannie does. He relates in a more distant kind
           of way. So I felt that Mannie was in a sense more of a
           warm, social type of interactive person.

Gerry: Yes, but you know I just had a thought. I was telling you
           last week I was down in L.A. for the ABEPP exams. One
           of the chairmen for one of my exams came downstairs and
           sat right beside me on a couch. There were a couple of
           other people there. He said hello, and introduced himself.
           I looked at his profile and he looked like Al.

Irv: You said he looked like Al?

Gerry: He looked like Al, because the look on his face, the way he
           looked off into space was like Al. I remember this from Al's
           workshop in January. Al has a distant expression yet at the
           same time I feel he is very friendly. I am sure that this in
           some way is related to feelings from the past with regard
           to my father.

Irv: I read over the transcript of last week's session and I noticed
           that the girl made some mistakes in terms of when Al was
           speaking and when Mannie was speaking. Then I noticed
           that Al said a few things and I was very surprised. It inter-
           fered with the fantasy I had, the stereotype. I thought,
           "Al said that?" I know he said it, but I thought he does not

talk that way. I feel that Mannie is close and more related to us whereas Al is more distant. Then when I read the transcript I knew Al said things and I almost could not believe it.

Gerry: Well, I wonder too. It occurs to me, of course, that we have a lot of feelings about competition between psychiatry and psychology. Al is a psychiatrist; Mannie is a psychologist. Maybe this is our own distortion; of course it is.

Irv: I know that when I saw that Al actually made these statements, I could not believe that he said it because—

Gerry: He is not that friendly?

Irv: Yes, that he was that friendly, so there must be some transference involved. Well, how did this whole thing start? We approached Al and not Mannie, and Al said, "Let's get together with Mannie, too." I know my initial feeling was, "Well, what do we want Mannie for?" That was before we knew you. Because we approached Al Wolf, not Mannie Schwartz, we did not understand this. And I felt, "What is he getting this guy for?" And then when we began to interact in our sessions, I felt we sure would have been way out if we had not had Mannie along. In other words, I felt that Mannie is really making a contribution. Maybe we tend to transfer to Al more as the father and see Mannie in a different kind of light.

Gerry: Good fathers and bad fathers.

Irv: You did mention, Mannie, some time ago when we brought this problem up, that you felt that traditional ways of training were not necessarily the best ways.

Mannie: I still feel that way because I think that most of us and particularly us, who are not medical people, have had to get our training in a variety of ways outside of institutions. That does not mean that getting the piece of paper makes any graduate any better or any worse an analyst than people who do not have that piece of paper.

Irv: Yet people do go through formal training in order to achieve a certain goal and they do have some kind of belongingness.

Gerry: That is true, Irv, but I think you are missing a point and I think I can see what Mannie is talking about. Our own training has to come, since we are in the part of the world that we are and we have the limitations. We are meeting our own need in this way and this is a very specialized kind of thing with only two of us involved. This cannot lead to any piece of paper. It can only lead to training where we can have some inner confidence about what we are doing. We are not going to be able to say to someone else that we have this piece of paper, but I think that as we go along and develop what we are doing here, it is not out of the question to consider this as a mode of training that could be set up in a formalized way, maybe for a bigger group of people or a different group of people.

Mannie: Every training institute, every educational institution by nature is conservative. It attempts to preserve and conserve and to perpetuate traditions to which it is committed. Our work here is quite revolutionary in that sense. This is a radical departure and I think that it can be useful in terms of increasing your own confidence and your conviction about your competence as analysts. To expect that the conservative organizations are going to recognize this is really not to perceive the nature of this experience correctly. What I am suggesting is that this belongingness that you feel you need may come later on by creation of your own training group.

Gerry: I think I already have it. I have a feeling of belonging to this unique experience.

Mannie: Exactly, and also even to larger groups when you begin to develop further elaborations of this and new directions.

Gerry: Yes, and when I was down in Los Angeles last week and I mentioned that we were engaged in this, people were really interested and I felt kind of good. I thought, we are first.

Mannie: In the long range you are going to have to come to the realization that you are in a very lonely profession because many analysts and groups of analysts are very isolating and cultist. This is in the nature of the work we are doing and we are especially lonely in analytic circles if we are non-medical persons, in that the medical professionals in the main will not accept us. They will accept you individually and personally, but not as groups and not as professionals, and you have to struggle with this reality for yourself. I share this with you in terms of my own experience. It reminds me of Kittredge at Harvard. He was the world's authority on Shakespeare and he never got a Ph.D., a professor of literature. They asked him why he never got a Ph.D. degree and he said, "I don't take them, I give them."

Al: I wonder whether what Mannie has said does not hold up. Many of the people who are our teachers were themselves people who had a three-month's analysis with Freud. As years have gone by they have become more demanding of increasingly extended training of younger colleagues.

Irv: But you have to have standards. That is a reality, isn't it?

Al: Yes, but my feeling is as long as you two are working and struggling and looking for teaching, that is the thing that really counts. It is always going to be a problem for non-medical therapists. I do not know about always, but it certainly is going to be difficult for some time, to get the kind of status they want in the community.

Gerry: Well, that is the old problem, somebody is always.

Al: There are exceptions, Erich Fromm, Theodor Reik, and others, who because of their asserting themselves and doing original, creative work have achieved status.

Gerry: I feel like this is the kind of thing I have already looked at as the way to get out of this bind for myself; that is, by what I do and by my own communication with people, maybe sometime I will be able to write down some of the ideas I have and publish them. This is the way I am going to get any external validation of what I am.

Al: I used to think that my being a certified diplomate in psychiatry and neurology, which I got in 1940, would make a difference. I do not think there has been anybody ever who has asked me whether I am or am not, whether a professional colleague or a patient. Nobody seems to ask me where I have graduated, where I am connected. It is a very rare thing.

13

Elaboration of
Feeling of Participants

What is reality? What is illusion? What is transference? What is the value of structure, spontaneity, activity, passivity, and conformity? These are some of the questions every analyst asks himself again and again, especially if he works with patients in groups. A discriminating response in the face of multiplicity of experience is more difficult. Often we must turn to ourselves, our own experiencing, to perceive what is happening.

Mannie: I felt rejected after last week's session. You gave me a working over.

Irv: Who did? Who gave you a working over?

Mannie: Both of you. I read the notes carefully.

Irv: Well, let's talk about that. What was the working over?

Mannie: Somebody had the feeling there that I was subservient to Al's authority. I think that was you, Irv.

Gerry: No, listen Mannie, you did not read them very carefully, because you did not see where *I* said that this is the kind of thing that *I* do. On the manifest level it is a statement like, "What do you think, Great White Father?" But all the time you have, as Irv accuses me, the banzai sword under your coat.

Mannie: Yes, but I thought that you were being very kind in trying to take the blame on yourself as being purely projective. Yet I have a psychoanalytic commitment that there is some reality to which we latch on when we make a projection, a transference. So I was disheartened by the reality that you perceived.

Irv: I did not think we gave you a bad time, Mannie. I thought that, as a matter of fact, a lot of motherly feelings were expressed.

Mannie: Mother with a beard! I think you fellows are wonderful! I am really only provoking you a little because I wanted to lead into a problem that Al and I have talked about in view of last week's session.

Al: What are your associations, Gerry and Irv, to this more detached, remote figure who surprises you by some warmth occasionally? This is partly real. I feel that I am much less reactive than Mannie. Partly, I think it is the interpersonal situation. Mannie is so interactive that I tend to take more of a back seat than I might if he were not so responsive.

Mannie: Or if you were here alone with Gerry and Irv.

Al: But you have some feelings about your own associations. Is it one of identification, for example?

Gerry: Well, for me it must be because you made a very good point at the end, as I read over the notes, Al. You pointed out about my being the sixth in the chain of seven kids and I must sit back and build this up. It comes out that way so many different times. And I know it does. I know often I have the feeling, like when Irv and I were back in New York at the meeting, that I am a kind of shirttail relative. You are a fluid, verbal person, Irv. You know how you are always quoting the literature. I feel like I am the little guy running along behind.

Al: But, Gerry, you are saying that there is some identification; we are both tails of the other siblings or kite. You are a tail to Irv and I am a tail to Mannie.

Gerry: Yes, but nonetheless—

Irv: In reality, of course, there is no basis for it and—

Al: Maybe there is reality to it too, as Mannie says. It is a position we assume. Why do we assume this retiring position?

Irv: For example, I noticed in looking over the notes of our meetings that I had been the one who was responsible a great deal for the structuring of the type of content that we dealt with. At least that is how I feel. I do not know whether it is accurate or not. But my feeling is that I was responsible for a lot of the discussion on transference and regression. This morning I brought up immediately to Gerry a topic with which I am concerned. Now I am wondering, maybe part of it is defensive on my part too, because I cannot stand to have an unstructured meeting. There is always something that concerns me, something I want to deal with when it comes to these meetings. Gerry does not seem to come with that kind of attitude. Do you, Gerry?

Gerry: No. Often I think, well, I ought to have something prepared, but I figure we will get something out of it anyway.

Al: Well, that is Irv's requirement for a formal course of training and a formal piece of paper. That is Irv's wish to structure all the time. Gerry is saying, "I do not need formal structure."

Mannie: I am glad Al stopped me this time because I was going to jump the gun. But I still would like to get into it, Al. I do not know whether you are satisfied with their associations to you.

Al: I am not satisfied. For example, a couple of things occur to me. First, I do feel, Gerry, you and I are identified in your mind and that in part in reaching this man—was it in L.A.?—who was me you are probably trying to reach yourself. But I feel somewhere I must also be a transference figure, that I am not just a figure with whom you consciously identify.

Gerry: Oh, I do not question that at all. In many ways you are a lot like my father in build, shape, size, and I suppose in the way he *is*, too. He was remote. But one who had the word, of course. That was his attitude. He was a person who was always right. But it is more than that too, because while he was a lawyer for the railroad, and the head of his department, an inexperienced relative of the railroad top management was put in over him as head of his legal department. Consequently my father was ghost-writing for this figurehead. I think this is what I was saying about Mannie last week, that you, Al, are the figurehead. He was somehow deferring to your authority but not really accepting it. I guess that is what my reaction is. Of course, I do not know to what extent it is true of Mannie.

Irv: I do not think we really have explored our feelings about the relationship between Mannie and Al. What do they do when they get together?

Gerry: Well, what difference does it make what the relationship is between them when, in fact, this is what I make it? Mannie really has his own ideas and convictions, but he uses Al to give some impression. Then he will go along and either agree with it or contradict or give his own opinion. It is kind of using Al. I have focused on it as that until now.

Irv: You mean he sort of calls Al into the picture. He is sort of a director, that is the feeling? Mannie is sort of the director and he says, "Okay, Al, it is your turn to come in again. You tell us what you think." Or, "I wish Al were here; he would tell us what he thinks." That sort of thing?

Gerry: I suppose so. I think of Mannie as one of my older brothers. "What is dad doing out playing golf with them? How come my brother goes to law school? How come Mannie can get through a formal analytic training? How does he get to be what dad is?" I am sure that is the involvement. "How did my brother have the courage to go to law school when my father was a lawyer and knows it all? You have to go somewhere else."

Irv: Some other profession.

Mannie: Like psychology.

Al: How does your older brother get to be your father?

Gerry: No, that is not what I said, but of course, that is involved. I am saying, "How does he get to go to law school like my father?"

Al: But you cannot get to be your father.

Gerry: Well, I can of course, but will not.

Al: Well, did something go on between your father and brother that did not go on between you and your father?

Gerry: Not that I know. I don't know.

Al: Well, look, it seems your father sponsored something in your brother which allowed your brother to have his kind of authority. I am the big authority. I have sponsored Mannie and he is as big as I am if not bigger. Where do you stand in this triangle of you, your brother and father, that is, Mannie and me?

Gerry: I don't know. I stand out in Seattle, that is where I stand.

Al: Towards the tail end, eh?

Gerry: It is like reality, too. They still live in the East, in Boston, and here I am in Seattle.

Mannie: You could not go any farther away, could you?

Gerry: No.

Irv: Although you did have your father living with you for a year or so. How long was he out here, six months, a year? One thing we have not explored, our feelings toward your beard, at least my feelings toward the beard.

Gerry: I heard a good joke about his beard from our secretary.

Irv: Our secretary has a transference to you, Mannie.

Mannie: Yes? Because of my choice language?

Irv: No, not because of that. I think because, well I don't know, maybe it is because of that. . . .

Mannie: Here we go again! I like your secretary, too. What is your reaction to the beard, Irv, since you raised it?

Irv: All right, I would like to talk about it. I remember I saw you with the beard and I thought, "What comes off with this guy?" I thought, "What is he trying to do, is he a Freud or something?"

Gerry: What came off with this guy, is that—

Irv: Yes, that is it! What has he got the beard for? It is kind of weird, you know. Then when I spoke to you, you sounded kind of reasonable, but I have always associated people with a beard like that as trying to act out something. I thought, "What is he acting out with this beard of his? There is something bizarre, something strange here. He needs that beard for some reason." That was my feeling about it.

Gerry: What reason?

Irv: I figured that he probably wants the beard to feel more important, to give him some stature, to give him some authority, to add to his appearance because he is short and a little chubby and I think the beard makes him feel more like the old man.

Gerry: I do not see any beard on Al.

Irv: No, I mean like Freud, *the* old man, Freud.

Mannie: Well, I had three people at a meeting the other night at which I was a discussant say to me that they were impressed by how much I looked like Freud. I was sitting there with a big cigar in my mouth and I said, "Of course, why do you think I did it?" What other motivation can you suggest?

Irv: Well, I wonder.

Gerry: You could be a rebel like all those Mexicans and South Americans. They wear beards too.

Mannie: Why does it bother you, Irv? You seem to be bothered more than Gerry. He did not have a father with a beard; he had a mother with a beard, he told us last week.

Irv: It doesn't bother me. Well, maybe it does. It does bother me because I am wondering if this guy is really well analyzed. What is he wearing a beard for, what does he need it for?

Mannie: But, Irv, it apparently distresses you and I think you might want to explore why it distresses you. Maybe there are other things about me that distress you. I think you at least ought to find some association to it.

Irv: I do not know if I am distressed by the beard. I think that when I saw you with the beard, the association was of a lot of the other characters I see in Seattle, the beatnik characters who are running around wearing beards. It reminds me of my Provincetown days when everybody was walking around with a beard and it was all an affectation.

Mannie: What were you doing in Provincetown?

Irv: I was walking around with a beard! No, I am only kidding, I am only kidding.

Gerry: You wanted to walk around with a beard, huh?

Irv: I wanted to walk around with a beard, but I never grew one. That is it. I was never able to grow a beard.

Gerry: So you are saying, how can he grow a beard?

Irv: I probably would like to have a beard myself if I had the guts to get away with it.

Al: You have to follow the structure too much.

Irv: That is it.

Al: You cannot be certified if you have a beard. I think every man would like to see how he looks in a mustache or a beard at some time in his life. He may not be obsessed with it, but we have all toyed with the idea.

Gerry: You know, it just occurred to me—I don't know why I had not thought about it. My father wore a mustache. I did not even think of it when I was thinking of Al and the man in Los Angeles and how they looked like my dad, aesthetic, thin, small structured people. I thought they looked alike, but it just occurs to me—my father always wore a mustache as long as I ever knew him. As a younger man he did not, but throughout all of my lifetime he had a mustache.

Irv: I think that what you hit upon, structure and this conformity, is quite correct. Actually I would rather be avant-garde. I would enjoy it. I like Provincetown and I would like to wear sandals and walk down the beach and read poetry and I would not mind having a beard myself. I would like to have a beret and—

Gerry: I almost bought a beret a month or so ago. It was a plaid one. It was really nice.

Irv: Apparently, Mannie, you are doing some of the things I would like to do and do not have the guts to do.

Mannie: Apparently I have already done some of the things you would like to do.

Irv: And do not have the guts to do.

Mannie: All right, including certification and position and a lot of other things in reality.

Irv: Right. And your way of thinking and your encyclopedic comprehension is the kind of thing that I envy. In a way, it is the way in which I deal with knowledge. In other words, the things I know, I know in terms of organization. I can cite a whole host of related references on the same thing and what leads to what. So I am sure that from what I see, I like your intellectuality and I like your warmth, humanness, and your interaction. This is the sort of thing I envy. I would like to have it. I would like to take over your position, be in your shoes.

Al: Maybe you can do it. Maybe there is a part of your desire for structure, rationality, knowledge, and recognition which is appropriate. But you know, you can leave room also for more spontaneity in yourself, such as Mannie has.

Gerry: And you can leave room for fun.

Irv: That is the thing that I love about Mannie, the spontaneity. It is just a wonderful quality which I envy in people. These are the kind of people I like, the kind of people that you get together with and they are very good conversationalists. They are very interesting; they are very warm. You get a good feeling when you are with them and it is a wonderful kind of experience.

Al: You know I have a student in analysis who is afraid of her spontaneous affect and of showing it. Mannie fascinates her because she sees that he is spontaneous and yet that he can at the same time be structured, reasonable.

Irv: I think that is the thing that surprised not only me but Gerry, because we were most surprised when we got together with you. We were most surprised when Mannie started talking, and I think that you had that feeling too, Gerry, didn't you? We felt Mannie was going to be all over the place, but he was not; he was well organized.

Gerry: I don't know if I can go along with that completely, Irv. When we talked to Mannie I was delighted in talking with him, but I was also incredulous that anybody could be that friendly to a shirttail relative from Seattle.

Irv: No, but I recall, Gerry, we both shared in the feeling. We wondered what it was with this guy.

Gerry: Well, he was very spontaneous. When we asked Al about having this kind of a session and he said, "How about having Mannie join us?" I thought I didn't like the idea because he is a very verbal man. He would smother Al and maybe we would never get anywhere with his spontaneity. It will explode us all over the place for an hour a week on the phone.

Al: Gerry, let's you and I struggle not to be shirttails.

Gerry: I am struggling with it; I am working at it.

Irv: This may be just projection on my part, but this morning as I was coming to the office, Gerry drove up so I waited for him. I said, "Good morning, Gerry," real friendly. Gerry gave me a murderous, deadly look. That is the way I felt. Were you sore or something? You did not respond in any—

Gerry: How can I respond at this time of the morning? You ought to get up an hour earlier next week.

Irv: Oh, you were mad about that. Okay.

Al: Gerry, is Irv a brother to you too?

Gerry: Oh, in some ways, yes. I think so. I have thought about that a lot to myself before. I think that the ability he has to be organized and encyclopedic in his knowledge of the literature awes me. I do not know why except in terms of my own family again because I think this identification with my father is more than I recognize. When I read something in literature I do not usually forget what evolves, the ideas that are involved, but I have to put them under my own name. Irv has the ability, he is rigid in having to have all this organized knowledge and he knows the sources. But at least he is not a plagiarist.

Irv: Oh, I would not say that.

Gerry: Well, comparatively. Sure I think that I relate to you as a father in that way. But then again, like with my own father or with Al or Mannie or you or anybody else, when I am relating with the father, it is always as a teacher. I am teaching them. Like in the last few sessions. Al says I sit back and get angry at being left out, or leaving myself out really. Then I jump in there. But when I jump in there I am not jumping in and saying, "Look you guys, you are leaving me out," or "I am leaving myself out and I feel bad." I jump in there and tell you how you are not seeing what you are doing, what you are talking about. And I start telling you what you are talking about.

Mannie: We are still here.

Irv: I would like to hear your reaction.

Mannie: Who, me?

Gerry: Whose voice is that? I think you ought to change the tape this week, Irv.

Irv: Okay.

Gerry: I am going to let Irv go change the tape this time.

Irv: See, telling me what to do. There he goes, he thinks he transfers to me as a father, but I wonder about it.

Gerry: Say, I have a couple of specific questions. Since we have spent about a half hour on these feelings, I wonder if we can turn to particular kinds of cases in regard to group.

14

The Borderline Patient

Frustrated omnipotence as countertransference; deprivation, anxiety, pressure to expose repressed contents; couch and immobilization; no major changes; activity versus passivity; motility; separation. Life must go on. Working through in life experiences based on insights gained in therapy; liking the patient. Identification/differentiation. The analyst is human, has values. Total reflectivity, perfect mirroring, is dehumanizing. The therapist working in a group must be committed to the idea that rigid control over all aspects of a patient's life is neither feasible nor desirable.

Irv: Hi Al. Hi Mannie. Gerry is not here yet so I am doing a solo. I suppose it is probably my fault because I asked him to get up an hour earlier.

Mannie: So it seemed last week. He was carrying it around with him.

Irv: Yes. He said last night that he was not sure whether he was going to be able to make it on time and I had fantasies of him not making it and sitting around for an hour and diddling my thumbs and not calling.

Mannie: It was your wish, was it not?

Irv: Which one? That he not come?

Mannie: I do not know.

Irv: That was probably my wish too.

Mannie: It was your wish that the hour be put up ahead.

Irv: Right. I am leaving for a four-day weekend east of the mountains and since it is quite a trip I thought that leaving early and beating the traffic would be a good thing to do.

Mannie: Great idea.

Irv: I would like to ask a question about what to do when someone in a group gets married. I have a patient that I have been seeing for about four years. When I began seeing him he was delusional and hallucinatory. He has really improved greatly. He was not heterosexually related at all, and now he is. To avoid understanding the transference, he acted out and impregnated a girl. I had already mentioned that he would be ready to terminate treatment probably in three or four months. The unconscious fear to which he later associated was that if he came in and said he was going to get married, I would take the girl away from him or take "mama" away. He is probably going to get married this weekend and I feel that he should have another three or four months to work through to termination. I am wondering about the idea of carrying someone in the group or in therapy after he has been married, you know, newlyweds.

Al: Why not?

Irv: Well, the only thing I thought about it was related to reading some of the material that Grotjahn has written. He felt that it is best that a therapist not meddle in a new marriage.

Al: Now look—

Mannie: Wait a minute. Don't forget, Grotjahn believes in meddling in an old marriage.

Irv: You mean getting them both in the group.

Mannie: Not only getting them both in the group. Read his new book, *Psychoanalysis and the Family Neurosis,*[20] in which he meddles in an old marriage a great deal.

Irv: Oh, yes, he will I know.

Mannie: It is only the new marriage he does not want to meddle with!

Irv: That is what he says, yes.

Mannie: He wants it to get a little seasoned before he deals with it.

Irv: I was just wondering about it.

Al: This patient is liable to feel your terminating as a very threatening thing. It is like the father abandoning him just because he married, which might be much more menacing actually. It might be more therapeutic for you to go and dance at his wedding. I generally have a policy that I do not go to weddings and parties and visit group members on the outside, because once I start going to one of them, they all start inviting me to one thing or another, and I just do not have the strength to keep up. Maybe if I were your age, I could do it. In some respects there is some positiveness in going, but if you go and dance at his wedding and are delighted with his relating to a woman, he will feel he has a right to the woman. If you remove yourself at his marriage, he may experience it as a condemnation.

Irv: I think he already sees my approval and sees the fantasy of my cutting him to bits as unrealistic, because that is what he has been working with in the group. He thought that I would just chop him to bits. He would not mention her name when I was around and he behaved quite differently in the alternate session. He told the group in the alternate session he was real happy and had a lot of emotions; he really loved her. He told the group in their alternate meeting first. When I was there he could hardly tell me and he was stuttering.

Al: This is a great opportunity for him to work this through by your taking a very strong, positive position with regard to his relationship to this woman and his marriage.

Mannie: But, Al, how can Irv take a happy, strong position if he does not feel that way?

Al: Yes. Well, why does it occur to you to ask about it? Maybe Mannie is right.

Irv: No, my feeling was, why didn't he wait four or five months? That was my initial feeling. Then when I thought it over I tried to understand why I felt that way and what he had done, and why he had done it the way he had done it.

Mannie: Maybe, Irv, he did it because you made a bad guess. Maybe

he was not ready for termination in three or four months.
With this much oedipal anxiety, I am not sure he was ready
for termination. What are your criteria that he was ready?
He sounds to me to be quite paranoid with regard to you.
He sounds to me as if he expects not only that you are
going to chop him to bits, but that he cannot even mention
his girl's name or you will take her away from him. This
degree of anxiety can occur. But from what you say, in
four years from a delusional patient to this position is a
great advancement. But I do not know that he is ready for
termination. I would like to hear your discussion about
how you came to this conclusion and then feel so terribly
hurt that he disappointed your omnipotence. He said he
was not ready to leave, but he said he was going to get
married. You are sore at him because he is getting out ahead
of your plan. Why are your plans so vital and precious to
you? Let's talk about it, Irv.

Irv: When I say three or four months, I did have plans. What
I had in mind was that maybe around December or so
he might be able to leave therapy. He has improved
greatly. When I first saw him in the group and in combined
therapy, he was really a machine. He was rigid, his posture
was rigid, he "heard people talking" about him. He heard
"voices coming through walls," and he gave off "an odor
that anybody could smell." The defensive purpose of the
odor was to rationalize his distance from people and his
isolation, to keep him isolated. The group members said,
"We don't smell anything." Then he went through a period
of elaborate experiments to see when he gave off the odor,
when people said he had the odor and when they said he
did not. As he began to work at the projective nature of
what was going on and as he began to confront himself
with his own fears of being feminine, relating to his own
feelings about his father and his mother, gradually he began
to lose this projective defense and began to warm up and
relate. It has only been about a year.

Al: You did a wonderful job with him.

Irv: I have a good feeling about him and the progress he has
made.

Al: You had a very positive, hopeful attitude towards him.

Irv: Right. And all this time he has improved in his work and was promoted. His boss just told him the other day that he did the finest job he has ever seen. He has really advanced very much.

Al: Well, are you sore at him?

Irv: I am not sore at him, no. I think my initial reaction was one of anger. I am not sore at him now. My initial reaction was, there he goes gumming up the works and, as you say, interfering with my omnipotent scheme. But I think it was based upon a misconception that I had that if he got married it would be best not to continue to see him.

Mannie: Why, Irv? I think you are trying to rationalize.

Irv: Okay, let me try to understand that.

Mannie: I think you are trying to rationalize your rejection of him for his having foiled you. Let us talk about at least the theoretical if we cannot talk about the deep-level feelings. Let us talk about the theoretical position from which you wanted to operate in not taking him into your group or continuing treatment with him after he got married.

Irv: Okay. I do not think I have a theory to support my thinking. The only thing I have is just some common-sense notions. I think from an emotional point of view what it probably represents is my hidden desire to take the girl away from him. Maybe that is what he senses.

Al: You have some competition with him as a father and—

Irv: Right. I think that is what it may be. It may be my own countertransference. Because as I think about it, I do not want to meddle with the marriage. Well, why don't I want to get in there and meddle with it and take the girl away from him? It must be that I am re-enacting an oedipal conflict with him. So I suppose that is the basis of it. It must be that I must want to meddle. I mean, that must be the emotional feeling I have been avoiding.

Al: He is hooking onto that nonverbal attitude of yours and really feels threatened by you.

Irv: Yes. In addition to that, at least from my knowledge of what I have read, if someone is in analysis and gets married, usually he stops the analysis.

Mannie: Now let's go over that. Let me tell you the historical aspect of that. The orthodox position has gone through a variety of changes. There was a period in classical analysis in which the analysand was forbidden to have sexual experiences during the period of his analysis.

Irv: Right.

Mannie: It was thought that if he was frustrated, the repressed material would emerge. This is the major technique of classical analysts; frustrate, regress, interpret.

Irv: Yes, the idea of deprivation to give rise to ideas—

Mannie: To give rise to the anxiety and give rise, therefore, to the pressure to expose the material and to cope with it. Now this was a passing fancy although it still is a pretty basic technique to deprive, to frustrate the patient. This is the nature of the analytic experience. One of the ways of keeping somebody immobilized is to use the couch. One of the movements, one of the directions of good analysis, in quotes, is to immobilize, to keep the patient passive, put him on the couch, do not let him move, do not let him act, do not let him do anything but talk. In introspection he tries to be conscious of his own introspection and thereby analyzes himself, in front of the mirror of the analyst. This whole trend toward passivity and immobilization is what makes the classical analyst opposed to any action, any activity on the part of the patient. This is why they are opposed to group therapy, for example, because there is too much activity and interactivity.

Irv: And the idea that anything that occurs stems from within the patient himself.

Mannie: No major changes in the patient's life while he is in analysis. Change was considered antianalytic. Therefore, if the patient made a large-scale change in his life, the analysis was terminated, because this was considered antianalytic.

Irv: And they have done that here at the psychoanalytic institute with some candidates.

Mannie: They have not seen change as something positive. They see large-scale change only as something negative, as the patient's acting out, on transference and in resistance. Obviously you cannot immobilize a human being and you cannot view all of activity, such as marriage, change of job, even divorce as being always exclusively and purely pathological, without any positive aspects in it. This attitude has to be rejected. It is really very punitive. The patient in the changed situation really needs you now more than ever before. Your patient has never experienced the anxiety he is going to experience in a close relationship with a woman who is already pregnant with his child. You are rejecting him at the moment he needs you most.

Irv: I have not rejected him. It is only in my own thoughts or maybe in my nonverbal behavior.

Mannie: You reject him in your thoughts when you take this position on an intellectual and theoretical basis. We have arrived at the position that you cannot stop living when you get into analysis. These are not people of upper-class Vienna, the aristocrats who did not have to work anyway. We believe life goes on and we must participate in life. I have a commitment, for example, that analysis is not what cures. Analysis provides the matrix and the catalyst for the cure which takes place in life. We have to be aware that the patient has other days of the week and twenty-three other hours each day, even when he sees you.

Irv: In other words, do you feel that the really reparative factors are the experiences he has in living as a result of the changes that he sees, or the insights he gains in analysis, and then he can really reinforce these things in living?

Mannie: Right. I think his cure comes through experiences with human beings and in life.

Irv: And exposing himself to them, you mean?

Mannie: I think the experience with the analyst provides the possibility of life in a more positive and constructive way; that he does not have to continue old patterns; that he can have human experiences in a more positive way; that he does not have to be resistant to these experiences, and so on.

Al: Irv, did he give any indication that he wanted to quit after his marriage?

Irv: No, he did not want to quit.

Al: He did not want to quit?

Irv: No, he wanted to continue.

Al: Well, by all means then, Irv, I would encourage—

Irv: Incidentally, I have not said anything about him quitting. He is just continuing, that is all. But I had said something in the group about a month or two ago about his improvement. He had been talking about feeling tied down because of his therapy and the fact that as soon as he finishes his therapy he would be in a position to take a better job some place else.

Al: That is, despite his wish to go on he shows a pull to get away from you.

Irv: Right, he does.

Al: Which is related to his fear of the father.

Irv: Incidentally, this boy's father died when he was seven years of age and he was alone with the mother after that. He is an only child.

Al: This would increase his—

Irv: And before his father died he openly remembers wanting to poison him, used to shoot darts at him and all sorts of things. And he just went into a frantic rage when his father died.

Al: Yes. Irv, wasn't it you in my workshop at the two-day annual institute of the American Group Psychotherapy Association who raised questions about activity and acting out, and doesn't this prevent the unconscious material from emerging? Didn't you raise a question like that?

Irv: I don't know if I did. I think that I may have. But I think I was of the opinion at that time, after having read through the material that your workshop had put out on sexual acting out, that there were positive and constructive aspects to acting out and that if one could learn from acting out, it often could be a vehicle for further insight. Now I think in general, my feeling is that if there is acting out all the time, you cannot contain it. So how are you going to work with it? But I feel that one episode of acting out or some acting out could be useful in trying to explore what is going on, like what I am doing with Sally and Leo.

Al: In his relationship with this woman there surely is both acting out and something constructive. He may be trying to castrate you and take the mother, but he is also relating to a woman.

Irv: Listen, this is a wonderful thing. He used to walk holding his head in his hands, covering his face; sitting on the bus he thought everybody talked about him. He used to sit in the group and talk about wanting to destroy the world, press the button and everything would blow apart. He was unrelated and he was very mechanical. Now he is warm, considerate, kind, and helpful to people. He is so warm, it is just an amazing and wonderful thing to see.

Al: Do you tell him how much, how positively you feel about his development?

Irv: I do. I mean I do not say to him directly, "I feel wonderful about your development," but I did indicate it by bringing it up in the group, how much he has improved, how members feel about it, what changes they see. When I brought this up, it brought up a tremendous rivalry problem which we explored too. One patient got mad. He said, "I am leaving the group right now. What in the hell did Hal do to improve so much? I can't stand it, you are praising him." We explored that in terms of what it meant, and in terms of his own past experiences. This represents a departure from classical theory in a sense because a classicist would say that I am provoking something by praising him. In other words, I am actually doing something. But my feeling about it now after exploring it with you two is that even though the analyst may say something which may provoke something, each one responds idiosyncratically in the transference. And it is the transferential response that you want analyzed anyway.

Al: I think you have done a marvelous job with him. I am very impressed.

Irv: I am very impressed. I just do not know how I did it.

Al: I think partly it is because—

Irv: I think I like him. I think that was it; I could identify with him.

Al: I think that helps a lot when you like the patient.

Irv: I liked him. I saw him very much like myself in a way, and I identified with him and I was eager to work with him.

Al: That is a very important issue for us to explore with all our patients, to ask ourselves, Do we like, don't we like them? Why do we like them, why don't we like them? We need to be able to like something about them that we can sponsor in them and I think it is appropriate to like a patient.

Mannie: You know Strupp's research on that, don't you?

Irv: I don't know his research on that, but I read an article by Charles Savage on countertransference with schizophrenics.[33]

Mannie: No! Strupp's research. Will you please write Hans Strupp and ask him for a copy of his paper. He is professor of psychiatry at Chapel Hill, teaching at the Medical School of the University of North Carolina. I will tell you essentially what he did in just a sentence. Showing a film of a first interview with a patient, he did a study of some three or four hundred psychoanalysts and psychotherapists of all schools and disciplines. He discovered that where they liked the patient described or shown in the film, they felt that he was healthier, the prognosis was better. Those who did not like the patient felt that he was sicker and that the prognosis was poorer. Those who liked the patient recommended more sessions per week. Those who disliked the patient suggested fewer sessions per week even though they saw him as sicker.

Irv: And I bet you the basis of liking is one's capacity to identify with the person and to accept oneself in a way.

Mannie: That is probably a big hunk of it.

Irv: Because I was reading what Savage was saying on countertransference: that if you cannot identify with the patient, in some way, you may as well not work with him. If you cannot do it, then you really cannot work with a schizophrenic. You might as well give up. I think there is a lot of sense to it.

Mannie: Watch that, Irv. You are shifting your conditions there.

Irv: Where is that?

Mannie: Talking about schizophrenics, yes. Where you talk about neurotics, watch out. Because with neurotics, if you are going to operate on the identification, you may actually create a borderline disorder in them as a solution of the neurosis rather than analyze the neurosis.

Irv: You mean in the countertransference, you may tend to see yourself in them totally and not see other aspects of it?

Mannie: You make them execute your wishes in your identification with them.

Irv: Well I know that would be a countertransference problem.

Mannie: That happens very often, if you work with neurotics this way. Whereas with psychotics this is a necessary preliminary stage in order to deal with them. I think the conditions of working analytically with a psychotic patient and with a neurotic patient are quite different.

Al: What about the problem of liking the different? I mean if we can only like images of ourselves and understand them and identify with them, how much are we not able to like the stranger? How much do we demand homogeneity, which I would consider as another derivative of the borderline problem?

Mannie: Yes, that is the diegophrenic problem of mother and child. The mother will not allow the child any degrees of difference.

Irv: I agree with you, I think this is one of my problems, I recognize it and am trying to work on it.

Mannie: This relates to what Al is saying, that when the patient moves in a direction other than what the analyst wants, we get anxious, we get punitive. The need to control becomes more important to us than the need to educate, to allow the child to grow and to love him.

Irv: I think this was what happened with Leo and Sally too, because it was a very threatening situation to me. Leo was calling her up at home, and her husband was calling me up, and the situation was disturbing me in terms of my own security.

Al: What has happened with them?

Irv: I have not seen either of them individually. Leo walked out of the Monday group meeting. He walked out. He just could not stand it and he came back Wednesday. He wants so much attention, he wants to devour the whole group or devour me. He wants to be the sole center of attention. He cannot stand it when anyone is talking about anything else. He says that he wants to destroy me and take over. The thing I am wondering about Leo is it seems to me that we are dealing more with a pre-oedipal kind of transference than an oedipal one. His desire for exclusive possession of me, I think, is really a mother transference. My feeling about it now is that he is angry at me only because he does not get the mothering, and that he would be happy if he got the mothering. Although he verbalizes consciously that he wants to take over, yet he does not really want to. He just wants to be mothered.

Mannie: He wants to be incorporated; wants to be fused with you.

Irv: I think that is probably the experience he had with his mother. Maybe this is a good association, the motility problem that you raised before, the idea of separation. I mean, the parent that will not let the youngster separate.

Mannie: This is based upon his conviction that he needs to be fused with the mother in order to survive. He is struggling for survival, to be fused to you. This goes then into other levels of development, although it starts in the pre-oedipal, oral stage, it also affects him both in the anal and the oedipal development.

Irv: Could you elaborate on that? Could you elaborate the translations into the anal and oedipal development?

Mannie: I'll try. In some ways he uses his anal development in a sadistic-masochistic, homosexual attitude toward you. One way to fuse with you is by virtue of having a homosexual relationship with you, and this is not exclusively an oral problem, although it has its roots in the oral fixation.

Irv: In other words, it is strongly related to the idea of separation and fusion.

Mannie: The basic damage is in the narcissistic relationship with the mother.

Irv: This is what I see now. Originally I was confused as I looked at it. I thought perhaps there was a lot of oedipal material here, but I think the thing is pre-oedipal primarily. There is oedipal material there, but I think that the real problem, I mean his real relationship to me, is in terms of mother and in terms of not wanting to separate.

Al: A week or two ago I said, "Why did you so erratically cut out the individual sessions?" Do you think that giving them individual sessions would be sponsoring their relationship to the mother and be inappropriate? Do you think it is good to frustrate them in this?

Mannie: The answer to that question cannot be made in general. It has to be sought by evaluating the individual patient and the patient's resources and needs. If this man can withstand the frustration, if he has enough ego resources to be able to maintain himself and struggle with this, then it would be better to keep him in the group and not give him the individual session.

Irv: That is my feeling about it.

Mannie: Individual sessions might encourage his regression. If he does not have the ego resources and needs the relationship of the mother to survive, without breaking down, then you have to give it to him.

Irv: Look what happened to Sally. She fell apart and has now pulled together again.

Al: But you saw her individually.

Irv: One session, just one session.

Al: How did the individual sessions terminate? Did she ask to quit or did you suggest it, or what?

Irv: We were doing combined therapy with many of the patients. My feeling after working with you was that in actuality these patients were doing their major work in the individual sessions. The individual sessions in a sense were detracting from the group because they would save material and bring it in to the individual session. Although it is possible to analyze it, I thought it would make a much more dynamic group session if they had to do all their work in the group. So I reached a point where I suggested the change to most of my patients. A few have narcissistic problems which are so severe, I felt that they needed the individual as well as the group relationship. Most of the patients whom I felt I could work with just in the group I see just in the group. I did this at the time that I added the alternate session. In a sense they were getting the alternate session right at the same time.

Al: Now Sally is less psychotic?

Irv: Yes, yes! She is back to where she was before.

Al: And do you feel that Leo can struggle with this?

Irv: He is struggling, but he was struggling even before in the individual session. He has reacted in the group like this before, except now I think it is more focused.

Al: Do you think he will continue in therapy?

Irv: Oh, yes, I think he will continue in therapy.

Al: Well, then, let him struggle with it. He is not going to go psychotic. Is that your feeling?

Irv: My feeling is that he will not.

Al: Yes, then let him struggle with it.

Irv: Good, good. Say, I wanted to raise a question which you raised some time ago. I just wonder where Gerry is. I guess he is really going to do me in this morning, you know, make me feel bad.

Al: Probably repressed the whole change.

Irv: I will tell you what happened. We talked about it last night. Then when I got home, I received a phone call from him. He wanted to know if I would bring my tape recorder down this morning so he could borrow it for a couple of days and do some work with it. Well, I was reluctant to do so. I have a lot of packing to do in the morning and it is going to be. . . . He does not know how to work the thing anyway and I felt I would rather get together with him some night, spend an evening, show him how to work it, or do it at some other time. I told him I would rather not do it this weekend. Why don't we get together later on and do it? I had a reluctance to bring it down and he may have felt slighted by that.

Mannie: The way he handled it was to withdraw and give you the whole session today. Perhaps this is characteristic of Gerry.

Irv: And we joked about it. Incidentally, he just got his diplomate.

Mannie: Oh, marvelous. It came through, and he was worried.

Al: Give him our congratulations. Have an alternate meeting with him and try to get him to talk about his feelings about what he did today.

Irv: Incidentally, our secretary . . . it is a most interesting thing . . . but our secretary found out that she was calling me Mannie, and Mannie me. She was slipping in naming us, and it turned out that she tended to see Mannie and me as the same.

Mannie: It is interesting that an outsider is also drawn into our identifications here.

Irv: I asked her why she did that and she said, she thought we are both Jewish, maybe that was a factor. Then she tended to identify both Al and Gerry together.

Al: We are more withdrawn.

Irv: Yes! So maybe that is the thing, you know.

Mannie: Al is less Jewish.

Irv: Well, at least from her perception; she did not know whether Al was Jewish or not.

Mannie: How did she know I was?

Irv: She assumed Mannie Schwartz is a Jewish name. I do not know. She even thought you looked like me. She was surprised. She had a fantasy that you looked like me, and then when we were describing how you looked, she was quite surprised and shocked.

Mannie: Maybe we ought to get her in on these sessions.

Irv: I asked her if she would write up her notes or her reactions and feelings and she said she might, but she never got to it. But she had a lot of feelings.

Mannie: Encourage her to do that.

Irv: I thought it would be very interesting because after all, one really should investigate the distortions the secretaries have when they are typing this kind of transcript. They are involved too. She said that she told Gerry that joke, perhaps, to get involved because she felt left out, she felt rejected. Here she is slaving away, typing up the transcripts, and all the time we are having a good time relating and she is left out.

Al: Do you feel, Irv, that you have a better time in these meetings than Gerry? Is he having a rougher time?

Irv: I do not know. It is hard for me to say. I know I alternate. I look forward to these meetings; let's put it that way. I am eager and always here early. It is the high spot of the week for me. Although at times I do not like being called rigid, even though I am. I think Gerry enjoys it too. I really cannot say. I get the impression from what you say that I am having a better time than Gerry.

Al: Yes.

Irv: I do not know. It means a lot of things to me. To me it means an opportunity to relate with people I like and the kind of people I knew in the past. So it has a lot of personal kind of feeling to it.

Al: Gerry sounds like one of the men in my group. My groups are mostly Jewish and occasionally I get a group with one Gentile in it and they come in feeling, much like Jews, a minority in a Gentile community.

Mannie: Like the Irish taxi driver in Tel Aviv who is living the life of Cohen.

Irv: You know, we have never explored this and I have often wondered about it myself. But I feel that this may somehow be related to your own feelings about him, about Gerry's being or not being Jewish. I think that, maybe it is because of my feeling about Gerry, but I think he really enjoys these sessions.

Mannie: I do too. I do not have Al's feeling. I think there is a real pixie quality somewhere in him. I think he has a real sense of humor and—

Irv: Oh, he is a real nice guy, no kidding.

Mannie: I must confess, Irv, that I had a much more positive reaction to him at our luncheon than I did to you.

Irv: I have more trouble relating than he does. He is a lot warmer than I am, you know.

Mannie: I felt that way. I felt that way at our luncheon. From your description and feeling about me, you felt I was swarming all over the place, but I was quite aware of both of you and what was going on.

Irv: And, of course, I was more anxious at the time than he was.

Mannie: I think that is true, too.

Irv: I am almost ready to terminate my analysis in another month or two. I was going through a pretty rough spot when I was in New York. There was a lot of inner conflict. But in general I think that Gerry is warmer than I am. Although I think I am willing to be more spontaneous now. Anyway, I feel more open, I feel more spontaneous.

Al: Tell him we are sorry he could not make it.

Irv: He may still be here, although I don't know. I am just wondering what is happening right now, is he just waking up and wondering, "It is quarter of eight; it is too late to come down anyway"?

Mannie: Yes, something like that.

Irv: You know, he missed two meetings, too. I mean he did not miss, but he was late a couple of times. So there must be some feeling. Maybe it is a family thing.

Mannie: Yes. I thought that he felt you were taking over and he was not getting enough. Then he felt that he had to sit back. Do you remember Al was working on that issue with him not to be the shirttail, being swayed by you and me. He identified himself as being a shirttail. Al suggested to him last session or the session before, remember he said, "Come on, Gerry, let's you and I not be shirttails." It may very well be that he feels he is not getting a fair shake out of this kind of an arrangement.

Irv: I think he did not get a fair shake in the beginning. I tried to monopolize, but I think as time went on we shared equally.

Al: Irv, maybe this is something you can work with. That is, it is true Gerry makes his contribution by feeling he is a shirttail. You suggest ten o'clock and he has to go along with it. Then he does not want to go along with being the shirttail. He gets resentful of being in that position and perhaps punishes by withdrawing. You describe with reference to Hal that when Hal wants to get in there with the mother, you get somewhat competitive. Maybe you want the woman and maybe there is a mother in us somewhere that you want to reach, and you are trying to push him out a little bit.

Irv: It is probably more than a little bit. It is more than a little bit, but I think that just being reality-oriented about this and forgetting about some of the psychodynamic aspects of it, I would do the same for Gerry. If Gerry said to me, "Irv, I have to go someplace, let's meet at a different time," I would do it. In other words, I thought it over and thought, "Gee, I would like to leave early in the morning."

Al: That is, he need not countertransfer this much.

Irv: Yes, it is only an hour. I would do the same thing for him anytime. And I want—okay, I could leave an hour later, but when you go on a trip, my feeling is I would like to get started early in the morning and get going. I did not have to. I could have left at nine o'clock, but we are going with other people and I thought if it is a nice day, I would like to get started.

Al: Is he going away for the weekend?

Irv: He is not going away for the weekend. I am taking Monday off; he is working.

Al: You have it again. At ten o'clock you are going away for the weekend. What has he got?

Irv: He has nothing; he has to work. But he got his diplomate and I have not, you see. So he should be on top of the world.

Al: That is wonderful.

Irv: So I don't know.

Mannie: You do not have to feel guilty about this. All you have to do is be aware of it.

Irv: Oh, I am aware of it and I think that the problem. . . . Well, sure I would like to monopolize, but—

Al: I would like us to discuss the patient staying from a group session, and Gerry, to explore, to understand it in himself and understand patients that stay away.

Irv: Very good, very good.

Al: Because we have patients who absent themselves, or walk out, or one thing or another.

Irv: Yes, that is very good. I think I am beginning to feel somewhat like a heel now.

Al: As I said, don't feel guilty now about this because you would have changed for him.

Irv: I would have changed for him anytime.

Al: Right. You are very fond of him.

Irv: We have our competitive businesses going on, but I think we like each other very much and we have a pretty good relationship. I think maybe that is him right now. No, that is not him. No! Say, while we have a minute or so I want to explore one problem that we are talking about. You said that the analyst in reality is not a mirror, that he is an interactive part of what is going on. To think that the analytic situation is one wherein the patient just produces and it all comes from within and the analyst in no way imprints the analytic situation is ridiculous. I think you cited the work on countertransference as an example to the contrary. Usually everybody has countertransferences, but isn't the idea to explore your countertransference and to try to avoid being in countertransference, trying to check it so that you don't get into that kind of situation?

Mannie: Yes, but in reality that is only one aspect of it. You can only avoid it after you have done it, and it is going to have some effect.

Irv: Countertransference already has an effect, even if it is just in fantasy.

Mannie: It is going to influence the way in which you respond, the kinds of interpretations you select, the material you will select to emphasize or not to emphasize, the nature of your interpretation, the feeling that you attach to the interpretation and so on. But quite apart from the irrational and the unconsciousness aspects of the relationship, an analyst has a commitment about what he feels is healthy and unhealthy, what he feels is constructive and nonconstructive, what his values are. Recently there was a piece which appeared in which the question of analyzability of patients was raised. In discussing the analyzability of patients, the point was made that if the patient refuses to accept the values of psychoanalysis—and remember psychoanalysis is committed to a set of values, such as freedom, autonomy, rationality, consciousness—you cannot analyze this patient. I think this is one of the problems that we come across when we attempt to work with Catholics. I think this is one of the real issues. I would like to see some analyst who had a lot of experience with Catholics who are in grace, not those who have broken away, discuss this.

Irv: This would be a good thing for you to discuss with Gerry.

Mannie: Yes, I think it would.

Irv: Because this is what I have heard other analysts say about the difficulty of analyzing Catholic patients. Gerry has a lot of Catholic patients. And you know from talking with Gerry that he certainly is committed to the values of psychoanalysis.

Mannie: No question about it. We know Catholic analysts who are wonderfully committed, but I would like to discuss it sometime. Maybe Gerry is the one to discuss—

Irv: I think so.

Mannie: —the problem of conflict of values. The analyst is not merely a mirror because of his unconscious and pathological processes, but he is not a mirror also because of his conscious and theoretical commitments, his real commitments and values, and as an analyst. I have written on what I call the eclectic view of Freud in which I attempt to extract from Freud those values all schools might agree upon regardless of their variation. For example, the values of freedom, autonomy, the family, consciousness and so on. These we communicate and reinforce, because otherwise there is no goal or direction in analysis. We obviously do continuous rewarding and punishing; that is, rewarding and unrewarding of learned attitudes, and so on. To view the analyst as a mirror is really to allocate responsibility away from the analyst.

Irv: They frequently try to do that, too, you know.

Mannie: Of course, and I think one cannot. The moment you accept the social contract with a patient that you will help him, you put yourself in a helping role. Therefore, as a helper you have to contribute something. I think every human being is both helped and helper. I think this is the nature of reciprocity. We also know that not only is there helped and helper, but there is also self-help. One of the contributions of the analyst is to liberate this potentiality, the helf-help resource. I do not think a mirror can do this. This is my commitment. I do not think the analyst is a mirror. I think the analyst, by the way in which he talks, the way in which he walks, the kind of person he is, the values to which he is committed, the way in which his room is arranged, the way in which his hours are organized, the way in which his office is decorated, and so on, all play a part in the nature of the experience.

Al: This being a mirror also creates an enormous amount of isolation in the patient. The mirroring therapist is not a human being. For example, I had this experience with a supervisee who told me of a young adolescent she is treating whose mother has recently completed seventeen years of individual analysis with apparently a reflecting analyst, reflecting the patient back to herself. She seems identified with this analyst because all she does with her daughter is try to get her daughter to analyze everything she does. She does not respond to her in a human way anymore. In a way she has been dehumanized. And this is considered a completed analysis.

Mannie: I am working on a paper called "Assumptions Behind the Helping Professions," all the helping professions. I am trying to get at what are the basic assumptions. One of the assumptions I think we make it that one cannot be a human being, and I talk about the human animal now, unless one is willing to play alternately the role of helper and helped, I think this is in the human condition.

Irv: You mean one has to be able to allow himself to be helped by someone and also be willing to help someone; you mean if he is going to be in a helping profession. So that you have to work through those kinds of problems within yourself. If you cannot take something from somebody or have someone give you something, apparently that would be the best . . . I probably take things rather than have anyone give me anything, but if you cannot accept something from somebody then you are in a bad spot.

Mannie: That is right. I think this is true of the patient as well. This is true of all of us. This relates very closely to Al's statement of the reflecting analyst, the mirroring analyst as a dehumanized position. By the way, I meant what I said to you a couple of weeks ago, that a most wonderful experience is to see this play on Broadway, *The Far Country,* in which Freud is shown as a very deeply human person. Some analysts have objected to the play because they say that Freud lost his dignity because he became too human. This is again our need to dehumanize the father, to dehumanize the authority and to say he has no human quality, he has no weakness. This is the omnipotent father; this is the narcissism problem.

Irv: Wasn't Freud more interactive than latter-day analysts have been? I mean even of the classical school.

Mannie: He was very interactive with some, and not at all with others.

Irv: Incidentally, speaking of what you asked earlier, you asked what my criteria for termination are. I think that is a good question.

Mannie: We ought to put that on our agenda as something for exploration.

Irv: I would like to do that for our structured course.

Mannie: Listen, Irv, will you leave a note with our love and kisses for Gerry?

Irv: I sure will. I am going to give him a call right now.

Al: Tell him we had a good time and we wished he could be with us.

Irv: Well, he will hear it on the tape. I will have him listen to the tape rather than read the transcript. Okay. Thanks a lot and we will see you next week.

15

The Nature of the Analytic Contract

The question recurs, Is supervision teaching or therapy? Is a control analysis analysis? What is acting out (transference or countertransference) in supervision? How do we deal with group problems such as anonymity and exposure, formality and congeniality? Is the objective of analysis equalization in differences (hierarchical issue)? Must regression be encouraged, or does the plea for help evoke it regardless? Is rivalry a necessary condition of group membership?

Mannie: Al and I told you that we had discussed what was going on among the four of us and we thought that there had to be a greater emphasis upon transference and countertransference, as in control analysis. In a sense control analysis is analysis. It is a different kind of analytic relationship, but we are analyzing one another. We are using our analytic tools to understand the nature of the interaction with the supervising person. It is an authority position, a learning situation, like analysis. Freud emphasized the need of the analyst to maintain the authority position. One of the things Al and I thought was that perhaps we should recognize that what you need is an experience with us of this kind, as a learning experience as well. It is approximate to what goes on in any group setting. It has been high-level group interaction that we have been having here these last three or four weeks. Before he left, Al asked me to tell you this.

Gerry: I feel it has been very helpful, very rewarding in many ways. I thought I learned a lot from the last several sessions. Of course, it scared me when my analyst implied all this material was leaking out. Which is true. I was using this experience against my own analysis, which is of course not appropriate.

Mannie: Of course not, but it is part of what has to come out and be analyzed.

Irv: This raises a point. You mentioned a long time ago that you were much more interactive, much more social with your patients. And Al said once, why not go to the wedding? My attitude always has been one of reluctance to have a relationship with the patient outside of the therapeutic setting, and I wonder about that.

Mannie: First I am sorry Al is away on holiday because I should like him to respond. By the way, Alexander Wolf, chairman of the psychoanalytic faculty at the New York Medical College, is going to be the commencement speaker at the annual graduation exercises of the Postgraduate Center next week, and his topic will be "The Future of Psychoanalysis." He gave me a short rundown of what he intends to include. He told me he will talk about what an analyst will look like in the brave new world of the future into which we are heading; that we need some kinds of boundaries and ego anchorages for understanding. That is, the analyst is going to have to get out of the office and into the community if there is going to be a future for psychoanalysis and that he will have to lose his anonymity more and more and recognize that if he has any value, if psychoanalysis has any contribution to make to men, he is going to have to make it not to a limited number of fifteen or twenty patients a year. The problems are much larger and much more intensive, and the analyst will have to deal with problems on every level of man's struggles to survive in this crazy world. There is a recognition and a vision in this attitude that we here in New York are seeing. I think this is part of the direction of Al's commitment. For example, in 1938 he was doing psychoanalysis in a group and introducing an alternate session. Now he is saying, "I would like to go to the wedding," and he does, but always remembering that we are conscious, planful, and purposeful, and that the patient's needs are central. Therefore we do not go to every wedding and to every patient's wedding, and we do not show ourselves equally and in the same way to every patient.

Gerry: Yes. I think I identify Al and Mannie much more with a man like Colby[8] than I do to some of the analytic people in this community.

Mannie: I am glad you had that association. And then compare Colby with Menninger.

Irv: That brings something to mind. In my supervision in this community some of my supervisors have pointed out to me that you should always refer to the patient by the title Mr. or Mrs., and never call him by his first name. In a group, of course, this is impossible. You cannot respond to patients by Mr. or Mrs. or something like that. But the supervisors feel you should never get that familiar with the patient because it interferes with his regression. They feel it puts you on a different level. My feeling about it is that it is not realistic in working with patients. If you work with a patient for five or six years, it is very sterile, very formal. It seems to me it is not human.

Mannie: Do you recall the paper Al and I wrote where we talked about this analyst (by the way, he was one of Al's supervisees) who said that if his patient ever called him by his first name, that would be the end of the analysis? This is another of those same kinds of rigidity that do not make sense. For me, and I talk only for me personally, the objective of the analysis is the struggle toward equalization of analyst and analysand. This is one of the objective outcomes that I strive to approach. It is never achievable in individual analysis because the roles of helper and helped are fixed and formalized by the nature of the social contract. But at least we ought to strive for greater equalization, otherwise you never resolve the authority problem.

Gerry: Just listening to that now, I wonder whether ideally or theoretically we should not be trying to use as a structure with the patient against which to see distortion is not analyst versus analysand or the authority vector, but the reality of two persons. With adults whom we see, there is a contract between two persons who share a horizontal vector, but they have different capabilities, different skills. We happen to have a skill with which we can help others.

Mannie: Exactly.

Gerry: So, in fact, in the group, using a first name does make sense.

Mannie: We are seeking equality in difference. This is the resolution of the homosexual maneuver; this is the acceptance of the heterosexual position.

Gerry: Yes. I was thinking that after all, we might see people who have the same levels of professional competences and skills in other areas. We are only an authority in the sense that they have come to us for help in an analytic way, by virtue of this particular social contract. Anything else that puts us into a vertical, authority relationship becomes a neurotic projection or distortion.

Mannie: Or a countertransferential demand.

Irv: I would like to add to that because it seems to me that regressing a patient is very important. I think at a certain point in analysis you try to deal with these fantasies and try to bring them out into the open and try to equalize the situation, but—

Mannie: We said the goal, the outcome.

Irv: Yes, but I think that initially you want to encourage regression, you want to use the authority vector to bring out some of the infantile, archaic—

Mannie: Irv, I want to take exception. You have been saying that for weeks and I want to take exception to it. You have a right to a different opinion, but I want you to know where I stand. In the beginning of an analysis you are always placed in this position without having to encourage it. In the analytic relationship initially you are generally *in loco parentis*. Patients come to you because they want to be helped by you. They project upon you the necessity that you be omnipotent. You do not have to encourage this.

Irv: You can attenuate the regression. And I think sometimes you can attenuate it prematurely.

Mannie: I agree with you on that. That, too, is a countertransference problem, in my opinion.

Irv: I do not think you want to attenuate the thing prematurely. For example, this patient Hal I was talking about last week is exploring why he feels I am going to chop him to bits. But when he got married last week, he had the fantasy that I was in back of the church dressed in a black cloak, and when he associated to it in the group, I was an executioner ready to cut him up. There the thing was out in the open. I could deal with that fantasy and try to point out that it is a fantasy. What I am saying is that if I had attempted to reduce this, if I had been friendlier all along and done a lot of other things all along to attenuate the regression, I do not think we could have gotten to this point where it would have been so out in the open. So now we can deal with it. Do you see my point?

Mannie: I am in accord with you. But let us not then substitute the notion of encouraging for accentuating. What I am suggesting is that it is in the nature of a person being a patient that he will regress, that he is in a regressed position.

Irv: Because he is coming for help anyway.

Mannie: Exactly, and because he is neurotic. But you have to be careful, particularly since we are seeing more and more patients who have psychotic components than ever before. A psychotic patient is already regressed. To encourage him beyond this or beyond what is necessary is a problem which we may be adding to the patient. This does not mean that I cannot conceive of a patient where you may encourage the transference. I think every time you ask for a dream you are encouraging the transference.

Irv: Why is that? Could you elaborate on that a little?

Mannie: Yes.

Gerry: He has done it before, Irv.

Mannie: I think it is a very important psychoanalytic point that telling dreams to the analyst encourages transference. First, because dreams are viewed by all of us as a piece of secret stuff; dreams are part of regressed material. We know quite unconsciously that it is related to childhood. In the first three or four years of life all of our experiences, all of our preverbal experiences, are images out of which the dream is made. It is primary process material. Therefore, we are entering into the world of illusion in the analytic contract by reinforcing, by sharing primary process material and entering into it as if it were a reality. The moment the patient begins to use the dream as the basis for communication of thoughts, feelings, and acting in an *as if* relationship with you, as if the dream had objective reality, then this, too, is something else we can talk about. But we are encouraging the regression and the transference neurosis. Do you understand?

Irv: Yes.

Gerry: Yes, I understood because you said it a month or so ago. I wonder why you do not remember it, Irv.

Irv: I remember that he made the statement, but he never elaborated on it.

Gerry: Yes, they did; Al did too.

Irv: Not to this extent, Gerry. What are you so angry about?

Gerry: I don't know.

Mannie: Who is angry?

Irv: Gerry is angry. He looks perturbed and he has an ugly face.

Gerry: I have just been thinking about why you shut off that machine for the first fifteen minutes.

Irv: Well, I was anxious to get in and I thought you were in here before I was. Maybe that was it. I was anxious to get in and I forgot to press the button to start the machine. Then I remembered it when I was in here.

Gerry: Yes.

Mannie: Irv has the same kind of anxiety to get in that I was talking about in myself, that I have to get in everywhere.

Irv: Well, here I am out in the other office. Gerry is talking with you in here.

Gerry: This could be a retaliatory kind of thing. I did not show up last week and made you feel bad. So you are going to make me feel bad because the first few minutes we got to talking, you were in there and you were shutting me out.

Mannie: And, Irv, do you have some guilt similar to what I talked about last week? Why does it distress you if Gerry has a long face?

Irv: At the same time I think there is another feeling. I feel, well, let's expose Gerry. I will squeal on him, you know.

Gerry: Tattletale.

Mannie: I think he wants me on his side, Gerry.

Gerry: There is no question about it.

Mannie: He wants to line us all up against you. He wants to keep you in that out-group membership position.

Irv: There is no question about it.

Mannie: We are going to fight him on that even though he wants me on his side.

Irv: You do not want to get on my side then?

Mannie: Oh, I am not going over to your side because I do not think your side is any different from Gerry's side. We are all on the same side. I think that is your distortion.

Gerry: That is the problem. We are all equipped the same.

16

Effect of Absence
of Face-to-Face Cues

What is this supervision all about? Multiple teachers and students complicate the supervisory process. We do not know the effects of distance, isolation, silence, tones of voice, number of words, separation, and deprivation of visual cues. We can only share our reactions and experiences with this kind of supervision.

Mannie: Al, do you want to say something about what you have in front of you?

Al: I want to thank you both for sending us the abstracts of those two papers. They sound very exciting and I hope you will send us copies of your presentations.

Irv: This is what we tried to do. They are calling a conference on mental health in this area and we got together to write a couple of abstracts for presentation. Along with it we were trying to conceptualize what our experience with you is and has been. We thought that this brief paper might be the foundation for . . .

Gerry: Shaping our thinking on what we have been talking about.

Irv: Yes, in the paper we will write together.

Al:	Both abstracts sound promising.
Gerry:	We cannot hear you very well, Al.
Al:	Both are excellent. They are filled with promise, make me eager to hear more.
Irv:	We do not have more to say, though. That is the problem.
Mannie:	I had some associations when I was reading the notes of the last session. I think you ought to use some of the transcript material to illustrate points. There was a point toward the end of the last week's session where I think Irv turned to Gerry and asked, "What are you making faces about?"
Irv:	No, Gerry looked at me.
Mannie:	Or Gerry looked at Irv, whatever it was. There was a series of exchanges of that kind.
Irv:	We were wondering—to do a really full paper, it would be interesting to get your perceptions, your reactions, how you feel. After all, you are involved in all kinds of training and it would be important to reflect your ideas about it and how you feel about being with one another and with us.
Mannie:	I think Al mentioned this last week. You recall originally when we started, about the second or third week I suggested that you were uncomfortable because you could not see us, and we discussed that. We thought that it was your wish coming through that you wanted to see us. But in last week's session or the one the week before, Al said he would like to see your faces. We had Al on the spot where he was somewhat anxious in not being able to perceive your reactions. Maybe this moves and shifts from person to person as the anxiety of the different participants comes into focus. Last week you were focusing on Al. The preceding week the three of us were working Al over and he read the material and he came in last week and said he did not feel like an "out person"; and it was in this session, I think, that he said he would like to see your faces.
Irv:	A friend of ours, a psychologist, looked over the transcript. Gerry showed it to him and he looked it over and said, "You know a good experiment on this would be to take a transcript and delete the phone references and have others read it. Then ask them, 'Where do you think this conver-

sation took place?'" He says from the way he looked at it, nobody would ever guess that it was a phone conversation.

Mannie: That would be very interesting. Also you might think of submitting it to twenty professionals who have had some experience in supervision. This is also an experiment in multiple supervisors. I have never had an experience with multiple supervisors. Al, have you ever worked together with a number of supervisors, supervising one or more supervisees?

Al: Only when I first started doing group therapy. I had a number of therapists who sat in. I welcomed them for a while, but it got to be too difficult.

Gerry: You are going to have to turn around and look into that mike, Al. We cannot hear you.

Al: I had a number of therapists who wanted to see what was going on and to learn. Each session would be devoted to reactions to the newcomers, and I felt that we could not get enough involvement with each other. The patients started comparing me all the time with the other therapists and we got stuck on that theme. I felt that there was too much of a change of population with these multiple observers. Maybe if I had had one there all the time or a co-therapist, it might have been more appropriate and could have been worked out. No, I never had an extended experience where there were two supervisors, co-supervisors.

Irv: Incidentally, our secretary is typing up the notes on her reactions. I think they are quite interesting. Rather than take the time over the phone right now, maybe we will just mail them in as soon as she finishes.

Al: One thing that occurs to me about my anxiety, my wish to see you, is the feeling I have that I am close to you and that you are pretty spontaneous and we are too. It reminds me of the experimental work where if a normal person is isolated from seeing anything in his environment or hearing anything or touching anything, he starts having to populate his environment with his own projections and sooner or later hallucinations. He cannot stand that much isolation, and in a sense I feel deprived of the experience of seeing you. I feel that as a deprivation.

Irv: Gerry and I were thinking about this the other day. We were wondering whether deprivation, too, may not be a very important thing for trainees because it makes us more aware of our own needs. It puts us more in perspective and helps us with our countertransferences.

Mannie: Exactly. And that leads us right back to one of the sessions that we had earlier. I have a strong commitment to the idea that supervision has to be done by working on the problems of the therapist and not on the problems of the patient. The problems of the patient represent merely the context in which we continue to explore the personality, the technical, the knowledge and skill problems of the therapist. Otherwise the therapist becomes merely a messenger, an intermediary between supervisor and the patient, and for me that is very bad supervision.

Irv: Then where does this relate to therapy? For example, in therapy or in one's analysis one is supposed to deal with his own problems, but it seems to me that I am learning a lot about myself or sort of sharpening up problems that I have within myself when I see that they are occurring in our relationship together.

Al: One thing that might be explored in your paper is the experience with us as a kind of group therapy situation. We are talking about attitudes and feelings we have towards one another and what impact it has had on your individual analysis. Another point is what your individual analysis tells you to bring to the group. That is, do you have an alternate session with us, as contrasted with your individual analysis? What is excluded in each? What are the differences in the experiences?

Mannie: I want to go back to what Irv just said, although I have an impulse to say, "Where is Gerry?"

Gerry: I have been listening, Mannie, and wondering why I am not talking.

Irv: You are tired, that is why you are not talking.

Mannie: What is that?

Gerry: I have been listening and wondering, here are the three of them really talking and I am just sitting here. I have not a word to say. Why? Irv says I am tired. I do not think that is all of it, but I somehow felt there was not something to say.

Irv: You were working on those papers and you had a lot to say Wednesday.

Mannie: Gerry, I want to go back to a point that Irv was making and I think you two will want to look at it. I think both of you have a problem or should have a problem. If you do not have it, I am projecting. You ought to try to struggle with it in regard to supervision. I think that you have had a misconception about the nature of the supervisory experience. I wish you would read Freud's paper on terminable and interminable analyses.[16] In it the whole concept of supervision as control analysis is described. It is not something that should surprise us that we in supervision are going to provoke problems which you will have to work out for yourselves. This is a central aspect of good supervision and it is not really therapy at all. I disagree with Al in seeing this as a group therapy experience, because my function and my wish here is not to therapeutize either one of you, Al, or myself, but rather that we explore together the kinds of problems and feelings and thoughts and actions, knowledges and so on that we have, and see how this either helps facilitate or impede our work with patients.

Irv: It seems to me that in this type of supervisory structure our own countertransferences really are exposed very glaringly.

Mannie: Much more, much more than in a one-to-one, face-to-face situation, I can tell you that.

Irv: That is the thing that we were trying to explore in our paper.

Gerry: This is why we put together the idea and I think we all can contribute to it. We felt that these papers we could read here at the meetings, but they were just the groundwork of our own thinking in terms of what we felt we ought to write, particularly for other people in the group therapy field.

Al: I ask you, Mannie, and you, Gerry and Irv, why you think countertransferences emerge more in this group situation than in individual supervision? Is this the sort of thing that you feel in the group, that multiple transferences are stimulated, that there is more health and more pathology stimulated in the group situation?

Gerry: I think it is a function also of the separation of us from you.

Irv: And the need it creates. In other words, the separation brings archaic needs into focus. And I think it brings archaic needs of the supervisors as well as the supervisees into focus.

Al: Do you think that it is the separation, our not seeing each other, the distance rather than the group?

Irv: I think the group is another dimension too, both of them.

Mannie: The telephone is another dimension. The fact that all of this is recorded and we later see it played back are other dimensions. Another is that we are being continuously provoked and stimulated, not by one another, but by a geometric increase in the number of people participating in this experience. That is, I do not think that it is in the nature of this experience that countertransference is provoked. I think all good supervision must ultimately work on the problems of countertransference. This is the central objective of the work of a good supervisor, but I think that much more of it is available here. And I think, Al, you answered the question a few minutes ago when you associated to the experiments in isolation where you thought that in the isolated situation the person must people the world around him with his own projections. The fact that we are separated and the fact that we are not able to pick up the clues and cues and confirmations so that we are continuously drawing upon our fantasy to fill in and fill out the material, always therefore also draws with it some archaic material.

Gerry: I think also that this supervision compares with analysis where you do not usually see the analyst. You see him when you come in the room and when you leave, but most of it is a production from within, without working face to face with someone. Usually in supervision you are seeing the person who is doing the control.

Irv: Yes. We saw a comparison between lying on the couch and this kind of supervision.

Mannie: The similarity.

Irv: Yes.

Al: One of the thoughts that occurs to me is that in our analytic school a great many of the supervisees who come to me, where I focus largely on their countertransferences, experienced this as a new approach. They have had one or two supervisors before and the supervisors concentrated largely on what was going on with the patients. There was some initial resistance to my way of working, but as they went along with it, they discovered something about themselves and their countertransferences. So whatever supervision they had had in the past, there really had not been a focusing on the nature of the involvement with the patient and the supervisor.

Irv: I know this is true in the past supervision I have had. Any time countertransference came up, my supervisor usually said, "You have to work this through with your analyst." And it was usually avoided. I had the feeling that my supervisors were avoiding my countertransferences in the supervision.

Mannie: There was an interesting chapter by L. R. Wolberg[49] on "Supervision: Is It Therapy or Education?" In it he talks about a combination of both as possibilities. The tendency in American analysis has been to deny control analysis and call it supervision, to think of it largely as being educational, a learning experience. Similarly Irv in his resistance to this experience kept calling for structuring, a lecturing, a covering of a stated curriculum rather than accept it as an experience in which he participated and grew in understanding and insight. Resistance takes the form of talking about the patient, asking for lectures, for information. This is also a resistance that we experienced here. I think that you asked earlier about our resistances. You must not forget that we too have been having a new experience here. For us this is new and I think that some of our functioning and some of our interaction might have to be seen in the light of its newness. One of the reasons why Al and I were able to function perhaps more easily in this kind of situation than two other supervisors might have been because we have been working together this way for several years. Over a period of nearly five years Al and I have worked with each other just the way we are working with you. We have done this every single week, every Saturday, without a miss unless we have been out of town. We interact with one another just as we four have been interacting. So we have had a long history of security with one another in exposing ourselves to each other.

Gerry: I wonder then if it would not really be very important when we jot all of this down, to compare your perceptions and feelings about the kind of thing you have been doing and how it compares to the face-to-face contact you had been carrying on. Though you are still face to face, there are more people involved in the interaction.

Mannie: I think my distortions are less effective and less frequent in this situation than they are in face-to-face supervision. I believe that I am freer of what we call supertransference, that is, the transferences of the supervisor to the supervisees. I think that using Al here as a buffer, using the telephone as a buffer, and using the distance as a buffer permit me a much longer period of hesitation and selection than I would normally take in a face-to-face situation with an individual supervisee. I am an interactive person and if you count the number of words I speak during the hour, you will find that I probably say more words and I may even use more time. This is my tendency anyway, but probably I am still using much more time to be reflective in order to use better the one hour we have on the telephone, knowing that it costs something and knowing that our time is limited, knowing that we are investing a great deal in this. I am much more reflective about what I will and will not say than I would ordinarily be in supervision. Therefore, less of my own transferential distortion and expression comes through here than when I am alone with a person. I am more exposed here.

Irv: More exposed?

Mannie: Yes, I think so. I think there is greater exposure by virtue of it being written down, recorded, and transcribed, by virtue of three other people, and therefore I am more selective. I believe I tend less to act impulsively or even spontaneously.

Gerry: I have a different kind of feeling which I think is a contrast to this. I have felt that in some ways the sting of self awareness is less painful in this kind of a relationship.

Mannie: That is true, too, Gerry. I think you can turn the phone off and run away from us, whereas with most of our supervisees we see every day or every other day the rest of the week. My trainees know that I am around even if I am not there physically. I am there as an authority figure, and they feel that their certification, their livelihood, their future, depends upon, in some degree, my attitude toward them. In a sense it does, and therefore, even though they walk out of my office after a supervisory session, they are never really free of the feeling that I am around and I know about them.

Irv: This brings up another factor that has occurred to me. In a sense, having supervisors that are out of our community lessens the threat. For example, our livelihood really is not dependent upon you people, and at this point anyway you are not holding us back or giving us anything like a certificate or anything else. What we do is really going to be dependent upon what we personally get out of it, how we develop ourselves, and I think it gives us a bit more freedom. If we were operating within the framework of a training center where you were the gateway to a degree or a certificate or something like that, I think that we would be more self-protectively oriented.

Al: That is one of the problems we have at my training center. Many students heave a sigh of relief when they are certified and say, now I can really develop my interest in psychoanalysis, now I do not have to worry about being certificated, now I no longer have to submit, now I can enter analysis.

Irv: You mean, now I can really talk to my analyst.

Al: They have the feeling that they are in a school, in a set of courses that they have to pass, and that the analyst at a faculty meeting will make a recommendation about them and all the teachers will, et cetera, in this tightly knit community. The sort of thing Mannie was talking about with people at his training center happens at ours. A number of people have come back to analysis, either the same one or very often another one on our faculty, after they have been certified and they are free of this kind of controlling intimidation. We are having an alternate meeting across the continent. We are not under that kind of restriction.

Irv: I think it provides more freedom and I guess it is very much like the alternate meeting in group analysis.

Mannie: It is different and I want to demonstrate that it is. I think the comparison between this kind of an experience and the alternate session is wrong. No matter how we would tend to deny it, I would like to—

Irv: You mean we cannot make some status denial here?

Mannie: Yes, sir. I think you are denying the fact that we are in a status difference, whereas in the alternate session real status differences do not exist.

Irv: Well, won't you allow us a little fantasy?

Mannie: Yes, but remember we were talking about writing down our experiences. Putting it down as a fantasy, I think is fine. But you ought not call it an alternate session.

Al: I felt that we are less in the authority vector.

Mannie: It is attenuated, but it is there.

Al: That is true of the alternate session, too. The authority is there, but it is attenuated.

Mannie: Those who are participating in it have no authority relationship except a symbolic one. It is true that in the fantasy of each patient in the alternate session the therapist is there. That is true. But among those who are present and who are interacting there is no status difference. They are all patients even though they may be in transference, be in hierarchical relations to one another. Here the fact that Irv and Gerry pay us, the fact that they expect something of us, immediately alters the nature of this relationship. They would be tremendously disappointed if they did not get something from us. They would wonder why they would be paying us if they did not feel that in some way they

are expecting to be helped by this experience. They are
still in the role of helpees, whereas we are in the role of
helpers. And to put it in the co-patient or horizontal vector,
I think, is to deny the reality of our experience.

Al: I think you have a point there, Mannie, but I still think
there is a point to this having some quality of the alternate
meeting which is not quite as authoritative as the setting
in Seattle.

Mannie: Correct. There is more freedom in this kind of learning
situation than there is in others, but I do not think, therefore, that every interpersonal situation that has greater
degrees of freedom is an alternate session. When kids go
out of the family setting onto the street and play with one
another, they have greater degrees of freedom than when
they are in the house playing with one another. Does that
mean that their playing on the street with their gang is an
alternate session from the household situation? I think this
is to misuse the concept of an alternate session. Do you
want to get into this fight or are you listening to Al and me
struggle this one out?

Irv: I was trying to . . . I was wondering what is going to happen
here, who is going to hit whom or what?

Al: Who is fighting?

Gerry: Say, this brings back the thought, who is on top or who is
going to win out here? The secretary was saying to me the
other day when she was typing out her notes that she
thought Al was the one who should have the beard and
mustache.

Irv: I just looked over her notes briefly, and she sees him with
a white flowing beard, almost like a god-creature or something.

Mannie: That is a characteristic fantasy of Al. Everybody has it.
Even I have a hunk of it.

Al: What does that mean?

Mannie: By the kind of person you are and how you speak and
how you use yourself, you tend to provoke in all of us
some kinds of transference reactions.

Gerry: You have a very quiet voice, Al. You are very aloof.

Mannie: You rarely use words the way I do and you rarely get in there and pitch the way I do. You do not say dirty words, even on the telephone the way I do. Obviously you provoke a kind of distance even though you are very close to me and we are almost touching face-to-face.

Al: I must be very omnipotent if I provoke this.

Mannie: No.

Gerry: Not necessarily, but I would like to throw in a reflection on this. I think that the quietness compels us to come closer. It is a control.

Mannie: Go on, Gerry, say some more.

Gerry: Well, this godlike figure can control us, can draw us closer to him by the quietness of his voice.

Al: Do you feel that way about me too, that I am this guy with the long white beard?

Gerry: No. I do not see the long white beard, but I do think of an element of control of some sort. I suppose it is the same sort of thing. I never thought about the white beard. I thought about the ascetic sort of "life is a fountain" type of muck.

Al: Sounds pretty depressing to me.

Gerry: I do not think it is depressing. I think it is a quality of . . .

Al: Contemplation?

Gerry: Contemplation! That is a good word for it.

Mannie: Al will never do what I did the other day with one of the patients that Al has in the group and I have individually. Al will never blow his stack with a patient the way I did with this patient in trying to break through his struggle for omnipotence. I said to him, "If anybody is going to be the omnipotent one in this situation, I am going to be it," and that he was going to have to forego some of his omnipotence. Al would never make a frontal attack on a patient's omnipotence this way. This is not the way Al works, not the way he functions. It is true that it scared my patient.

Irv: Al did it though. He did it I think to a fellow at our session. Remember that, Al?

Al: What was that?

Irv: Remember when we had this group session for a couple of days at the annual meetings and a fellow was sounding off? You really cut him down and you showed him who was boss right then and there. You did not mince any words and you were really quite forceful.

Al: Sometimes I can be tougher than Mannie thinks.

Irv: You were certainly tough that time.

Gerry: Boy, I'll say.

Mannie: He is not tough in the same way.

Al: No, I am not tough in the same way.

Mannie: Of course, you are firm. You can be very firm and assert your authority. You do that very well, but you are not tough in the same way. I am sure he did not raise his voice when he cut the fellow down.

Gerry: No.

Irv: Well, I don't know. Of course, I was threatened to beat the band when he was in there.

Gerry: No, this fellow was very loud and very gross about wanting a process group, and Al very neatly turned the push aside by this element of quiet control that I am talking about. This is his way, but it is very solid.

Irv: But what you said, in essence, to this fellow was, Now grow up, behave yourself; we are not children here; you are supposed to be an adult in this situation.

Al: Mannie may not know this, but the fellow had described a previous workshop of a year before in which there was a "therapeutic" session, people expressed their feelings. I knew the group therapist they worked with and he had a "Whitaker-Malone" orientation. Maybe I was reacting to the group therapist who wanted to convert this into a subjective process experience.

Irv: You mean Whitaker, or the fellow in our workshop?

Al: The workshop. A group therapist conducted it a year before and was also only interested in having a subjective experience all the time. That had to take precedence over any kind of reality boundness or rationality or appropriateness or a learning experience. I was resisting that orientation as much as the fellow at the workshop was promoting it.

Irv: I went through a period of depression this week about group therapy and I go through this very often. It may be related to my feelings in this session, too. I have several patients who are very resistive, who are very silent, who do not interact, and I try to bring them out. They do not talk much. I keep thinking that if I had them in individual therapy it would be different. I would have more information or they would talk more. I would be able to deal with their defenses more effectively. I would know what is going on. That is the feeling I have. I felt I am not close enough to them and they are not close enough to me. They are being lost in this large group. This may, in a sense, parallel a feeling that I have here, that I would like to get Gerry out of here.

Gerry: Exactly. I was going to say, yesterday you said you hoped I did not show up this morning. Not in those words . . .

Irv: You were teasing me. He was teasing me last night and he was sort of saying, Well, it is so late I probably will not get there in the morning. And you were sort of trying to provoke me a little. But yet, I go through this feeling very often. You get a person in a large group and he does not have the opportunity to have his associations dealt with; you miss quite a bit. For example, the compulsive usually is one who can hardly make a statement without wanting to take it back. I am sure you can see this in group therapy very often in the way in which he will do the same thing in group in his limited free associations. But in the individual session it is seen in a more dramatic fashion. Anyway, I just wanted to get this thought across, that I feel quite depressed. A couple of silent patients had been acting out. I did not know what was going on with them and I felt that if I had been seeing them individually in intensive individual psychotherapy, they would be in closer contact with me; I would be in closer contact with them and things would be working along much more effectively. I think that perhaps . . . well, I know very definitely it is a need of my own which I feel I have to work through.

Al: To identify with them.

Irv: Yes, yes. The identification is there and, of course, it brings up the other question and that is, What is really therapeutic? It brings up the whole question of, Can you really work through effectively with a patient in the group? It raises another question: What about termination? When you have a patient that is terminating, do you see him alone for the last session or do you just say goodbye to him in the group?

Al: I say goodbye to them in the group.

Irv: You do not have an individual session with them?

Al: Occasionally, rarely, a patient may ask to see me alone in the final visit, but that is unusual. One of the associations I have is that maybe for some of these patients a private session would be indicated, but my first preference would be to ask the silent members to start associating to their silence and to ask the group to free associate to the silence.

Irv: Then I get into the problem of doing individual therapy in the group. It is a hard thing to get away from. For example, someone is resistive and then you focus on the one member and try to get the group to interact to it too, but yet you are focusing upon one person.

Al: You do not focus on one person. You work with other people's reactions, too, while they are reacting to him.

Irv: You mean try to work it all through at the same time?

Al: Why are the active members leaving the extensions of you out? You seem to identify with these people. What is there in their silence that active members let it go on? Why don't they want a relationship? Who is the silent member to them that they don't even relate to him, and who are the active ones to the silent members?

Mannie: I want to get into this.

Gerry: You are in.

Mannie: There is only individual treatment. I want to go on record that there is only treatment of individuals. Maybe we have you gun shy saying do not do individual analytic work in a group. I think there is only individual analysis. You cannot analyze a group. You analyze individuals in a group setting. Let us keep this straight. There seems to be some timidity about working with the resistances of a single patient, for instance.

Irv: Let's take an example. Let's take a patient who has not said much. When I ask, "How do you feel about this?" he says, "I don't know." I could ask the others to associate to it. I can ask the group to talk about it, but this is a lot different than the silence that comes up in the individual session because a person can hide in the group more easily, it seems to me.

Mannie: That is right.

Irv: The silent patient in the individual analytic session is almost forced to participate or leave. The silence becomes so striking that there is more pressure on him to do something, even though he may not. In a group session he becomes obscured because there is a lot of activity going on most of the time.

Mannie: Yes, but the pressure in the individual analytic situation is largely internal, whereas the pressure in the group arises out of the provocation and reaction of the other members. Al suggested that you might ask the others why they are willing to tolerate the silent members in the group, how they feel about it, what their transference provocations are, what their transference reactions are to the silent provocation of the silent members. I think that there is a qualitative difference. Moreover I think that both patients are resistive, but they are resisting in a different way in the two different settings. There is pressure in both settings upon the silent patient. However, there are differences in the qualities of internal versus external pressure. It is possible for the internal pressure to be considerably increased in the group. The individual analyst does not tend to put pressure on the silent patient, not the same kind of pressure that other members do and can and should.

Al: I think as therapists we tend to get caught up with the patients who are more verbal and more interactive and who seem verbally to be exploring interpersonal and intrapsychic processes. There is a tendency to neglect the silent patient. I would take the attitude that the patient in his silence is in some kind of transference relationship. This may be to the group as a whole or the group as one parental figure and the therapist as another, and individual transference reactions to other individuals in the group. The patient who disregards the silent member is also in transference to him in his disregard of him and indifference to him. He is in some transference relationship to him that should be explored.

Gerry: How would you do this, Al? How would you go about it in the group? I mean, of course one can do it. It is not the technique of how, but I am saying you bring it up once, you bring it up several times, then what? I suppose you have to keep working at it until it does not exist because it is a resistance or a defense against exploration. But you can go on for quite some time with a silent patient getting the group's associations, their feelings, reactions to this, without a budge.

Al: Well, look—

Gerry: It is even a gratification to the silent patient.

Al: Maybe we can learn something about an approach. Gerry, let us say you are experiencing yourself as a more silent member of this group and perhaps a more silent member in your own family. What would enable you to participate more? Maybe we can learn something from this about a possible approach. What would help you?

Gerry: I do not know, but I was just thinking as you got started that there must be some real gratification to the silent person in having others exploring, reacting, expressing feelings about his silence. Now I do not think I was particularly a silent member in my own family. In fact, I was a very vocal one. I was very active in the family, but there was also some element of being a person who provokes father indirectly by chopping down his position, getting him to stick his neck out instead of sticking my own out. I do not know what in the group or in here would enable me to talk more. I think in some way there is real reward in you fellows saying, "What do you say, Gerry?" I do not think I was particularly nonverbal as we started these sessions. I do not know if we went back and checked it and whether or not I was, but I know since we have talked about this, when I am quiet, now I think, "I wonder how long this is going to happen." There is some kind of control.

Al: Just waiting there maybe for your father to stick his neck out. But maybe you are entitled to go after him a little more, stick your neck out, to break with this pattern.

Irv: The thing I do not understand is that when I am in a group I am always thinking. I have needs to be met, there are things that I want to ask, that I want to do, that I want to talk about. Yet in my groups I have patients that come in and they just sit and have nothing to talk about. It seems, as if I were a patient in a group asking help, I could not sit through a session without asking for something, demanding something, bringing up a feeling, a need. Yet they sit there as if they are not troubled by anything, and it is hard for me to see this because I do not see it in myself.

[a pause]

Silence! What happened?

Mannie: I think a lot of things have happened. Obviously we are going to be ourselves no matter where we are. You cannot help but be yourself in your group or with us or in your own personal life. You cannot expect that you are going to be able to function the way Al does or the way I do, or that I can function the way Irv or Gerry does. All you can do is to try to utilize the techniques that are available in your consciousness in struggling with the whole problem of dealing with those patients who in some way are more difficult for me or for you or for the next one. There are some group therapists who are perfectly willing to let a silent patient be silent for a long period and let him hide out. There are other therapists who cannot tolerate a silent member. There are some who cannot tolerate the over-active, and over-interactive patient. I think this is a very personal matter. We all have our preferences for and in patients. We all have our identifications. We make our countertransferences and we struggle with them to the best of our awareness. Just talking about it this way is in itself a movement toward greater awareness of the necessity to find ways and means for struggling with patients who are, themselves, not struggling. Irv just a moment ago was talking about patients who have nothing to say and that they are not troubled by anything. They are so troubled that they are not speaking. It is not that they are not troubled. They do not have the freedom you have.

Al: Let me tell you something of my own life. My mother was more passive than my father. When my father got sore he would break dishes. My mother never broke dishes. I think that when Mannie is more interactive and vigorous, I become more passive. I tend then to retire in the face of the broken dishes, Mannie's assertiveness. I feel protective toward my mother and somewhat identified with her because she did not know how to cope with this and I did not know how to cope with it. When I have a silent member of a group, not infrequently there are schizoid qualities in this patient. They are not outright schizophrenics and I tend to be overprotective of them. That is, I think to myself, "I am the only guy in this group who knows this patient is schizophrenic and whatever they are doing with him, they do not know that he does not have enough ego strength to take this." In one group all the members, spontaneously on their own, after four months of experiencing a silent patient, went after her for three quarters of an hour and demanded that she talk. After they kept this up, I found myself getting anxious. My father was breaking the dishes in front of my mother and I was taking care of my mother and myself. As soon as I said, and I tried to put it diplomatically, "We do not seem to be accomplishing our purpose of getting her involved. Why don't we come back to this another time?", the group turned on me en masse and told me to go jump in the lake, that she was either going to talk or get out. The patient herself turned on me and said, "Leave them alone; this is the first time they have shown any interest in me." So I was reassured. The patient (and my mother) could cope with this, could take it, and the patient was not in trouble. Actually she then broke down and wept and began to talk. I do not know whether anything like the same possibility occurs with other people, but I am telling you that I can be overprotective toward a hurt or silent member who, for me, gets into the mother position or my position. Somewhere, Gerry, you also identify with this person, whoever it is in your family.

Gerry: Silent person, huh, the uncoping one? My mother used to break dishes over our heads, so I do not think it was she.

Mannie: Your father was the silent member there.

Gerry: Yes, he was the silent man.

Mannie: Listen, gentlemen. This may be our last contact with Al for quite a while.

Irv: Isn't Al going to be here next week?

Al: No. I will not be here until September twenty-third.

Irv: Oh boy, we certainly shut that out. This is our last contact for a while.

Al: We will be looking forward to a reunion.

Gerry: We sure hope you enjoy your trip.

Al: Thank you very much. I hope you guys have a wonderful summer. Mannie will be with you, won't you, through the month of June?

Gerry: We are very envious of your chance to go on tour. That is something I would like to do in a year or two.

Irv: Are your groups going to meet during the summer, Al?

Al: Yes, all but one. One is breaking up for the summer because there are too many young people going away, out of town.

Irv: Al, so long.

Al: So long guys. Have a marvelous summer.

Gerry: Bon voyage.

Al: Thanks a lot.

17

Supervision:
Education or Treatment?

The absence of visual cues in this teaching-learning setting gives rise to more exposure, more anxiety, more countertransference analysis. A geometric increase in interaction and activity seems to occur in four-way supervision. Learning is emotional as well as intellectual. In this field it approximates holistic involvement. The meaning of classical terms, the couch, the dramatic effect of the group on patients, are all needed in becoming a group therapist. Community consultation efforts are somewhere related to the group therapy movement.

Mannie: I thought I would let our telephone ring a third time just to make you anxious.

Gerry: Well, you did. Yes. I thought, he always answers on the first ring and that makes three. He must not be in yet.

Mannie: No, I was gathering my material to bring it over. Since Al is not here today I am sitting in his seat. You understand. That is the way it has to be. This is the hierarchy you understand.

Irv: Al will get a kick out of that when he reads it.

Mannie: I am sure he will. But I was moving over and that is why it rang an extra time. I thought surely you would think I am not here, but I was taking all my stuff off my desk and moving over to Al's chair.

Gerry: How do you have it set up there in the room? You say moving, grabbing the stuff off the desk and moving to his chair.

Mannie: Well, you see, I work at a long table. I do not like desks. I have a long table and it is all piled up. The thing that amazes and amuses Al is that I can stick my hand into the pile and pull out what I am looking for. I am that kind of a piler. I have a pretty good notion about where the stuff is and so I work at that desk and I have a swivel chair. Then right next to it against the wall, I have a nice deep, soft chair that I am sitting in, with a hassock in front of it. Al usually sits in this soft chair and works on a clipboard and I sit up at the table on my swivel and so we sit face to face without anything between us. The table runs north and south and the two chairs are face to face parallel to it.

Gerry: The reason I was asking is that I wondered where Al was sitting because his voice sometimes is so much more quiet, but yours is coming through clear.

Mannie: We usually put the mechanism on a small table, one of those end tables, between us.

Gerry: Well, you are coming through clear as a bell.

Mannie: I think it is because I am sitting in his seat and that always helps me. That reminds me, I want to say good morning to your secretary this morning. She always waits apparently for somebody to say good morning to her so I want to say good morning and I am glad to meet her too. I got her comments, which I think are tremendous in view of the other material I got from you two.

Irv: Did you get the letter we wrote?

Mannie: I sure did and I am going to write a letter to John Bell because your letter was so formal, Gerry, that I had a feeling that John might think, "What is this?" I have known him since who knows when. I know his son and I know his wife and we have been quite good social friends, so I thought—

Gerry: I have only met him twice at business meetings.

Mannie: But seriously, I thought I would write a follow-up letter on it and say, "I am very much interested in your help." As I told you last week, I think that it was through me that he met Al and that Al stimulated him on his first family group project.

Gerry: Well, as you said, my letter is a formal thing. That is the way I am.

Irv: But it is a natural kind of letter to write to someone you do not know.

Mannie: Yes, I think that is quite right, except that if you wrote it from Gerry and you, that would be one thing. But you included my signature and Al's, and I just think I have to follow it up. Besides I am not that kind of a formal guy.

Irv: Even to someone you do not know?

Mannie: Someone I do not know, yes, I think so. I do not know, but I do not think I would write a letter like yours although I was very impressed. In fact, I must say to both of you that I am stimulated, I am impressed, I am provoked. I am really quite involved and have been doing a lot of thinking since I got the material, and even before. Last week's discussion of all kinds of training and research possibilities in terms of our experience was provocative. I think what triggered me was the ingenuity with which you wrote up your papers to be read at the Western Mental Health Institute.

Irv: They look pretty good to you then, huh?

Mannie: They look tremendous, but what looked best to me was the thinking, the ingenuity as I say, of getting an angle on this. To me, angles are always the creative things, the data and the research and all the rest are often quite plebeian. It is the new twist, the adding something new of yourself, that is so important, and I think that was what triggered me.

Irv: Looking back on our experience of four or five months, I think it has been tremendous.

Gerry: I do not think it is utilized by other people the way it could be. The telephone company tries to sell the use of phone conferences between business people, but here are all of these professional people who can use this kind of inter-action with one another and they simply have not capitalized on it at all. I do not think colleagues of ours or those in other fields fully realize how useful a phone can be, just a phone itself without the newer developments, like the real exciting idea of a television phone. That seems like it would really change what we have been doing here, would add a whole new dimension to this.

Mannie: I wanted to share a few associations with you, even though I tend to monopolize, according to your secretary. I want to talk about her feeling and your feelings that I was depressed on June tenth, the day before my birthday. Maybe I was, but I want to talk about this research outline that you wrote to John. There are two things especially I just want to underscore for our future thinking. . . . Excuse me, I was lighting my pipe. Incidentally, it is interesting that I explained to you so that you would have some visual cues. I am so hepped now on the idea of not having visual cues. I am really quite conscious of it now, as you will see in a moment. I had two ideas in terms of the possibility of doing a research follow-up on some of this material. One is a training problem. I would like to offer the hypothesis that by virtue of the nonvisual clues that more emphasis in our supervision with you is devoted to countertransference problems than in any other kind. This idea came out of your write-up and our discussion. It is my impression that it is probably true. You remember I provoked this about the fourth or fifth session. I said I had discussed with Al the wish on our part not to deal with our own interaction. The tendency was to deal with patient dynamics, which I thought was a mistake. I always do supervision by emphasizing the therapist rather than the patient. Otherwise you make out of him a messenger boy between the supervisor and the patient. I have the feeling nevertheless that there is a great deal more countertransference material discussed here in our phone sessions than in any other kind of supervision in which I have been involved. I have been doing this now for umpteen years, so this is an interesting question. It is related to a hypothesis that is implicit in something that you wrote in the letter you sent to John; namely, that in some ways there was a parallel in this four-way supervision to group therapy as the two-way supervision is parallel to individual therapy. That is a fascinating idea, that there is a geometric increase in interaction and activity on the part of all the participants, and also that the content becomes more personal. The individual analyst can remain so aloof, so removed, so secret, so anonymous, that he does not have to show himself as much as in a group. The absence of clues creates a great deal more necessity for exposing oneself to provide for better facilitation of communication. One more item and then I will be through. I have a patient who is completely blind in one eye and has about ten per cent vision in the other. He has been in treatment with three other therapists before me. They contributed something to him, but I think they never quite faced the issue. In all three therapies he has had before, not one of the therapists discussed his blindness with him. They analyzed him as if he did not have any problem in vision, and I have concentrated in the year I have seen him on the fact that he has a great deal of anxiety, he denies and projects, he has paranoid kinds of reactions to people. I suggested that this was largely due to the fact that he had limited visual cues and that, therefore, he was always extremely sensitive to other kinds of cues and always responded by defending himself by attacking first. He had a relationship with his brother whom he did not understand, who was somewhat difficult because he was only a kid. Largely he always anticipated his brother jumping out from somewhere and attacking him. He could not see him, and therefore was always startled whenever the kid brother appeared and confronted him.

Gerry: Yes, jumping out! When you said jumping out and startling him, I reacted. Even someone coming up to talk to a blind person on a wall-to-wall carpet, well, everything jumps out of nothing, literally.

Mannie: Right. That is because hearing and sight are the two distance cues that you get. And sight is very important to us. We all use our vision in order to get anchorages in reality, and without vision we are bound to have more anxiety. We might ask ourselves a training question, whether increased anxiety on the part of the trainees actually facilitates learning. There is the belief that anxiety is an important component in furthering patients in analytic therapy. Adolf Meyer believed that you have to maintain what he called therapeutic pressure. As a psychobiologist he held that if you diminished the therapeutic pressure too much, if you gave relief from it, there would be no movement toward change.

Gerry: This is an analytic conception, too.

Mannie: The analytic conception is that anxiety exists, that you must bring the anxiety into awareness and then you work with it, not in terms of pressure. That is a psychobiological word. Psychoanalysts do not talk about it as being pressure, as therapeutic pressure and the judicious handling of it, evaluating it in terms of the ego of the patient to see how much he can tolerate and at what point to increase the pressure or decrease it. Some people call it the manipulation of the transference, which means dealing with the anxiety in a judicious degree. This is certainly another parallel. I think we draw a very interesting analogy between this kind of supervision and therapy and deal with what is one of the central problems of American analytic training. There is much in the literature about the question, Is supervision therapy or education? This fits directly into it and gives us a new dimension to at least bring some new material into this issue. The more historical view is that supervision is control analysis. It is therapeutic; it is analytic. The American view is that this is supervision, not control analysis. It is education and teaching. And, of course, the straddlers say it is a judicious, harmonious combination of both.

Gerry: Yes.

Mannie: Those are my associations and I have monopolized—

Gerry: It has been very good. It stimulates my thinking a lot. I do not know how it strikes you, Irv, but I think you learn when there is pressure or anxiety. There must be a disequilibrium of some sort in order for you to want to do something about it. In a class with a teacher who teaches something you already know you go to sleep.

Mannie: Unless you have a relationship with the teacher and then he can teach you craft. That is the strange part of it. You see that is the analytic view, that it makes no difference how much you repeat the material. If you have a really good transference neurosis going, it does not matter. It is one of those things. Because as you know, working through can be boring, bilaterally boring, particularly if you have a really entrenched repetition compulsion going. And yet somehow we struggle with it because there are narcissistic gratifications involved in the transference neurosis.

Irv: I am not following you exactly, Mannie. Do you mean gratifications for the analyst or—

Mannie: No. I mean gratification for the patient. The analyst has not any right to demand gratification except in being paid a fee.

Irv: But do you mean gratification? You mean it is really dry and boring and the patient goes over and over and over again because it is satisfying him in some way?

Mannie: There is some gratification involved in terms of the transference relationship. I think that Gerry was saying that in class if you know the material already, you go to sleep. I say except if you have a certain kind of relationship with the instructor. Then it does not make any difference what he is teaching and whether you know about it or not, because you are dealing on a different level; you are getting symbolic gratification.

Irv: In other words, you mean—

Mannie: In the analytic position you are dealing with an emotional relationship which is quite a process, which has nothing to do or very little to do with content. It is not from the eyebrows up; it is from the eyebrows down.

Gerry: Yes.

Mannie: What has happened here is that we have some bilateral or multilateral transferences going and that at times it does not really matter too much what the content is that we are talking about. We are going to be involved as long as these multilateral transferences keep going. I did not want to lose the analytic view of why the student does or does not get bored. He goes over spelling, like the kid in Six-A going over the spelling of the same words week after week. It can be boring and yet he is motivated to persist in this, not only because it is a familiar pattern, but because he has a relationship, an emotional relationship, with the authority.

Gerry: Of course, that is true with our conferences here too, because we have gone over and over some of the things and I have—

Mannie: You even entered in and interpreted this to Irv on occasion.

Gerry: Yes. But I have said that I am still here and I think I am going to break through this. Maybe the guy in the classroom who has this special kind of relationship to the teacher that he will put up with the repetition of the spelling words for the fiftieth time does so because he thinks he is going to make some change. Sometime he is going to—

Mannie: Graduate. He will get promoted.

Gerry: Or that sometime he is going to get the teacher to give something else.

Mannie: Right. By the way, that is one of the bases for the problem of addiction to analysis. I think that hidden behind this is a problem of the analyst not analyzing the transference neurosis and working it through, encouraging it and then not knowing what to do with it and then you get the twenty-three-year-long analyses.

Irv: I was reading a 1959 article by Phyllis Greenacre in the *Journal of the American Psychoanalytic Association*. It was on transference and she was saying, Be very careful and do not gratify the patient and do not gratify the patient's transference demands. She cites several cases where giving in would have prevented the analysis of what was going on. I think she critically refers to some of the work of Berliner, who said that in dealing with the masochistic patient you have to side with the patient; you have to be friendly. But according to Greenacre, any activity outside of the therapist's anonymity would be interfering with the transference and the analysis.

Mannie: That is the rigidly classical position. A training analyst recently said quite boldly and bluntly that if you liked your patient, this was already the end of the analysis. In fact, he thought that perhaps you had to dislike the patient a little bit really to be an analyst.

Irv: You really have to maintain neutrality.

Mannie: I said it runs against my grain. It goes against all of the experimental work that we have done. It is probably a correct position if we are dealing with healthy people, but the world of analytic patients has changed considerably on the American scene.

Irv: If you are dealing with a healthy neurotic, he can make demands and you can just let him fume and have tantrums.

Mannie: You can frustrate such a patient and not be concerned about doing him damage.

Irv: Yes. And you go on and on and then eventually you can analyze what the transference repetition is all about. But you cannot do it ordinarily with very disturbed patients who have needs, demands, and all kinds of problems. You stir them up to such a point that they really decompensate.

Mannie: They do not have the resources. I would say that in my analytic practice and at our clinic we do not see twenty per cent that look like good neurotics.

Irv: Incidentally, do you people use a couch? What do you usually do?

Mannie: I am quite flexible. I know Al is. Of my individual patients, about two thirds or three quarters of them use the couch, somewhere around a quarter of them do not. I have mixed feelings about it. First of all, I have no magical view of the couch. I use it where I think it is appropriate and I do not require it where it is not. But I think I sometimes use it defensively and sometimes I use it punitively. I think there are some patients who are so difficult to handle, particularly if they are a certain kind of disturbed patient with good ego resources, who are nevertheless quite hostile, resistant, and attacking, that I tend generally to want to get them out of my hair, so I put them on the couch. Sometimes I struggle against this when I think that this would be to entrench the isolative drive in the person, but sometimes I do it and say it will not hurt; besides it will give me a little breathing room.

Irv: That is the reason I brought it up. I have one patient I am seeing three times a week and she makes me uncomfortable. She is jumping around, she is anxious, she can hardly say a word, and she is peering right down at me.

Mannie: Put her on the couch. I will give you an example. Maybe

I have mentioned this young man. I have a twenty-three-year-old college senior who ran out of college. He has grown up in a family where they gave him too much and expected too little from him. He has a Corvette speedster. He is a car racer, and he has a yacht. He has been given everything with no demand upon him. He has everything and he is somewhat sociopathic. He drinks, plays the horses, he gambles, he does everything. He is so busy you cannot grab hold of him. He will not stop.

Irv: That sounds like us.

Mannie: He just will not stop; he is always on the go. He is continuously active. He bowls, golfs, swims. He drinks, he is promiscuous, and he never stops to think or to feel. During the early sessions he kept talking in a loud voice and he was active; he squirmed around in his chair and kept on moving. I put him on the couch and said, "Look, I want you to know why I want you to use the couch and I want you to co-operate with me as best you can. You are so active that you have not had time to do any thinking. And this is a thinking job we are doing together. We want to see if we cannot think about why you are functioning the way you are, why you have been living the life you have been living, and why you finally wind up in my office. We need a little time to think. I want you to make some conscious effort, to do a little thinking and to be a little less active." Well, he has improved in his struggle with his problems over these last three or four months and I feel that the couch was tremendously important for him. In the beginning he would squirm around on the couch, turn around on his belly and look at me, and stay face to face with me even on the couch. But by and large it has quieted him down considerably.

Irv: The reason I bring it up is that with all we have been talking about, interaction and everything else, I have been wondering whether the couch is necessary.

Mannie: Maybe it is not necessary if I could work out all of my problems and prejudices. You may be quite right that I have been trained as an individual analyst and lay on the couch so long, that I have to be like the teacher who felt she was a student so long and took all the discipline from her teacher. Now she has a chance to dish it out and pass it on to her students. Maybe the problem is that I am committed too strongly by my own training and my own convictions despite my protestation of flexibility.

Irv: This patient makes me so nervous, I know that if I put her on the couch or got in back of her or something where I did not have her peering at me all the time, I would feel a lot more comfortable. She is so jumpy that I have tried to analyze it. I have asked myself, "What is it? Why am I so disturbed by her?" She is a nice woman and yet she is so busy that I just cannot sit still when she comes in. She comes in, she starts dancing around, she squirms around and before long I can hardly sit in the chair.

Mannie: Anybody who takes the absolute position that you do not need a couch at all better be willing to handle some of the kinds of patients that in my experience I was unable to handle at all until I was able to get the patient to use the couch. I want to give you one more example. An analyst-in-training, a psychologist, a trainee of one of the analytic training schools here, came to see me and he paced my office for nearly three months, afraid to lie down, afraid to sit down, afraid to turn his back. In my office, he paced like a lion or a tiger, back and forth, for fear I was going to attack him sexually from the rear. He would pace back and forth keeping an eye on me. I got him at least to sit down on the couch and finally to lie on it. I would never have been able to reach him so long as I continued to allow him to keep his eyes on me. The breakthrough came and the sign for me of his own control over himself was when he was able to lie down on the couch. Maybe I could have done it with a chair, but someone will have to demonstrate to me that for some of these patients where clinically the use of the couch becomes the central issue for establishing a working relationship, that it can be done otherwise. Perhaps it can, but I have limitations.

Irv: Gerry and I both have loungers or whatever you call them. We have a chair which, if you push back on it, straightens out and you are flat on your back. The chair folds back.

Do you think that makes any difference as opposed to a couch?

Mannie: No. I only think it makes a difference as to where you sit and what the symbolic meaning of it is to the patient.

Irv: But if the patient comes in and actively pushes the chair back and is in a relaxed position, that would be the same as a couch wouldn't it? If you were in back of the patient?

Mannie: If you were in back of the patient, yes. That is, provided you analyze the symbolic meaning of the couch. Remember, the couch symbolically is a bed. On the couch you are in a horizontal position, which means the infantile position. You do not see. Just as in the infantile position you do not see the authority, the source of supply. You also associate this position with infantile sexuality and with adult sexuality. You also associate it with vulnerability. These are some of the symbolic meanings of the couch that need to be analyzed in any good analytic relationship.

Irv: Do you use the couch even with once-a-week or twice-a-week patients?

Mannie: Even on a once-a-week basis provided again you recognize that such a relationship requires a different kind of activity on the part of the therapist. I think it requires him to be somewhat more active especially with regard to resistance. Resistances tend to arise too greatly over a week's lapse and the therapist has to be especially aware of his activity in breaking through. Otherwise too much time is wasted.

Irv: I would like to bring up something else. I have an article here in *Psychiatry* on "Conjoint Family Therapy" by Don Jackson. Have you seen it? It is in the May 1961 number.

Mannie: No. I know his work. We have been in touch.

Irv: He talks about his theory behind family therapy with schizophrenics and he concludes the article by talking about what the effects have been on the therapist's individual practice as a result of this family therapy. The therapist becomes more active in individual therapy.

Mannie: Probably.

Irv: But even then he raises a point that is quite interesting and I disagree with him. He has a discussion on transference and countertransference and interaction and he says the

terms transference and countertransference are troublesome.
They refer strictly to aspects of a very special situation in
psychoanalysis. He says, "We have no doubt that our
therapists have feelings about the family members and vice
versa. On the other hand, no clarity is achieved if we label
such states of mind transference and countertransference."
He says transference is something that is related to the activity prescribed for standard psychoanalytic treatment, and
I think this is where he goes wrong. He says in conjoint
family therapy there is a lot of activity and consequently
he does not like to call this phenomenon transference. If the
wife is chopping the husband to ribbons instead of trying
to focus on the transference aspects of it, he focuses it back
to the other party. In a sense he does not really deal with
the patient's feelings about the therapist or the therapist's
feelings about the patient. I am getting kind of obscure
here, but it seems to me that in not looking at it from a
transferential and countertransferential point of view, I
think he is really going wrong.

Mannie: Al and I have this difference of opinion between us. Al takes
the same position as you do and I subscribe to the position
of Don Jackson. Let me state briefly what the problem is.
It is necessary that we not be bound by historical definitions
and words within a theory. What happens is we become too
limited by using a word that has a very specific meaning and
we then begin to use it in this kind of new meaning. I think
we are in a new phase of psychoanalytic work and maybe
we need some new words. I believe that "acting out" and
"transference" and "countertransference" ought to be restricted to their classical meaning. I do not believe that
groups "act out" or nations "act out" or husbands and
wives "act out." I think "acting out" should be restricted
entirely to an analytic relationship in which the patient
"acts out" rather than recalls or verbalizes the feelings and
thoughts which relate symbolically in the analytic relationship to the analyst. With group therapy and modern variations, such as transactional psychology, we are dealing with
other aspects of the problem. We are dealing really with
activity which must be viewed either as protherapeutic or

antitherapeutic. I think this is what Don Jackson is struggling with. I call acting out in this modern view any kind of activity which is antitherapeutic, which is based upon resistance and transference. That is, if it is on transference and in resistance it is antitherapeutic, so I call it acting out. But if it is protherapeutic—and there are some kinds of activity which are on transference and distorted but which nevertheless are therapy-facilitating or can be utilized or analyzed in a therapy-facilitating way—I would not call that acting out. The same is true of transference. Transference and countertransference are specific terms in the historical sense. Al uses them this way. There is a movement even in classical analysis to deal with this problem because it causes difficulties. A man by the name of Badouin, a member of the French Psychoanalytic Association, has written an article in which he talks about lateral transference. Lateral transferences are transference reactions to all others than the analyst. He uses the term lateral transference, meaning anything but the transference neurosis, that is, vis-à-vis the analyst. That is an interesting attempt to deal with what looks like very similar activity with similar kinds of distortions in relation to another, to a person other than the analyst, which we see in analytic group therapy and we know exists in the family and the life outside. One way of escaping this problem that the Horney followers and some others take is not to use the word transference at all. I think this is to avoid a very useful term and a very useful concept, but you see the kind of conflict we are in at this moment.

Gerry: I have the thought then that in traditional analysis you are taking the experiences you call lateral transferences and focusing these on the therapist, and this is where we usually use the word transference. Maybe this is manipulation; maybe it facilitates and emphasizes distortion and unhealthy or antitherapeutic things rather than being therapeutic itself.

Mannie: I do not think transference is therapeutic. I do not think acting out is therapeutic. I do not think it is healthy. It is distorted; it is pathologically motivated. But I think it can be helpful in expediting therapy if the material comes up. Before you can understand whether behavior is acting out or not, even in a classical sense, your patient has to reveal his dynamics. It only becomes acting out if you know his psychodynamics. You may not know whether a piece of activity is acting out until the end of analysis, just as you may not know the full meaning of a dream until the end of analysis. So all activity has to be evaluated in terms of an hypothesis we have about the nature of the psychodynamics of the patient. Are you with me?

Gerry: Yes.

Mannie: Am I getting too involved in theory today?

Irv: No, I do not think so, not at all.

Gerry: I was just struggling with some of these ideas. I do not think it is too theoretical. I suppose it has some personal meaning. You know Nicky. Well, Monday I got a call from her mother and she said, "I want you to know that things have changed since last Wednesday, since Nicky came out of the group, and she really looks good." I am confused by this because it is such a dramatic and sudden change in her. I thought we might have some ideas about it. Nicky, you remember, was the one who was mute, so to speak.

Mannie: Yes, and who would not go to the alternate session alone.

Gerry: Going only with some duress. Her mother is getting her there really. She talked a little bit in the waiting room and a little bit at the meetings, but not much. She really stayed out of treatment, but last Monday the mother called and then later Nicky came in and was full of gab from the time she hit the door. She was like she was when I first saw her in the hospital, when the doctor who was treating her asked if I would see her in group. She was really talkative and animated. She is a bright girl. She is a schoolteacher. Her mother said that a week ago Wednesday she did not want to come to the group. Her mother brought her down and when she came out of the group she said her eyes looked different, she looked alive. Then Nicky told me that she felt pretty good on Thursday and Friday, got active, was doing some housework, was out mowing the lawn, was interested in things, and she wanted to go to the alternate meeting

on Friday. She drove herself over to the alternate meeting.
She came down to the meeting on her own on Monday and
she is very, very active. But it is such a sudden kind of
change, I had the reaction, as did Irv when I mentioned it
to him, that it was like spontaneous remission.

Mannie: Could be.

Gerry: Then I tried to get her to associate to this. She did not know
why she suddenly felt this way. She explained that she
really did not want to be here, she really did not think
treatment was necessary for her and she had therefore
stopped talking. Though many times she wanted to associate in the group or bring up her own thoughts or feelings
and was impelled to do so, she would hold back and not
do it because she was afraid that it would be expected
of her that she was going to talk in the group and that
she was going to co-operate in treatment. Another association she had was to Ethel, the volatile girl who is promiscuous, drank and jumped out the windows and left the
group. Ethel kicked up a fuss, did not want to continue her
treatment, was not paying her bill, and that sort of thing.
So I saw her for an individual session. She was not going
to continue and I could not work it through with her at all.
She left the group, and a new man came into the group
who was very passive. He has been talking about his mother
who was so domineering all his life, and he had been very
actively assimilated into the group. It was after his second
or third session and the loss of this other woman that Nicky
became so animated. She associated to Ethel and said that
she just felt like she could not talk with her around, that
Ethel would not accept anything Nicky would say and she
just had a very negative feeling about Ethel. I said, "Well,
that would explain it except that you were not talking even
prior to being in this group with Ethel." Nicky had been in
another group and I made some changes when we started
our phone conversations here. She said, "Yes, in the other
group I think it was David that made me feel this way."
I felt like this did have something to do with her own
transferences or lateral transferences in the group and her
own problem with her dominating mother. The fact that

this patient came in and so actively talked about his mother and how domineering she was and then let this girl, Ethel, push him over seems to me to be the precipitant of the change in Nicky. Ethel got up and went over and pushed him right over in the chair. Of course, he must have used a push off the floor to get the chair to turn over backwards and end up on his rear, because Ethel weighs about a hundred pounds and he weighs two hundred. My feeling is that it was this kind of interaction which enabled her to begin talking in the group, but I do not know. It seems such a sudden change.

Mannie: The important thing is that you attempted to discover what brought it about. All these changes are multidetermined. You have a number of hypotheses, of hooks which you might try in the event she does go back into her silences. You have already mentioned a half a dozen of these hunches, like getting rid of the mother; like hearing this man talk about his mother in some way encouraged her to talk for she fears she might say something about her mother; and seeing the violence of the mother did not destroy this man, therefore, maybe she would not be destroyed either. There is also the possibility that because she has this symbiotic relationship to the mother, in which she is submissive to the mother's will, even to the mother's unconscious wishes, maybe she has made a mother of the group as a whole.

Gerry: Yes, this was Irv's reaction.

Mannie: And that in some way perhaps is what is happening. She was afraid that once she began to talk, the group would compel her to conform to this procedure in the future.

Irv: That was my thought.

Gerry: That is what she said.

Mannie: Therefore, she is saying that in some way, the way you have conducted your group she recognizes that even if she speaks at one time, she does not have to speak the next time, that she has some autonomy within the group even though she does not have that autonomy vis-à-vis the mother.

Irv: I thought that this girl has a tremendous fear of the fact that in her relationship with the mother she has no individuality, nothing of her own. Her fight in the group is to maintain herself, to prevent herself from being eaten up, from being devoured.

Gerry: This is true and I think back now on the last two sessions and the things she has been talking about. She brought in a book on mental health and gave it to one of the other patients. I noticed in these two sessions that she was talking about ideas from her own reading, she was taking the role of assistant therapist. She was taking over in the group and assuming the analyst's role or the therapeutic role. She was questioning the others and she was getting really involved with them, telling them what she thought. Really I suppose somewhere in this she has decided that she could compete with me as mother.

Mannie: Perhaps she can relate to you as father. We do not know because you have not talked about her relationship to the father. It may be that the group permits her to relate to the group as a whole as mother and you as father, and she can relate to you and have some feeling of an identification with you.

Gerry: This is a problem of hers. Prior to her psychotic episode upon leaving college and getting her teaching degree, she went out and was living in a homosexual relationship with another woman teacher.

Irv: Were they actively homosexual?

Gerry: Yes, actively homosexual, and she made a suicide try. It was during the course of this episode she was going to leave there and go somewhere else and teach. She really made a serious attempt at suicide by carbon monoxide gas.

Irv: I would like to bring up something that concerns me. I have a little conflict about it. It may be that I will get sponsorship from the Council of Churches in this area to work with ministers, cutting across the various denominational groups.

Mannie: Wonderful.

Irv: I am having a meeting on Monday. You know I ran a couple of ministers' groups a couple of years ago.

Mannie: I did not know.

Irv: For two years I ran a group for ministers where I did a type of group psychotherapy. Each one did what he wanted to do in the group. Some wanted to deal with their dreams and fantasies and some wanted a lot of help and others did not. Well, they are asking for help and they want something, and I have some conflicts. I do not know whether to give them a group experience and try to run it just like I would run an ordinary therapy group, or to use the group process as a way of letting them learn something about their interactions, providing didactic material, dealing with the kinds of cases they have and give them some lecture material on pastoral counseling. I think what they are interested in is gaining more sophistication in their work with their parishioners, particularly with their pastoral counseling relationships. I can take the position, which I think is a valid one, that if they understand themselves better and their own interaction, their impact on one another, they will develop sophistication and will be improved in terms of how they deal with their parishioners. But the thing that bothers me is this idea of working in a therapeutic relationship with a group of individuals who know one another on the outside and who also have a dual relationship with me. Some of these people I know, and they even refer patients to me. It is not the ordinary kind of relationship I have with patients.

Mannie: You two are repeating the history of group psychotherapy. You are going right through the same developmental sequence. As I said, there is conflict about the use of the terms, and Al and I have different points of view. In this Al and I share a point of view, and we had a struggle with Leo Berman, who died recently in Boston. Leo was doing work with teacher groups.

Irv: Who knew one another too?

Mannie: Who knew one another. They were in the same school.

Irv: Yet he worked with them on a group level?

Mannie: He worked with them as a group experience and he gave them a limited number of sessions. He limited it to fifteen sessions because he thought that he did not want this to develop into the kind of therapeutic experience which would be converted into group therapy. I think it depends upon

how much work you want to do, how much time you want
to invest, the nature of the group that is going to come in,
how large a group and how many groups you are going
to conduct. I think it is possible for you to take a tip from
Leo Berman and give them a group experience, an interactional experience. Follow that or precede it, however
you want to plan your curriculum, with group discussion
and group interaction, presenting the materials, educating
them about mental health, and even showing a film that
you will discuss. There is something about getting them
out of their isolation, giving them information as well as
an emotional experience, that can only do them good. I do
not think I would put them in group therapy because I do
not think I would make a long range or ongoing group
therapy experience for them. If you want to give any one
or any group of them a long-range group experience, I
would insist that they join one of your heterogeneous
patient groups.

Irv: What about the idea then of giving them a combination
of education and group experience, where they have an
opportunity to interact with one another and talk about
the kinds of problems they are having in their relationships
in the church and with the parishioners and sort of cut
across therapeutic and educational lines, giving them both?
That is what I had in mind and the thing that bothered
me—

Mannie: Even concurrently or consecutively, whichever one you
want.

Irv: That is what I had in mind. The only thing that bothered
me was the fact that I have a relationship with some of
these people other than just the teaching or therapeutic one.

Mannie: As long as you do not get into depth analytic relationships
with them you may avoid big trouble. After all, I have a
relationship with every one of my training students and it
sometimes complicates considerably my life with them and
theirs with me. It is a problem that has to be worked on.

Irv: Yes.

Gerry: I don't know. Just listening here, I was wondering.

Irv: What were you wondering, Gerry?

Gerry: Two things. I have thought a lot about having some kind of pastoral counseling workshop for priests and ministers whom I know, where I thought it would be a helpful thing for them. The other thing was that last night I was talking with a neighbor friend who is an internist at a prepaid medical group, who was asking me what kinds of people we work with, and talking about the goals of their prepayment plan for medical care, and what the problems are of offering this kind of psychotherapeutic help to their patients because of the financial problems involved. They can set up actuarial prices and know how to set prepayments on certain of the strictly organic things. Yet he realizes that sixty to seventy-five per cent of their practice are people just like in any medical practice, people with psychogenic, functional problems. He was very interested that we are doing group therapy because it is something that people who are involved in the kind of work they do are interested in too. I think it is a fruitful place for further talk. They do have to refer these patients elsewhere for psychotherapy and they do have problems of screening.

Mannie: I think it is worth exploring.

Irv: I think this ministers' thing will work out.

Mannie: Why not! See to it that you handle properly your own necessities in the situation. My association now is that I would be interested in your secretary's reaction to this session without Al here, because of her comments. We must all three of us have a certain kind of transference to Al that she believes he is the Great White Father.

Irv: You are in his chair you know.

Mannie: That is what I am saying. You saw her comments to us. Al is the Great White Father. Well now, having gotten that view of us, it comes not only from the two of you but also from me that indeed he is that in some way.

Irv: You very frequently spiel off and then you turn to Al and say, "Now, Doc, how about a word from you?"

Mannie: Yes, because this is the only way to get him to come out, because he is not going to fight me. He never fights anybody, not even in a group. That is the kind of analyst he is, the kind of person he is. Now with me, and she reacted quite right, you have to fight in order to get a word in edgewise. So knowing that this is true of me, I continuously invite others in. But let us do some thinking. If you two have any special commitments or problems for next week, get an agenda up and I will do what I can with it.

18

The Physical Structure
of the Treatment Setting

We have already touched on the importance of the physical setting.
How is the office furniture arranged? What is the office layout?
Where does therapist sit—in a special chair? What is the seating
arrangement for patients in the group? Do structural issues create
different pressures on patients and therapist? How do the physical
arrangements affect hierarchical and vertical vectors? What about
status denial? equalization? and its opposite, omnipotence? The
therapist as a model of good living seems also to be a factor in
treatment. Modeling is an important factor in the efficacy of the
teaching-learning alliance.

Mannie: I want to say a word about having the alternate sessions in
your office, Irv. We tend to take a fairly arbitrary position,
urging that it be done in the patients' homes. It has certain
advantages and values in the home, because it is easier on
us the way we practice, having our own offices in our own
homes. We have office and home combined, both Al and I,
so we tend not to want to have somebody take over our
apartments.

Irv: We are talking to you in your home now?

Mannie: Yes.

Irv: For crying out loud, why didn't you say so?

Gerry: For five months I thought we were talking to his office and
           we are in his house.

Irv: Why didn't you tell us?

Mannie: Al has been working in his home ever since I have known
           him, since he got back from the army. I used to have my
           office separated from my home until about 1951.

Irv: I thought his address, Al's address, is the same place where
           Nathan Ackerman has his office.

Mannie: Al lives in an apartment house in which there must be
           twenty-five analysts, and I live in an apartment house in
           which there are only eight analysts.

Irv: What kind of business is that, for crying out loud?

Mannie: Al and I have our offices in what I call, in my socially aware
           way, the Analytic Gold Coast. There are more analysts per
           square mile in the area from Fifty-ninth Street to Ninety-
           sixth Street from Lexington Avenue to Fifth Avenue than
           there are in the rest of the world.

Irv: Listen, give us a little bit more of a feeling for this. How
           big an office do you have? Do you have an office large
           enough for groups?

Mannie: Yes, of course. Al has a different setup from mine. Al has
           an individual room and a group room. Al has a much larger
           apartment than I have. Al runs quite a large establishment
           in that he believes in having his group room separated
           from his individual treatment room. I do not have any such
           need. Maybe I am rationalizing my wish not to spend that
           much money for the landlord. I have a large waiting room
           about fourteen by twenty with six or eight chairs around it
           and a good-sized office in which I have my couch and a
           bench and two comfortable chairs. For the group I bring in
           one or two additional chairs and that takes up to ten or
           eleven people. I have never had more than eight or nine
           so far. I have never run my groups even up to ten. Al some-
           times runs into eleven or twelve. He is more courageous
           and more perceptive. I do not usually do that. I do not
           have a large round table in front of my two benches, but
           Al does. Al has individual chairs rather than benches.

Irv: That is what we have.

Mannie: Al has a series of these chairs with a table, a large coffee table, and they surround it and he has chairs for all of them and he has a comfortable chair for himself. Otherwise he would have a busted back.

Irv: Does Al sit in the same chair all the time?

Mannie: Al sits in the same chair all the time. I do too, by the way.

Irv: How come, how come?

Gerry: So do I most of the time.

Irv: You guys, you guys.

Mannie: You have been shifting around, eh?

Irv: That is the way I feel about it. My office is arranged differently than Gerry's. I have a round table and ten chairs arranged in a circle and I take any chair and, of course, this brings things up in the group. This brings up a lot of flexibility in the group. Someone wants to sit next to me; someone wishes that I would sit next to him, and they talk about it. I shift around.

Gerry: They talk about that with me, too, although my setup is different. We have about the same office space, but my chairs are spread around the room in a much more open way, more like a living room than the circle you have.

Irv: Yes, I have a circle.

Gerry: And my chairs are spread all round here.

Irv: If you were to walk into Gerry's office, you would see about fifteen chairs all around the room. That is how it looks.

Mannie: Great. I want to finish about Al's office because Al has quite a distinct setup, and for a group analyst probably an ideal setup. As you walk in he has a very, very large waiting room area with lots of chairs around and magazines. This is a kind of waiting room off which two rooms go; one a smaller room which is his private individual therapy room in which he has a couch, desk, and a couple of chairs. Then he has this larger group room surrounded by books and he has this large coffee table, a low coffee table in the center on which there are ashtrays and so on, and these dozen chairs all around with the one comfortable chair that he uses. Sometimes, since I use the same chair and Al uses his own chair all the time, you will get a patient who will head for your chair. It is quite clear that this is your chair. It is the only one that is different from the others and that, of course, is an interesting piece of material to work on. But generally we do not shift around.

Irv: Why don't you?

Gerry: You know how that came up, Mannie? Nicky got so lively and competitive, she is really trying to be the leader in the group. She is giving people things to read and all that. I came out the other night to get a drink of water before the group started, and I told them to go in. I came back in and Nicky was parked over there in my chair. The group just laughed and she jumped up, got off and said, "I'll go sit somewhere else." I walked over, picked up some smokes off the ashtray stand, and was going to sit somewhere else but she jumped up and ran off. But we then had an opportunity to talk very directly about her competition with me and what she was doing.

Irv: I want to get back to this chair business. It seems to me that if the analyst takes the same chair all the time, this establishes a different type of relationship with the patient than if you shift around all the time.

Mannie: I am sure it must.

Irv: Because if you take your own chair or the same chair all the time, you are saying you have a chair that is identified as yours, then you are in a sense repeating for them an experience they must have had at home and you are in the vertical vector there.

Mannie: I think that is true, we must remember that the vertical vector is always there whether we like it or not. Maybe this is an accentuation of it.

Irv: I think it is. Now I am just wondering. I suppose you could work with it either way. It seems to me that if you take the same chair all the time, maybe this is a pressure toward regression or maybe this enables you to get more transference material.

Mannie: It may be. In fact, I have always felt that it is important to know whether there are shifts in the seating arrangements of the patients.

Irv: There is a recent article incidentally on this in the last number of *Psychiatry*.

Mannie: I did not see it. Who wrote it?

Irv: Two therapists in New York. It is on group analysis and the seating arrangement.

Mannie: It is a very interesting aspect and it is closely related to sociometry. Moreno has done a lot of work along these lines and I am sure conscious preferences and transferences and distortions all come through in the seating arrangement.

Irv: I am just thinking again that you said something important, Mannie, a week ago, that really struck me.

Mannie: When was that?

Irv: What I wanted to say was that you were pointing out that in the group as opposed to the individual analytic situation, the pressures are different. In the group a lot of pressure on the patient to respond comes from group members. There is a structural difference with regard to where the pressures are. If the analyst has a chair that is identified as his chair and everybody sees it that way, this creates a certain kind of pressure and structures the group to a degree.

Mannie: This is a repetition then of the kind of pressure of the couch and the chair behind it.

Irv: Yes. Maybe that is a good thing. Maybe this fosters regression. In other words, maybe this facilitates things when someone works through oedipal competitive dynamics. Perhaps he will begin to verbalize, "I want to sit in your chair." If you do not have a chair and you shift around all the time, then they do not have that to focus on. They have to have something else.

Mannie: They will find something else. I think you are quite right. And it would be an interesting piece of research to investigate it.

Gerry: It brings up another point. I now know what was happening in my own group a week or two ago. Thelma was so very disturbed. She was sitting over here in this chair next to someone, one of the women she said she did not like. She said she felt very uncomfortable and wanted to sit in the chair beside me where Sarah was sitting. This was the time when Thelma threw the ashtray and got very disturbed. I think really I was looking at her lateral feelings and transference to this girl, whom she sees as mother. She has some underlying homosexual attraction to her and in wanting to get over near me, she was trying to tell the group that she was really interested in a man. But actually the competitive portion of it was there and I did not get to it at all, that she really wants to change seats with me and she is talking about it in this other way. It is all part of the same problem.

Mannie: Right.

Gerry: I got only one facet of the thing by saying that she wanted to convince the group she wanted to sit near me because I was a man and not near mother because she is a woman and that is homosexual. She wanted also to take over my chair as a man.

Irv: This is terrific. I never thought of this. Is your chair distinctly more comfortable?

Mannie: I think mine is. I think Al's is too.

Gerry: There is an interesting point here, Mannie, because in my room there are two comfortable chairs. There is the Stratolounger and there is that Dux chair that I have. So we have an empty mama's chair.

Irv: Now what does that mean?

Mannie: But my two couches are comfortable and upholstered as my chair is. They are comfortable, but they are quite different.

Gerry: I think my chairs are comfortable.

Irv: We all have comfortable chairs.

Mannie: I meant that Al's are not upholstered.

Gerry: Yours are not upholstered either, Irv.

Irv: I have some upholstered ones.

Mannie: There is quite a difference if you start thinking about the seating; many dimensions begin to come out.

Gerry: You know this chair here. I have a straight chair that goes with my desk. It has a foam-rubber seat with a cane back, a very modern kind of chair. It has an arch in the back and the group always talks about that as the most uncomfortable chair in the room. It is kind of a dunce chair. And the newest member in the group—

Mannie: You put the person you do not like in that one.

Gerry: The person who thinks the group does not like him takes that chair, and I just thought about that.

Irv: Hey, listen to this. I have a plastic chair, one of the bucket chairs. I have one real rigid, obsessive-compulsive who always sits in it.

Mannie: All right. Now that becomes a piece of behavior you can analyze.

Irv: He said that he likes it. Nobody will sit in that chair except him and they say to him, "There he is on the toilet again." For some reason I want to talk about this more. I am just thinking if I were a patient and in your group or Al's group and I came in and you gave me one of those lousy hard chairs, I would be angry with whomever is sitting in the throne. Boy!

Mannie: If you pressed Al, I think he would agree with me, but he would tell you also that if you have three or four groups running, you need a softer chair or you will bust your back. The low back pain has become the analyst's occupational hazard.

Irv: Yes.

Mannie: I do not have that much complaint because I do not sit that long in any one place. I tend to try to get up and get out and go over to the clinic. Al usually stays in his office from morning till night. I spend a big portion of time over at the center so I do not have the same kind of complaint. I know Al would tell you that this is a necessity for him, but I think he would still agree with us on our theoretical and clinical implications.

Irv: I have been thinking about this, that maybe it is more important for the analyst, for the group analyst, to have his own chair and to have a chair that is identified as his and is in focus. This in a sense reinforced regression. As you pointed out, Mannie, there is going to be regression; there is going to be transference to the analyst as an authority figure. But it seems to me that having the same chair all the time, possibly even a softer chair, in many respects duplicates the kind of pressure you have in the individual analytic situation.

Mannie: It is a beautiful use of the symbolism and I think it establishes a whole series of questions for experimental design. It is a fascinating problem.

Irv: I am just wondering though, I am asking myself the question, What would I do if I had a chair of my own and someone sat in it?

Gerry: What do I do! I come in and my smokes are on the smoking stand next to it and there is someone sitting there. I go over and pick them up and I take another chair and then it does not take more than a half second for them to say, "Well, what are you doing, taking Doc's chair or Mac's chair?" They get their hostility towards me out too and we begin to work on it. You do not always deal with it because many of the people are not really that prepared to look at this kind of a wanting to take over from me. They rationalize this.

Irv: Has it happened to you, Mannie?

Mannie: Sure.

Irv: What do you do?

Mannie: Sometimes I have said, "Hey, what is cooking here?" or sometimes I have done what Gerry suggests.

Irv: Have you ever kicked them out of the chair?

Mannie: Not actually, but I think that I have conveyed it by my manner. You see I am different from Al. I do not have to say anything or do anything to kick somebody out of the chair. I seem to provoke in patients their transference, their authoritarian transferences onto me that make me always authoritarian even if I am trying to be gentle and kind. So it is pretty hard for me to answer whether I have ever kicked them out of a chair. I know that some patients have felt that I have kicked them out, but it occurs only rarely. In individual analysis sometimes when there has been considerable resistance, particularly among trainees, for example, young analysts in training with me, I suggest that they would like to get into my seat. They have brought up fantasies and dreams in this connection. I have said to them, "You know, there is a chair like mine right next to me here and I would like you to have it. But you do not need to have my chair. There is plenty of room here for another chair." Often there is a rejection of this offer or interpretation because the wish is to get into my chair. And, of course, you quite correctly pointed out, Irv, this is oedipal in a most undisguised form.

Irv: I think it is undesirable in group therapy when the analyst does not have a definite chair. Some patients look for solidity, look for support because they are fragmented and disturbed. The fact that the analyst is in the same chair and same place all the time may have a reassuring quality for them.

Mannie: Exactly. Just as having the same session at the same time every day or the same day every week.

Gerry: There is something else that you are not looking at, Irv. How can the patient respond to your changing around, your moving from chair to chair? They are going to feel that you do not want to have any stability, that you do not want to stay where they can get hold of you.

Irv: Yes. Well, I thought that would—

Gerry: We can look at this also as a transference either in terms of authority or in terms of friends in the group. Moving from chairs, what it means for them to move and sit next to somebody, then what does it mean in terms of counter-transference from you that they may be picking up at some level.

Irv: Let me say this—

Mannie: Right. It obscures their activity because it is initiated by your movements.

Irv: Let me talk a little bit about myself here.

Mannie: Go ahead.

Irv: At times when I have been very anxious and doubtful about the merits of group therapy, I have sat in the same chair because sitting in the same chair every time has made me feel more secure. As I have felt more confident about what I have been doing, I have been moving around more. The evenings that I move around and shift are the evenings when I do not feel as anxious. The evenings when I am rooted in the same place all the time are the evenings when I want some solidity. I want some support.

Gerry: Could it be that you are putting the cart before the horse?

Irv: All right, go ahead.

Gerry: Well, could it be—

Mannie: Oh, you are a mean one.

Gerry: Why?

Mannie: It is a wonderful question. Respond to it, Irv.

Irv: I am so dumbfounded, I do not know; I feel like I was hit over the head with a mallet.

Mannie: He did it! He did that!

Irv: Am I putting the cart before the horse? Now I am saying that sitting in the same chair has made me feel more secure and when I am confident, I move around. You are saying that it is the other way around.

Mannie: Right. Maybe you are anxious about sitting in the position of authority.

Irv: Ah, good, good!

Mannie: Beautiful, Gerry.

Irv: Good point. In the particular situation I am describing, I do not think it is true. Although I think that generally speaking I would be scared to be identified as having the same chair and somebody could find me and castrate me.

Gerry: You said that when you feel real good and you do not feel anxious, then you move around. I wonder how you can know, I mean, if it is a simultaneous kind of experience, and you seem to be saying that it is this way, when it may be the other way.

Irv: For a long time I would sit in the same chair all the time. I have a chair in my office that is low and it is an upholstered chair and different from the others. For a long time I occupied that chair all the time and patients would associate to it. That would be my chair and if someone would try to sit in it, they would say, "What do you want to take Doc's chair for?" But I felt that this may not be appropriate. I felt that shifting around and not taking the same chair all the time was a way of introducing equality in a sense and highlighting the transferential aspects. If I would take a different chair all the time, then if they would transfer to me, it would be clearer. They would really see it as contrasted with the situation where I have the comfortable chair. If that is the chair I take, if that is my chair, then I am asserting something. I am asserting my authority and am imposing it in a structured way.

Gerry: Sure. But what is wrong with that?

Irv: Apparently—

Gerry: Unless you are not an authority.

Irv: I can see now, I think this is very important—to have the same chair. To deal with it that way is important for many people. If you structure that way, they can work through their authority problems. Maybe shifting around the way I have been has hurt some people in the sense that—

Gerry: Maybe it hurts you too. Maybe it keeps both you and them from working through their authority problem, because I do think that you have to have both sides to it. Why else would you be so comfortable? It might be a technical question whether it is better to have your own chair or better to move around in the group and this might be something you are experimenting with, but it sure is not clear-cut when you feel anxious sitting in the authority chair and comfortable moving around.

Irv: If I do feel anxious sitting in the authority chair—

Gerry: That is what you said, usually when you need stability that is when you sit there.

Irv: No.

Mannie: Irv, you connected it with anxiety. The moment you do that, it is more than a conscious experimental or technical device.

Irv: Wait a second now. I said that for a long time I occupied the same chair in the group, that I did not move out of that chair.

Gerry: I am not talking about that. I am talking about what you first brought up. Some ten minutes ago you said that you were interested in this matter of the chairs. You said that when you feel the least convinced and the least sure about what you are doing in the group, when you feel anxious, then you take the same chair and keep it and it is some sort of a stability for you.

Irv: Yes.

Gerry: And when you feel pretty good about what you are doing and you feel comfortable, then you move around in the group. That is anxiety, isn't it?

Irv: Of course, it is anxiety, that is why I said it was anxiety.

Mannie: Therefore, it may not be fed as much by a conscious wish to use this as a technical device, but the result of counter-transference needs and demands.

Gerry: Which was why I said, "Aren't you putting the cart before the horse?"

Mannie: Right. The question that you are now struggling with is one of the central issues in group therapy today, the problem of the analytic therapist versus the nonanalytic therapist. The nonanalytic therapists call this status denial. They are a group of therapists who believe in what Irv was calling equalization. Actually, it is a denial of their authority and responsibility. They tend to want to deny as much as possible the vertical vector. But in denying it, they reverse the vertical vector and make the patient more important, more responsible, have more authority than the experts. They not only move around from chair to chair, but tend to move around physically during the session. One such therapist tells the story of when one of his patients suicided, he came in and lay in the laps of two or three of his students. They patted his head and consoled him. I said students; I did not say patients, even though they were his patients. And they consoled him on the suicide of this other person.

Irv: That is certainly a piece of sick behavior as far as I can see.

Mannie: Sick behavior or not, they can rationalize this very well by saying that they believe in the equalization. I think Gerry's point is very well taken, Irv, and it is what I am trying to say.

Irv: I think it is well taken and I can see that. I was aware of it when I mentioned it, that certainly my attitudes toward all of this have to do with my own feelings about authority.

Gerry: Yes. I am not saying you did not. I just thought that you seemed too convinced that you were comfortable moving around rather than avoiding anxiety moving around.

Irv: That is right. This is a very interesting point we have brought up because this relates to what Mannie was mentioning a week or two ago; that there are different pressures in the group and if you understand what the pressures are, then you are really more conscious of what you are doing and how you are working. It seems to me that having the same chair all the time is saying something very important to the patient. One other thing, Mannie, remember that patient I told you was schizophrenic and paranoid and was going to get married? Well, he got married. He was about two weeks late in paying me about a month or two ago, and his associations to it in analyzing it were that he was trying to grab my penis, trying to render me impotent, trying to show himself more powerful than me. Anyway, now he has been away for these three weeks and he has paid me for a whole month. He is going to be back in the group probably in a week or two. It happened again that he did not pay me. He does not say anything to me about it. He does not write me a note saying for some reason or another he cannot pay me. He just holds off paying me for a month. I am angry with him. My feeling is one of anger. My feeling is that after we worked this thing over, then he repeats the same thing again with me. Now my feeling is one of personal anger. What I am wondering about is when he comes back, it seems to me that I should set a limit: "This is the second time this has happened and you do not even say anything about it." Of course, my feeling is one of anger; when he comes in I would like to say to him, "What do you think you are doing?"

Mannie: What are you so angry about?

Irv: Because he did not pay me, you mean?

Mannie: I don't know. What are you so angry about?

Irv: That is what I am getting to. I am angry because I feel he is actually teasing me. He is depriving me of my money for that month, making me wait.

Mannie: How about reaction from the other quarter there?

Gerry: Ethel did this, the girl who acted out. She did not pay me until the end of the month a couple of months in a row and it was just before she terminated. She was holding out in the group, did not want to talk and I said, "You are holding out in the group, just like holding out the money." We talked about this and she said yes, she wanted to hold out; she thought I was a no-good bastard and she was not going to pay. We tried to analyze it. We worked on it and did not get anywhere. So finally this one night in the group I said, "Well, this has to be said, we cannot continue on this basis.

Unless the bill is paid tonight by nine o'clock, I will have
to stop seeing you." I let it go at that. The group went on
from there and she sat down and took out her checkbook
and wrote out a check and gave it to me.

Mannie: Yes. But were you angry, Gerry?

Gerry: I was not angry, no.

Mannie: What is your reaction?

Gerry: I do not know why I was not angry.

Mannie: What is your reaction? Irv repeated in about four sentences,
if you will look at the transcript of this, you will see that
he kept saying, "I am angry, I am angry, I am angry."
Gerry, what is your reaction to that?

Gerry: When he was saying it, I thought, "Why not be angry,
but what are you going to do about it when you are angry?"
I thought, "What is wrong with saying, Look, this makes
me angry, you are holding out on me, you are not paying
me; what are you doing? I am angry, but we have to work
this thing out."

Mannie: Yes, but he is not angry. Irv, I would like to interpret this
and you can say it is my projection, but I do not think you
are angry because the patient did not pay you. I think you
are angry because the patient indicated that you were not
omnipotent and that you did not work through, having
discussed it once with the patient.

Gerry: Oh, you know what my association was while Mannie was
saying that? That you are not angry because of the money.
I thought about the marriage, because that was what you
started out with: "This patient of mine that I worked so
long with and then he got married."

Irv: It could be that unconsciously, I am sure. Haven't you ever
gotten angry at patients?

Mannie: Lots of times, but I try not to act on it until I have worked
through my own anger.

Irv: I wonder.

Mannie: An analyst who is now dead used to boast that he had never
lost more than two sessions' fees with any one patient in
all of the twenty-five years he had been practicing. He said
that he never allowed a patient to owe him for more than
one week's sessions. He collected his fee at the last session

of a week, every week, and he had been doing that for twenty-five years. If they do not pay at the end of the week, they do not start their work the following week. This is a pretty rigid, authoritarian person. I would be concerned about it. I do not think there is another analyst around town who has not been cheated out of money by some patient. Part of why the group has its validity and part of why so many individual analysts are afraid of the group is that there is more activity, also more acting out in the group setting. And you have to let the material emerge if you are going to get to the psychodynamics. One of the ways that patients act out is with time and fees.

Gerry: I wonder if the greatest concern here and the greatest anger is that you in some way feel that you are co-operating in his acting out.

Irv: I feel that when—

Gerry: I mean, that sounds like it makes sense to me, that you said, that he is using me in this acting out. If he was using someone else . . .

Mannie: And he is toying with him.

Gerry: You are teasing too, if you are letting him tease you.

Irv: Yes, of course, I am involved in the process, but there is some reality too. For example, if a couple of months goes by and you do not get paid, you have to work with the issue.

Gerry: Right.

Mannie: I do not think I ought to try to deal with the situation until I try to work it out because if I let my anger through I am pretty surely always doing this beyond what is appropriate for the patient. I have sometimes done it, as everybody has. I have sometimes blown my stack with patients but I do not think that this is always necessarily what is best for the patient although it can be used analytically and very well.

Irv: The reason I brought it up today is I recognized that my feelings toward him are more than the money.

Mannie: Exactly.

Irv: And that is why I brought it up and I brought it up also because I am trying to get some consciousness on this.

Mannie: Maybe you are having too great an expectation, that you think that once, by having analyzed once, therefore, it is done.

Irv: I do not—

Mannie: I think you do not recognize that the most boring aspect of doing analytic work is working through.

Irv: Yes, but let me say this, Mannie, there is a difference between a patient acting out and acting out involving you directly. In other words, it would be different if we worked on something and worked on something and we kept on doing it and kept on doing it. But this time he is using me; it is involving me directly. In other words, I am not getting paid.

Mannie: But you are getting paid. You are getting paid a little later.

Irv: Of course, I will get paid.

Mannie: Therefore, you are really over-reacting to this. Do what Gerry did. Terminate. Irv, you have a right to be angry, but let us hope that the extent of the anger is appropriate to the extent of the threat to you.

Irv: Of course.

Mannie: That is the only point. You know you will get paid; but it is delayed a month. You know that this is an acting out and you know it needs to be worked through again. The group offers an opportunity for you to work it out, not only for this patient, but also to work it out for the rest of the group because the area of money is one of the most neglected in American analytic work. We are perfectly willing to talk about sex in its most intimate aspects, but we tend to shy clear of discussing money with patients or asking the patients to discuss money with us.

Irv: Say, that brings up a point about pregnancy and illness. I have a patient who is going to have to leave the group for maybe two or three weeks while she has her baby and my thinking about it is, I would like to give her three weeks time during which I will not charge her while she has the baby.

Mannie: Why not?

Irv: That is what I am going to do, but I was wondering, this brings up the point that we raised before about charges, charging people when they are sick and charging them when they are hospitalized for operations.

Mannie: You are apparently wanting to give her a gift.

Irv: Yes.

Mannie: If you want to give her a gift, why can't you?

Irv: I want to establish this generally for patients who are in a situation . . .

Mannie: Are you trying to sponsor the population explosion?

Irv: Yes.

Gerry: How do you determine? It is easy with a pregnancy. At least they are not acting out this month; maybe they were nine months ago. How do you determine whether this illness is in resistance to treatment or is one in the normal course of events?

Irv: A new patient came in yesterday and I told her what my charges would be. She said, "Well, are you going to charge when I cannot come in because of my migraines? I get real sick and I cannot come in." And I said, "Yes, you will be charged. I charge whether you get here or not. We will try to work with the problem of your migraines, but you are going to be charged." This is how I generally feel, but Al was mentioning some time ago about a patient that was in the hospital and he did not charge him for those two weeks. Apparently it has to be an individual kind of matter.

Mannie: Entirely individual, highly individual. And I would mostly respond the way you did. This is a general principle which also always has its exceptions. In general I do not alter the mechanics of my work. I do not initiate an alteration. I would not say to the patient who is pregnant, "I want to give you a gift." I consider this a countertransference implication. I would ask for you to explore yourself. But if the patient initiates it, then on the basis of your knowledge of the individual and the psychodynamics, as Gerry said, I would decide whether I wanted to accept some more flexible arrangement or not. But I would let the patient initiate the matter.

Irv: In other words, she might say, Well, I am going to be gone for three weeks and I do not feel like paying during that time.

Mannie: I say, let us talk about it. What do you feel about it? Why and how do you et cetera?

Gerry: It just occurs to me, that patient may want to pay for that time. She may want to have herself symbolically present even though she cannot physically be present.

Mannie: Yes, indeed. She may also be well able to afford it and think that you have it coming to you and that she is going out to have her baby or illness or whatever else it is and wants to pay for her time in order to reserve the time for herself. In general I would tend not to alter the mechanics of the relationship on the basis of my feelings about the issue, but rather to let the mechanics of the relationship be altered only upon my determination as an exception, based upon individual psychodynamics and initiated by the patient. In other words, suppose you think that it would be nice if we would all meet out in the park next week. I think this is your problem. I would not initiate it, but if the patients initiate it and you have the feeling that this is appropriate and so on, you discuss it, get their feelings, and you might decide to do this next week. Then it is a conscious determination based upon your own decision.

Gerry: Going on a class picnic, huh?

Mannie: Listen—

Gerry: Time is up.

Mannie: I am leaving on Monday for Lisbon, you know.

Gerry: Have a wonderful trip. I really like the idea of that. My wife said this morning, "Are those fellows married? How can they do this? What is the matter with you, you clod?"

Mannie: Of course, we are, you know that.

Gerry: I said, "Yes they are." And she said, "I do not know how they do it."

Mannie: You will do it too. That is not the point either. The basic principle so far as I am concerned, which I hope I am not rationalizing too far, is that if you are going to be a model of good living, of healthy living, you ought to be a model for your patient and part of it is to fight against this puritanical compulsion to have to work twenty-four hours a day, seven days a week. "If you are not working, you are a bum."

Gerry: Good idea. I like that. Have a wonderful summer, Mannie.

Irv: Mannie, we are going to miss you.

Mannie: Do you have our itineraries and how to get in touch with us?

Irv: We do not have your itineraries; we do not have anything, we do not know anything. Why didn't you invite us to join you in Paris?

Mannie: Come on, you still have time.

Irv: Hey, I would like to go. But if I went to Europe, I would like to go for three or four weeks. I do not want to go for three or four days.

Mannie: Come on.

Gerry: I would like to go for three or four months. That is what I would like.

Irv: I might just fly over for a couple of days, just to be together with you guys.

Mannie: Come on. We will both be at the same hotel and you will find us easily enough. Come and join us and we will appoint you as a member of the delegation.

Irv: Listen, I would really like to. I probably will not do it, but next year let us do something like that.

Mannie: Great. We are already planning next year. I ought to be in Rio.

Gerry: Group psychotherapy with a samba, huh?

Irv: Okay, Mannie, have a nice summer.

Mannie: Have a wonderful summer yourselves. We will be in touch.

19

Transference Theory:
Excerpts from the Later Years

Transference work is at the heart of psychotherapy, yet it must be done judiciously. Transference interpretations can be utilized as mutual defense by therapist and patient. Intrapsychic or interpersonal psychoanalytic models need to be contrasted to group dynamic models. Modifications are required by group realities. Choices must be made between different theories of transference; id psychology and ego psychology; and phenomenological or latent focus.

Irv: I came to a discovery this morning as I was thinking about our meeting today. I would like to share it with you. Remember we were talking last week about not wanting to hurt Al? I said that our relationship is different than it would be in an analysis. What I was trying to say was that in an analysis you feel that you can say anything to the analyst. He acts as if whatever you say has no real reference to him as a real person. Since it is all transferential anyway, you can cut him up and down and yell like hell and this is fine. During the week I happened to read an article by Thomas Szasz in the *International Journal of*

Psychoanalysis.[44] He was writing on transference. One important aspect of his article was his discussion of transference as a defense and as a defense from the analyst's point of view. He said that originally, when the concept was developed, it was considered a defense. Otherwise psychoanalysis would have been impossible. As long as the analyst can feel that whatever the patient says has no reference to the analyst's personality and character in any way, he can stand the kind of bombardment that he gets all week long. The analyst can walk out of the situation unscathed. This was what I was trying to formulate last week. It is different for us. It is not like an analytic session. If we say something bad about Al, whom we know as a real person, it is personally offensive. This morning I was thinking about this and wanted to talk about what happens in a group. The transference is rationalized as a defense. It is used by both the analyst and the patient in orthodox analysis. It can also be used as a defense by group analytic patients. However, as a game in a group, and this depends upon the group analyst, how he structures the situation and may help it become less of a game. It becomes less of a game when someone in the group really speaks up or stands up to someone else. I think it has more real meaning than when he stands up and plays the game of spouting off against the analyst in the individual orthodox session, and patients and analyst regard the remarks as transference manifestations, not here-and-now phenomena. One of the criticisms of group analytic work is that there is no neutrality. You cannot develop a transference.

Gerry: We are waiting, Mannie.

Mannie: This idea of the utilization of the transference mutually in the service of defense is one of the basic criticisms of individual analysis. It is no more a criticism of group than it is of individual analysis.

Irv: Wait. I was saying that it is more of a criticism of individual analysis than it is of group.

Mannie: It is a criticism of both. You cannot lose yourself in illusion in the group as much as you can in the individual session. Ezriel is the only group therapist who interprets everything as transference to the leader.[11] It is poor therapy if the analyst always interprets all aspects of the reaction of a patient as an "as if" reaction. At some point there is the whole value of the interchange between analyst and patient in the confrontation with reality. One criticism of analysis is that the analyst tends himself, too often, to see all behavior as illusory, and then makes the illusion the reality.

Irv: I think this is important. . . .

Mannie: The patient learns to hate you if he knows that he has made a fool of you. He knows that you have accepted the gentleman's agreement that this is all a fake, when you say this is all transference. "I don't mean you, Doc, it's my father I mean." And you say, "Yes, that is true." He knows he has made a fool of you and a fool of himself, and he hates you for it. We must not let the patient make fools of us and of himself by virtue of our acceptance that everything he says is rationalized away as if it were transference. He must take responsibility for his current behavior, here and now. To find the excuse that "This is my mother" or "This is my father" or "This is my transference" is a defense against the facing of reality.

Gerry: Obviously. But then that is just poor analysis, that is all. Freud would never do what some of our orthodox analysts do. We have been talking about this ever since we started— it seems to me that there are far more anchorages in reality in the group than there are in the individual situation.

Irv: Yes. It seems to me that when we want to analyze a person who is very obsessive and passive, who sees all authority people as fathers and who hates them and is subversive in his activity against them and at the same time is afraid to interact heterosexually because he thinks he is going to be beaten, slaughtered, and castrated any time he gets close to a woman, you have to bring this delusion or this fantasy into the patient's awareness. What is a better way of doing it than by analysis of the transference.

Mannie: He has to do it in the relationship with you, but not in the relationship to his antecedents. You discover the etiology by the analysis of history, but you don't solve it except in the relationship with you. It is by the human experience

Irv: with you, and your human interaction, by the confrontation with reality in the situation with you, that reconstructive change is possible.

Irv: But you have to give the patient an opportunity to have his illusion come out strongly. For example, a patient of mine for months walked into the group backwards. He would walk in as if he had placed a bomb under the building. He had a smile on his face, a guilty smile. Finally I confronted him and said, "You know, you are behaving like a subversive. You come in here and you give me this look as though you want to come over and kill me. What has it got to do with you and me?"

Mannie: All right. So what are you talking about? I think we have a problem in definition. I think you are using the total relationship as equal to transference.

Irv: No.

Mannie: The total therapeutic relationship is not transference. This is a misuse of the word.

Irv: I picked up Whitaker and Lieberman's book[47] and began looking at it. For the most part what they seem to do is to homogenize the group. They talk about the focal group conflict as Bion[6] and Ezriel[11] do. They speak of the whole group responding to some unconscious group conflict. They homogenize the whole group and identify a central conflict for the whole group and then treat the whole group with group interpretation.

Mannie: This is Bion's basic assumption, the idea that there is a fantasy life that the group shares in common, not that each one participates in a common experience, but that they are all involved in this basic fantasy which they share.

Gerry: Rather magical, isn't it?

Mannie: Very magical. There is no empirical evidence for it.

Gerry: It sounds like a collective unconscious kind of nonsense, no?

Mannie: Talking about collective unconscious, if you have not read it, I am putting on the "must" reading list C. G. Jung's memoirs.[24] In it you discover that he must have been very disturbed when he was working with Freud. He was involved with hallucinations, and a lot of what he later systematized was hallucinatory. It is really a must if you want to understand the development of psychoanalysis.

Irv: Another book which I think is a must—I haven't seen it yet, but it sounds very exciting to me—is this new book that Harry Guntrip put out.

Mannie: Never heard of it.

Irv: You must know Harry Guntrip.[21] He has overdeveloped Fairbairn's object-relations approach along the Melanie Klein tradition.

Mannie: Yes, but I did not know that he had a new book out.

Irv: He has a new book out that was just announced. In it he does a review of Horney and Sullivan and criticizes them for being too interpersonal without developing a concept of internalized psychic structure. At the same time he criticizes the ultra-Freudians and gets away from the instinct approach. So he does a job that really had to be done. He gets away from libido and instinct while at the same time developing a comprehensive intrapsychic orientation as well as an interpersonal one.

Al: You were speaking about the book by Dorothy Stock Whitaker and Lieberman and their homogenization of the group. Mannie and I were looking at the program of the American Psychiatric Association for their meeting in Los Angeles May fourth to eighth. Thomas Szasz is presenting a paper on the fifth called, "The Moral Dilemma of Psychiatry—Autonomy or Heteronomy." So this is one of the big struggles in group therapy, the struggle between retaining individuality or homogenizing the group.

Irv: Whitaker says in her book as her main criticism of you two that there are two main groups of group therapists. The first, with which she identifies you, retains the treatment model of the two-person dyadic system and applies this to group phenomena. The other group conceives of the group structure as requiring a different kind of conceptualization and a different psychotherapeutic model. She identifies herself with this latter orientation. She criticizes you for taking the psychoanalytic model into a group situation and treating the individual patient while neglecting the group forces. In her model she does not even use concepts like transference or resistance. She says there is no need to use them because they are subsumed under the general structure of focal group conflict.

Gerry: That is not new though. That is just the question of group dynamic versus individual dynamic.

Irv: Yes. I think that this is an important area to discuss.

Mannie: Right.

Al: We do not object to people doing the group dynamic type of therapy. We draw the distinction that it is another kind of therapy. Apparently, they think that they have the group feeling. We point out the negative aspects of it, but there may be some positive aspects of it even though it is non-analytic.

Mannie: Yes. Nowhere do we suggest that even though doing this kind of therapy is nonanalytic or antianalytic, that all other things being equal, group living is destructive of human beings.

Irv: Mannie, they quote you people as saying—

Mannie: Saying that group process is destructive of the individual.

Irv: Yes. Now where do they get that quote? It is unbelievable. I don't know where that comes from.

Al: They make that up because we say that the individual submitting to the consensual position is diegophrenic. We made a number of negative statements about submitting to group will.

Mannie: We emphasize the necessity for the individual to be encouraged in his autonomy. Nowhere do we say that group living is not in itself a positive thing. We are encouraging of the group as being extremely important for the adaptation, the development and the survival of the individual.

Al: We do not usually say "the group." We say "other people."

Mannie: But we also say "the family" and "other groups." It is not that we do not say "the group." We know that joining a group may in itself alter the development of a human being and be significant in his development. But we say this is not analytic therapy as we conceive it. By the way, I just want to add another fact to this discussion, since you quote Dorothy Stock Whitaker and her hostility to us. I do not know whether you know that all through the book she refers to Alexander Wolf as "Alvin" Wolf.

Irv: Yes, I saw that. There were a lot of mistakes. For example, Norman Locke was called something else.

Mannie: That's right.

Al: I am homogenized with Alvin Wolf and Locke is homogenized with somebody else.

Mannie: A Wolf is a Wolf regardless.

Irv: I was wondering who Alvin Wolf was. I thought of Alvin Zander, you know.

Mannie: Yes. It might be, because she does quote Cartwright and Zander.

Al: There is an Alvin Wolf at the center.

Mannie: Yes, there is, but she wouldn't know that. He is one of the students there.

Al: Individuals must have no identity in her group therapy.

Gerry: Were her references—I did not see it—were they bibliographical references?

Irv: In the book, in a couple of places, it was Alvin, and Norman Locke was called something else. But I thought that she raised a lot of interesting issues that we ought to talk about.

Mannie: What I am most happy about, and I would like to reflect my feeling on that, is that you two have picked up the enthusiasm that I have had all along. The whole idea of providing clinical material, that is, the life material, the dialogues, the interaction, is for me most exciting. I know Al felt that way and others have criticized us. One of the most exciting chapters we have in our book is on dreams.[51] It is the most human, the most living, the most touching aspect of the book. This is the nature of group interaction. It has a living quality.

Irv: I would like to get back to this idea about using individual psychology or the individual psychotherapeutic model when you treat people in a group. I would like to evaluate this.

Gerry: We have talked about it a million different times here. We keep going back and back and back to it. What it amounts to is you are either going to treat people as human beings or you are going to create a Frankenstein that is the group and try to deal with the group. Apparently, some treat "the group" because they have to deny that they are doing what they would be doing if they saw a person on an individual basis. It is a denial of their desire and a defense against intimacy.

Irv: What you are saying, really, is that the psychology of the human being does not change whether he is in a group or whether he is by himself.

Mannie: Oh, no!

Irv: No?

Mannie: I would like to talk about that.

Gerry: That is not what I was saying. I am saying that they create a fictitious "group" to treat, with a system to treat the "group" and thereby avoid treating the individual patient.

Mannie: The model of individual treatment is that you treat the individual in isolation. You do not even treat him as a related human being. The classical analytic model is to isolate him so that he becomes more and more introspective, more and more aware of himself. Ultimately this is the model even of the Rogerian client-centered method. If you isolate him sufficiently, if you force him by virtue of your presence and your technique to become more and more aware of himself, then he will be compelled in some way to change himself. The objective is to make him conscious of himself by his own turning in upon himself. It is a study in isolation. It is an experience in frustration of relatedness. It is an experience in moving him into a desocialized, dehumanized position. This is the model of dyadic therapy. The concept of doing therapy in a group setting is the opposite of this model. The human being exists, he lives, he functions, he develops, he adapts, he exposes himself, he experiences himself only in regard to other human beings. Even if he is alone, he is in with the unseen group. The human being develops as a member of a group. He develops in relation to other human beings and not in isolation. There is no such thing as a human being in isolation. Since this is a fact of life we might as well use this setting in our attempt to influence him. This is the essential difference in the models as I see it. What do you think about that, Al?

Al: It makes a lot of sense.

Mannie: The human being modifies his behavior, changes, adapts to the experiences he has in reality. The individual alone is thinking, feeling, and behaving differently than when another person is present, differently when two other people are present, differently when three others are present, and probably still differently when four other people are present. We think that when a whole crowd is present he thinks and feels and acts differently. This is what the difference is. Not that he is always the same and his psychology is always the same, regardless. Psychology has to do with what he feels and does and acts and thinks.

Irv: When I said the psychology was the same, what I meant was that the person's internal structure does not change if he is by himself or in a group. All of a sudden he does not become a different kind of being. I agree with you that a person may relate differently with one person than he may relate with two or three or four or five or six. But, as I see it, we have to consider, and I think this is the reason why I brought up Guntrip's work, that Guntrip, utilizing Melanie Klein's ideas, talks about interaction and at the same time talks about the unconscious internalized images which influence a person and which create inner conflict. He is saying that the culturists, Horney and Sullivan and that group, believe that people get anxious because of what happens in their interpersonal interaction. Guntrip maintains that the reason why their interpersonal interaction creates anxiety is that it triggers off some instability or some conflict within the internalized image at the same time.

Mannie: I heard Gerry trying to say something.

Gerry: I don't know what it was.

Mannie: Do you want me to react?

Gerry: Go ahead.

Mannie: We have to be careful about this, Irv. We can say empirically that there is evidence that a human being develops a way of adapting, ways of relating, ways of thinking and feeling as a consequence of his human experience from birth on. He does this by incorporating, adapting, reacting on a very basic level. He imitates, he learns, he picks up and he follows the demands of the social institution called the family. He responds, with the dance of life, to the mother and the father and the other members of the family. These learned experiences are based upon whatever biological trends and capacities and tendencies he has when he comes into the family at birth. Beyond that he develops all kinds of things. He watches the way his father smiles and what his father smiles at. He watches what his mother feeds him and so on, and learns these rituals, these ideas, these adaptational and maladaptational patterns of behavior, which take on, then, a kind of functional autonomy because they are not in his awareness. They are imitative, they are learned, they are deeply repressed. They often, as a matter of fact, are just sheer living and experiencing. But whatever these things are that you are calling "structures," you have to be careful because these structures are hypothetical. They are our effort to try to describe them. But we can only know them phenomenologically, descriptively, and clinically in terms of the ways in which they tend to manifest themselves. In a sense, every human being is a series of syndromes, a composite of adaptational areas which are a consequence of the varieties of human experience he has had in the course of his life up to this point. This is what we see and we know. We do not know this structure, whether this structure is a Melanie Klein structure or a Freudian structure or a Sullivanian or anybody else's structure.

Gerry: Yes, the structure is on a metapsychological level of abstraction and not an empirical reality.

Mannie: Exactly. Any more than we have a structure for a mind. This is again a metapsychological concept, a group mind, a group theme, a group assumption.

Gerry: Yes, but a group mind, a group dynamic as a metapsychological construct is a different kind of conceptualization of what a person is or the nature of the human being. I mean, it is saying that somehow the boundaries between Irv and me, as we sit here, and between you two and us sort of disappear and we become no longer four individual people, but a group.

Irv: I think that what they are doing—

Gerry: And that that group has some kind of a function.

Irv: For example—

Mannie: Sure it has a function!

Gerry: Yes, but there is no group; there are four people here.

Irv: Yes, but—

Gerry: The group is the way of describing the four people.

Irv: What Dorothy Stock Whitaker is saying is you get a whole group of people and they all may be experiencing the same primary need or wish at the same time in the group setting.

Mannie: The need to relate to one another and to have a common set of objectives, goals. They may enter into a social contract consciously or unconsciously or both simultaneously.

Irv: All right, so that a group sets into motion, or that the very presence of one another sets into motion certain needs and wishes that may be common to all at one particular phase or one particular time.

Mannie: The needs or wishes may not be common to all. But they are saying they are willing to cooperate with one another in the pursuit of an objective because it is in my and your benefit to do this.

Gerry: Yes, but the individual benefits are highly tinged with the individual history of automatically learned and consciously learned material that you talked about.

Mannie: Right.

Gerry: You cannot talk about intervention and working with this sort of common interest or goal of the group because it is only common on the outside. It is only common in a very . . . I don't know how to put it. . . .

Mannie: We can jump even further on this, Irv, and get you even further riled up. We might even suggest that the individual's pathology is socially derived, if you want to put it that way, and that it does not occur in the individual in isolation, but occurs on the basis of his human experiences in a social situation, in an interactive situation.

Gerry: That is my position anyway, Mannie. I think that's well stated. I like to hear that.

Irv: Why would that be getting me riled up?

Gerry: I think Mannie is teasing you a little bit because of our knowledge of the—

Al: Isn't his mindfulness of his consciousness or his reality perception also sociogenic? Wouldn't the patient be an idiot or wolf-child or a humanoid if he wasn't brought up in the family?

Mannie: Of course.

Gerry: It is part of the monkey studies where their vision is influenced by what they see. In their first weeks of life their development of retinal functions, the function of the lens and the transmission of light in the eye are influenced by what they are looking at.

Irv: I was just reading an article on Martin Deutsch, in *Life* magazine, where he points out that intelligence, intellectual development in certain skills, is related to experiences; and if you have deprivations, the skills are not there. He is now having therapeutic classes to try to help develop skills that were lost as a consequence of deprived experiences.

Gerry: It is the same sort of thing that Karl Pribram did with the studies on rats. Some rats were given cages to live in where they had toys to play with, spinning wheels and all those goodies, and some rats were placed in isolation. The ones that had the playroom developed an ability to learn mazes and developed a different brain weight. Actually, a different ratio of cortical materials and enzymes developed than the rats that didn't. So actually anatomical structures were being influenced by the activities.

Mannie: This is the position we have taken again and again, Al and I, that you cannot develop a human organism unless he is stimulated. The organism requires a phasic alternation of stimulation and rest. Without the stimulation, you are not going to get any development, just as the monkey studies demonstrated. Studies of the culture-bound nature of intelligence in the intelligence testing is a piece of this.

Gerry: Although it is only a comparative argument that we have now because nobody sacrificed children and looked at their brains, I would wonder if there is not a difference in the development of actual cerebral tissues and enzymes in those children in the Spitz-type studies that were deprived of stimulation from normal stimulated children.

Mannie: It would suggest that. I don't know whether they did any autopsies, but the marasmus Spitz describes that these three-year-old infants went into looked like an organic condition. It resulted not from lack of food but from lack of human contact, the lack of stimulation. It looked like an organic condition. This would relate to what Gerry is saying. Al, what do these infants with marasmus actually look like? I have never seen them.

Al: They look like starving children. They are completely skeletonized like Auschwitz prisoners.

Mannie: Like prisoners from the Japanese camps. They were starved, undernourished, seventy- and eighty-pound adults. When I was in the army, we got a group of them in at the hospital, even talking to them was like looking into my cat's eyes. I felt that there was nothing behind their eyes. They were unrelated. There was no human quality.

Gerry: Yes. Of course, you are talking about people who have grown up, have developed intellectual functions and then have been seriously deprived. In a sense I suppose it's like not using a leg muscle, it atrophies. Apparently, if a child is not stimulated—no, take animals. If they are not stimulated and we sacrifice them, ninety days later they are different in psychophysiological functions in the brain and in actual brain weight and comparative weight.

Mannie: We have gone a long distance from the original question, haven't we?

Gerry: No, not so far at all, because we get back then to the question, Does the group dynamic approach have any meaning?

Irv: I would like to discuss this issue a little further. Whitaker and Lieberman[47] raised the question of the transference and the primary and the secondary transferences and how you classify them. If you use a group model and if you use transference theory, then who is the most important transferential figure? They try to put it on that basis.

Mannie: The therapist is primary; the others become secondary.

Irv: Yes. They say that the therapist is always the primary transferential figure in the group and in my experience I think it varies.

Mannie: In our paper on countertransference,[37] Al and I describe what we think can be seen as a model, that there is a qualitative difference in the relationship to the therapist and the relationship to others even though you may get a father transference or a mother transference onto the therapist, and the same transference reaction to a number of other members in the group. We think there is a qualitative difference when it is projected onto the therapist than when it is projected onto a peer in a lateral direction.

Irv: In what way?

Mannie: Let's say the intensity of the investment, the amount of reality or nonreality that enters into it.

Irv: I disagree with you. I have a patient that was going to leave group treatment. She already had left and when I analyzed the resistance to the group with her in a couple of individual sessions, it became apparent that as she began to develop strong sexual feelings toward me as father, she became fantastically fearful of one of the females in the group. She became so fearful that she was constantly concerned in the group about the other patient liking her, was she looking at her sternly, et cetera. She then began to realize that she had a tremendous mother transference on this patient, intense, intense as could be.

Mannie: Enough to scare her right out of the group.

Irv: Enough to scare her out of the group and it came in the context of the triangular projection with me involved as well.

Mannie: I think you misheard my communication. This would only confirm my assumption. Let me describe it to you; and this can only be answered hypothetically. Suppose she had had a father on one of the other members of the group, would she not have a triangular situation with this woman equally as well? But isn't it conceivable that she might not have been forced to leave the group because she might have been able to see the reality or not feel as intensely about the father in the patient, that is, the co-patient, as she felt about the father in you? In other words, I am suggesting that there is a difference when she incorporates you into the fantasy than when she incorporates a co-patient. This is what I am talking about. What do you think about that? I am suggesting that the same triangle which drove this patient out of the group might not have driven her out if the third member of the triangle were not the therapist, but another male in the group. We need your thought on this, Al.

Al: You need my thought. What if it was a person other than Irv?

Mannie: Because I think that there is a difference. The reality of the relationship with the therapist is always present, even in the projective system of the psychotic patient. He knows or she knows the difference between who is the therapist and who is a co-patient. One cannot entirely deny the nature of reality and the relationship to the reality that every human being is involved with, no matter how deeply projective they may be at the moment. The relationship with the therapist is qualitatively different from the relationship with the patient at any and all times.

Irv: Let me toss something else in on this.

Mannie: Wait a minute. I would like to get Al's reaction. We don't give him a chance to talk. He knows more about this than the three of us put together. Or would you like to argue that one?

Al: I think it is easier for the patient to handle a "father" who is a co-patient than for the patient to handle a "father" in the therapist.

Mannie: Why?

Al: And a mother in the group.

Mannie: Why? You asked me why. Why?

Al: I think that the therapist is much more loaded with authority than that patient's projection on the co-patient. The projection is always diminished by the reality that he is a peer.

Mannie: So you are confirming the argument I am making.

Al: Yes.

Irv: As it turns out in this particular situation, this woman for two months wanted to leave the group. I could not budge her. Finally the day before she was to leave, I said, "This is your last session in the group and I want to see you for one last individual session." When she came in, I asked, "What do you think it is that is driving you out of the group?" She said, "I can't think of anything unless it is you." She could not think any further. She then related a couple of dreams which facilitated the resolution of this resistance and I got her back into the group. Here is a good example of an oedipal working-through, or the beginning working-through of an oedipal struggle. Some people say that oedipal material cannot be worked through in a group. Here is a good example of the emergence of it and the real intensity of it.

Al: Here is an illustration to illustrate what I said. A member of my workshop, a male, has invited a female of the workshop to be a co-therapist with him in a private group. He wanted to bring her in without announcing it to the group. I said, "Why don't you first explore the group members' reactions to her coming and ask them how they feel about it, so they have some choice in the matter? Otherwise, they have no choice or at least they can't ventilate their feelings about it."

Mannie: Of course, you know they don't have any choice in reality.

Al: They don't have any choice with this therapist.

Mannie: So let's stop kidding ourselves. At least let them ventilate their feelings in advance.

Al: Two women objected to this other woman coming in. The therapist never consulted the group about bringing in a co-patient. He may or may not announce that a new member will be coming next week, but here I suggested that it be explored about another therapist coming in. Now these two women both projected the woman who was coming in as the mother. They objected to her, they were afraid of her, they threatened to leave because she was in the hierarchical vector. They would not do this with a peer.

Mannie: In other words, another female patient might be acceptable to them.

Gerry: But that is not always true. I know I have had many examples of patients having as intense a feeling as that, as intense a threat of leaving, just about another patient.

Irv: Let me emphasize that this last example of transference repetition happened in the group. This relates to the neutrality and the anonymity issues. The fact that people in a group, despite all the reality going on, develop intense transferences despite all the activity, sheds light on individual analytic theory. The maintenance of neutrality in order not to mar the transference material is a lot of nonsense.

Mannie: Exactly. They are going to develop intense transference regardless.

Irv: No matter what. The patient who bolted from the group because she was afraid of Sally, afraid that Sally would kill her, came back to the group. Sally was scared to death and angry. It turned out that Sally had a mother on the very patient that had a mother on her.

Mannie: Fascinating.

Irv: So they both had a mother on each other.

Mannie: Marvelous.

Irv: They both were relating like children. Sally projected to Flora as her mother and Sally was the child and at the same time, while Sally was feeling like a child to mother Flora, Flora was terrified of Sally and feeling Sally was her overpowering mother.

Mannie: That may be what happens in a family with a schizophrenogenic mother and daughter.

Irv: How do you mean?

Mannie: The borderline child is often used as a mother by her own mother.

Irv: Oh, yes, yes.

Mannie: And the child is using the mother as a mother and is also resisting the role of the child.

Irv: Like many of these borderline patients, many relate a history of having to have been a mother to their mothers.

Mannie: Yes, or the demand of the mother that the child be a mother to the mother.

Irv: Yes.

Mannie: It forces the relationship to the father into a new direction which intensifies the fear of the self and of the other on the part of the child.

Al: This is very common in psychoanalysis in groups among women. With me and with other male therapists where there is a positive transference to the therapist as a father, there is very often a mother figure or an older sister figure who is terrifying patients. In fact I had such a patient once who was so terrified, in such a panic, that I had to take her out of the group for a while.

Mannie: Did she develop this, then, with your wife or the projected

wife? They sometimes do. They do that in individual treatment as well.

Al: They do that in individual analysis. For example, I have a
patient in individual treatment who gets disturbed any
time she comes into the waiting room and sees a patient
walk out of my consulting room, particularly a female.
She goes wild. She now comes about five or ten minutes late
so she will avoid any patient coming out of my office. Also,
she makes me wait for her rather than her waiting for me.

Irv: Let's talk about this transference notion, okay?

Mannie: What transference notion?

Irv: We told you about what our former analyst brought up
and the articles he recommended when we met him at a
meeting of the local orthodox analytic society, when Leo
Rangell spoke.

Mannie: Go ahead.

Gerry: Our former analyst, at the meeting a couple of weeks ago,
brought up the distinction between the common conception
of transference in terms of the analysand re-experiencing
feelings, revivals and intrusions of early feeling towards
the parent now towards the analyst, and the more generic
concept of transference as an endopsychic process. He referred to a couple of articles, one a book called "Concept
and Theories of Psychoanalysis," by Heinz Kohut and
Phillip Seitz.

Irv: No, that is not the book. That is the article in the book.

Gerry: This is an article from a book; that is what I said.

Irv: *Concepts of Personality.*

Gerry: Right. Only I did not get to that yet. It is in a book by
Wepman and Heine, *Concepts of Personality*, published last
year in Chicago. A very brief and clear summarization of
most of the theory I would say.

Irv: Of classical psychoanalysis.

Gerry: Right, and—

Irv: Before you get to that, because it was written later, Gerry,
let me talk. In *The Journal of the American Psychoanalytic
Association*, Volume III, 1959, there is an article by Heinz
Kohut on "Introspection, Empathy and Psychoanalysis," in
which he reviews the field. He gets to a discussion on trans-

ference which I thought that I would bring out here because it is very short, and then maybe we could discuss it. He says many people maintain psychoanalysis is not interpersonal enough or that it uses a one-body frame of reference instead of the social matrix. He says that a view like that fails to take into account that the essential constituent of psychoanalytic observation is introspection. Therefore, if you are going to talk about psychoanalytic meaning, the term "interpersonal" as connoting an interpersonal experience has to be one that is open to self-observation. Any interpersonal experience which is not open to self-observation or introspection is one which you cannot handle psychoanalytically. Psychoanalytic use of the concept interpersonal differs from the interaction/transaction concept used by the social psychologists. The analyst uses empathy and his own introspection to understand the introspective processes of the analysand. He makes a definition of transference. "The phenomenon of transference [is] the particular influence which the unconscious exerts upon the introspectively more accessible part of the psyche." He says, "The analyst, to the extent that he is a transference figure, is not experienced in the framework of an interpersonal relationship, but as the carrier of unconscious endopsychic structures; that is, unconscious memories of the analysand." The analyst as transference figure is, as persistent introspection with analysis of resistance reveals, an expression of unconscious superego forces, the unconscious father image in the analysand.

Gerry: You are getting off, you are just reading it there, Irv. What is the point?

Irv: Here it is. He says, For the neurotic the analyst is a screen for the projection of internal structure which is called transference. Then he goes back to the original Freudian definition in his dream theory and says, "Transference is defined as the influence of the unconscious upon the preconscious across an existing although often weakened repression barrier."

Gerry: You are getting so damned redundant there, Irv. The point is that very often in treatment what is considered to be transference is more appropriately termed a characteristic form of object relationship. Transference as such comes up where unconscious material uses preconscious content, as in a dream the day residue is woven in to carry the latent content. The feelings and reactions to the analyst mix together the unconscious and preconscious material. Transference refers to that endopsychic process, not what we observe. What we commonly talk about as transference in the analytic session is just one example of the occurrence of the transference.

Irv: Yes, which is one example of the occurrence of a transference because other endopsychic processes—

Gerry: What it adds up to is that our former analyst brought this up in relationship to group therapy. He said we should understand this issue more clearly. The more neutral, the more abstinence on the part of the analyst, the more he is capable of becoming, in the patient's unconscious, similar to a day residue, a nonvalenced object, so that the unconscious will use him for transference. The unconscious content will use preconscious content that is nonrelated to other loaded preconscious content just as it uses the occasional happenings of everyday—

Irv: I don't think he said that. He didn't say—

Gerry: Kohut does.

Irv: Kohut does, but our analyst does not say that. Kohut is taking a classical position that the analyst has to be the blank screen and he is using this as a justification for the neutrality of the analyst. But all our analyst was trying to say is that there is a difference between characterological object relations and a true transference. While it is true that all transferences are repetitions, not all repetitions are transferences. To be classified as a transference there has to be a present influence of the remnant of the past that is still in actual existence. If someone has characterologic behavior that is patterned after a childhood model, then this would be called an object relationship or a type of object relationship. A true transference is something wherein there is an actual striving, a breaking across the repression barrier into the preconscious. It is a more active, fluid, structural kind of conflict; whereas an object relation is patterned after some model of experience in history, but is not a true transference.

Gerry: Yes. Do you comprehend this? Have you read either of these, Mannie or Al?

Al: I have not, no. Does this mean that Kohut and Seitz or your former analyst are attacking group therapy because group members cannot be neutral?

Gerry: No, I don't think so.

Irv: This is Gerry's bit.

Gerry: No, I think he was saying that much of what Irv and I classify as a transference reaction is really a more static characterologic object relationship. What appears and what might be called by many people a transference is not classically a transference. It is a character pattern. Transference applies more to an endopsychic process and that the more the analyst or the object of the relationship is known, the more of his personality that is known, the more he is a valenced object, the less available he becomes for transference, for true transference manifestations.

Irv: Gerry, I differ with you. That is what Kohut said. All our analyst wanted to point out to us is that—

Al: You find this to be true in your own group.

Irv: No, I disagree with this, but I think that this—

Al: Transferences to one another?

Irv: What's that?

Al: The fact that they are valenced?

Irv: No. I think this is a different point. I think Gerry is focusing on something else and I thought that it deserves a paper by us on this. This is something I have been thinking about for some time, but all our analyst was trying to point out, although Kohut is justifying classical theory by his position, is that what you call transference is essentially a projection of endopsychic structure and that you have to distinguish that type of phenomenon from characterologic object relationships which you frequently see, which are not really projections, but which are characterologic maneuvers by the patient. Very often they are called transferences or assumed to be transferences when there is really no active projection of endopsychic structures projected onto the therapist or onto the group. Rather, this is a characteristic way in which the person behaves. It may have originated originally in terms of old transference, but now it is autonomous and built into the character structure. What our analyst was saying is that very often in analysis it is only after you have worked through resistances and gone through various levels of character armor that you finally get transferences to occur in the relationship to the analyst.

Al: How do you deal with these characterological things that are built into the patient that are not transference? How do you deal with them?

Irv: That wasn't the question that was raised. The question was to distinguish between that and transference. He says that many people—and he felt we are doing this, and he included his own candidates—failed to make this distinction. How you handle it is another question. That is all he was saying. Is that right, Gerry?

Gerry: Yes. He also said that it has a direct bearing on what we are doing in groups.

Irv: Yes. He said that, but he didn't follow up on it.

Gerry: No, he didn't follow up. He just was making the distinction. But I think we have to make the distinction because it is related to the idea of activity versus neutrality or abstinence.

Irv: Yes, and this is—

Gerry: This is where it gets fuzzy to me because I can follow this and it seems fine, but then you get into the problem of does the transference—

Mannie: I have been sitting here and listening to this for fifteen minutes and wondering why you let yourselves get drawn into something which is essentially nothing new. A lot more words said about something which is very old. Why don't you cut through the words. This is not a new theme. You are rediscovering electricity. What we are hearing here it seems to me, with all the fancy words, is an attempt to understand the difference between classical analysis, which is id psychology, and ego psychological developments within more modern formulations of psychoanalysis. If you continue to work with the ego structure, you are dealing obviously with character armor. Reich wrote a great contribution.[31] What did he discover about ego? He talked about it in the form of character; he talked about the character armor. This was the beginning of ego psychology in psychoanalysis. If you are talking about ego, you are not talking about transference because we, by definition, talk about transference as an unconscious mechanism and an unconscious process, an unconscious operation dealing with unconscious material. You are not talking about ego material or ego function.

Irv: Yes, but ego material can be unconscious.

Mannie: Object relations have to do with ego function. This is what we are talking about here. You are saying you have to make distinction between what are ego functions and what are not ego functions, and I am completely in accord. The fact that some people make a mistake and call ego functions one thing or another is obvious. If you view transference as coming from unconscious forces, then the more ego you introduce, the more reality, the more activity, the more valence, the more ego becomes involved. Therefore, the less unconscious material becomes involved theoretically. This is a plea for regression and that only in regression does transference appear. And the deeper the regression the more transference. This is the argument. Where are you working? Are you working for regression and the depths of regression in order to get to these deep transferences? Or are you working in an ego-psychological way?

Irv: I am glad you brought in this regression point because this is what he was saying to us about a second analysis. He felt patients don't regress enough in a first analysis. He said you really need a second analysis to get down to basics.

Mannie: That is right. You have to regress them back into the womb. This is the big argument. I think that we are struggling here between libido theory, old classical forms, energics and ego psychology. This is the big struggle that Hartmann tries to reconcile. I don't see this as being new or different from anything you should have known or do know at this point. You become threatened the moment a reformulation of old ideas in new terms is presented to you. There is nothing really new in what you have presented here, in Kohut, or any other material so far as I can see. I think this is what has been happening to you. You obviously know, and I am sure you will agree, Al, that if you work with manifest content and the repetition of phenomenology, you are not dealing with transference. I do not think either you or I and I hope neither one of you two would see that as transference. We would look for what is transferential in what is being carried from unconscious or preconscious into that phenomenology. You would look for the latent. This is what we do all the time. We do not call phenomeno-logical behavior transference. So this is all that you have been presenting. If you deal with the phenomenology you deal with the reality, you deal with ego psychology, you deal with the manifest. You are dealing there with reality and not with what is being carried out of the historical past. You are dealing with phenomenology, the here and now, the characterological repetition of patterns of behavior. If you want to deal with the transference, you have to work not with the here and now, but the then and there, which is now playing a role in the here and now, which is influencing it in terms of its character, its emotion, its distortive ele-ments, and so on.

Gerry: At any rate, you are only going to see the phenomenology because you never really see the unconscious content that is underlying it. You only see the result of it.

Mannie: We never see the unconscious material.

Gerry: At the same time it raises this whole question of regression versus activity or the influence of activity in terms of regres-sion and getting at walled off unconscious content.

Mannie: Wait a minute!

Gerry: Wait until we finish it. Then I will wait. All right?

Mannie: All right.

Gerry: You have the material which has been walled off, which bubbles up. That's transference. Now, does that come up and can it get associated with preconscious ideas about the analyst, about other people, members of the group? Can it become attached and expressed in that way? Will it not become attached, or use those preconscious contents be-cause they are too valenced? That seems to be the question that is raised here.

Irv: Yes. That is the secondary question. I want to comment on what Mannie said. In talking about ego psychology you pose that the ego always operates on a conscious level. Ego operates unconsciously too.

Mannie: Then it is not ego process by definition.

Irv: Oh, no; not at all. Many of the ego operations that Anna Freud[15] is talking about are unconscious, if you look at the ego—

Gerry: Many of the defense mechanisms are considered to be—

Irv: Yes.

Mannie: Those are ego mechanisms. We are not conscious of them any more than we are normally conscious of the beating of our heart.

Gerry: Yes, but they are ego functions.

Irv: Yes, ego functions. That is ego psychology.

Mannie: That is ego psychology and these are ego functions.

Irv: And unconscious.

Mannie: It is not an unconscious process; it is a mechanism! You are talking about mechanisms. These are mental mechanisms, psychic mechanisms. You discover that the organism utilizes certain mechanisms in order to deal with its life. Of course, all of these operations are mechanical; there is no conscious activity then. Even my thinking at this moment in talking to you is not entirely conscious.

Gerry: That is right.

Mannie: I have not picked a single word out of anywhere. I have not preprepared this idea. I am reacting here quite without consciousness of what is going on in my head.

Gerry: Right. Consciousness only refers to that introspective eye looking at our current activity. More or less what I am doing right now is preconscious activity because only when I focus back on it as I am saying it, is it a conscious activity.

Mannie: But we seem to be confusing a whole series of fairly simple operations by this kind of involvement. This is the kind of thing that Irv presented first so complicatedly and you stopped him, Gerry. Then you repeated it in an equally complicated way, it seems to me, because you are struggling with trying to make a theory of energics operative in areas where it no longer represents operation. I think Al's response to you, "What do you do with it?" in terms of his immediate clinical and empirical necessity is the proper question to ask. I think when you get caught up in this kind of theorizing you really get lost. What is basically being discussed here today? It is not the clear question of interaction or noninteraction; not the question of transference or nontransference; but the whole issue of the libido theory, of energics, of a mechanical concept of the nature of psychology. This is what you are getting at. If you stop for a moment to ask yourselves whether you misuse the word transference, you will discover it is not really the central issue here. I can hardly imagine a clinician not recognizing the difference between phenomenology and latency. The moment you begin to talk in depth-psychological terms you are getting away from phenomenology. Introspection is to get to depth. For example, a dream provides you with transference indications. Is the dream unconscious? Why does the dream provide them? It is not analytic utilization of the dream if you deal with the phenomenology of the dream only. But if you undo the dream work you will get to the transference material. The dream is what may be the carrier of feelings and thoughts out of the past which are projected onto the present object. The dream itself does not tell you anything about the transference; you must analyze.

Gerry: The dream, then, tells you again what the clinical interaction tells you; namely, something about repetitive forms of object relations.

Mannie: It tells you—

Gerry: You have to analyze.

Mannie: —the mechanisms. The dream, in a sense, represents, like any other mechanism, a way in which the nature of perception is altered by the organism in order for the organism to maintain some constancy. If you want to know the mechanics, if you want to know what motivates, if you want to know the tensions, if you want to know the anxieties which make for this alteration of perception in this particular form and this particular dream of this particular patient, you must undo the dream work. You must then go into introspection. You must then analyze.

Irv: I am a little confused, Mannie.

Mannie: I am too. We all are. That's all right.

Irv: I am a little confused when you talk about ego operations and ego psychology dealing on a conscious level rather than the ego as unconscious defense mechanisms.

Mannie: Yes. That is the big conflict. Read Gill's book,[18] whether the ego is structure, process, or object. This is another big problem now, a tremendous confusion provoked in the American psychoanalytic movement, since Gill wrote that book. "Ego" like "transference" is used in a variety of ways. I would much rather see you deal with this problem in terms of phenomenology versus latency. It think it is much easier to understand in this way. Character structure and object relations deal with phenomenological processes. Transference deals with depth, with latent processes. If you approach the problem in this way, you make it easier because these words are distorted, loaded. They confuse us because they are being used in a variety of ways in order to make do with an incomplete theory. We have no complete theory, neither the old theory nor the new theory, nor the modifications of the theory. Transference has always to be inferred. It is always an implicit thing. It is always that which is hidden away and carried. It is not there consciously. It is not there phenomenologically. We must look for it. We explore for it. We associate to it. We introspect about it. We speculate about it. We build it up and build it out. We undo it. We undo the dream work. It is a reconstruction, or even a new construction.

Gerry: I would like to use an example that came up in the group the other night. See how that fits in here. I have a patient, you remember her, the one who has the baby and who nearly died. She has an interest in a man in the group, a new man. He took her home from a group session a couple times and in going home with him, she became attracted and so she put all her packages on the seat between her and him. She talked about it in the group, how she was building a barrier because she was afraid of her own feelings about him. We talked about this in one group session. The next session she came before the other members arrived, except the same man. She took a seat, one seat away from me;

that is, there was an empty chair intervening. She put one of the packages she was carrying on the chair. Then she went on to talk about some things. A few minutes later, she was dealing again with these feelings. She wanted to leave because she was afraid of her attraction to this man. Then I said something about, "Maybe this is related to why you put the package on the chair between us."

Mannie: You were handling the barrier.

Gerry: She was building the barrier.

Mannie: All right, now that is an object relationship, building the barrier is phenomenology.

Gerry: Right, but—

Mannie: Character structure.

Gerry: But wait a minute. The fact that she was behaving in an object relationship with the man to express feelings that were displaced from me, which in the first place, was transferential material.

Mannie: You only know that if you imply motivation and history and latency.

Gerry: Right.

Mannie: If my name is Wolpe, or Skinner, or even Sullivan, I do not look for this and I deal only with the characterology, the phenomenology. There is no transference.

Gerry: But isn't the transference here where the unconscious struggle with her feelings about her father, that he would rape her—

Mannie: Only if that is there, and you can only know this by getting to the introspective material, the history and the latency.

Gerry: Right.

Mannie: Transference is to be found in the latent; in what is not manifest, not phenomenological. What is phenomenological is her characteristic behavior, the object relations; namely, whenever she comes into contact with a man in this kind of proximity, she builds a barrier. That is phenomenology. That is object relations, character structure, character armor. The way in which she characteristically deals with anxiety. That is mechanics, mechanism. If you want to know why she has to have this kind of character armor for dealing with her anxiety, you will have to go to the conflicts involved in the anxiety. You will have to look at the inhibitions and the symptoms that condensed the armor that this is, by digging behind what is manifest. For that you need the introspection, for that you need the history, for that you need psychodynamics, for that you need analysis. Then you will get to what is transferential, what was carried in this behavior, in this character structure. You will get this. Al, you wanted to say something.

Al: I only wanted to say that I felt that Irv's and Gerry's former analyst was doing something a little antianalytic.

Mannie: I agree with you.

Al: I think that—

Mannie: He is projecting onto them that they were doing something antianalytic.

Al: I think he is being antianalytic.

Mannie: Absolutely.

Irv: How is that, Al?

Al: I feel that he is making a transference. He is diluting. He places an unnecessary emphasis on transference. Getting you to look at what is defensive on the part of the patient, this is character armor, this is important too. I think that in some respects he is rejecting transference.

Mannie: And he is rejecting you two as analysts. If you do it in the group, you are not analysts because what you think is transference is not. And you are accepting his criticism as if it were so.

Irv: I think we are going to struggle with this a little more.

Gerry: I know I am. I haven't got it in my head yet. I guess all I've got it in is my unconscious.

Mannie: I urge you to try not to get involved with words in this matter. Try to get involved with process. Try to see this in terms of your clinical work. Try to see how you would use it. What ways and means do you have of dealing with the clinical material as it presents itself to you? I think the moment you do that, as in the case you presented, Gerry, if you look at this matter only in the way she relates herself to a man, if you see it only in these terms, that she builds a barrier repetitively; this is not transference. It is repetitious behavior of a defensive order. This is part of her character. These are long-range attitudes and long-range behavior.

Al: But based on transference.

Mannie: Behind this, if you believe that there is something behind this. If you believe that this is based upon something, if this is your psychological commitment, then it is based upon what we would call transferential motivation, based upon history, based upon psychodynamics. If you do not believe it is based upon anything, it is only what you see. If your psychology is this, then it is not based upon anything. This is a conditioning viewpoint.

Gerry: Yes.

Al: Your former analyst is rejecting the unconscious.

Mannie: For them. He is saying, "The unconscious belongs to me, but it does not belong to you. Remember that. Your unconscious belongs to Daddy."

20

More Transference Theory: Excerpts from the Later Years

Transference is at the heart of psychoanalytic theory and practice. What it is and how it is manifested are always difficult to describe away from clinical material. One misconception is the purity of transference. Does activity attenuate transference? The bilateral aspects of transference are especially to be seen in the group. The influence of the analyst's personality and style must also be taken into account. Bilateral aspects of reality and projection in behavior becomes the bases for investigating the interactional nature of group psychotherapy.

Irv: When I came back from vacation, the local psychiatric clinic called and asked me to come in and start a lecture series on group therapy. I gave my first one last Monday and it was very well received. I took your suggestion and I talked about the comparisons of individual and group treatment. But my basic thesis was, Why do group psychotherapy? Is there any basis for treating people in a group more than just expediency? I went on to give a variety of reasons. As I was preparing to talk, a criticism, something

I did not quite understand, occurred to me. It also came up in one of the questions from the clinic staff. I raised it with Gerry and I would like to raise it with both of you. I know we have talked about it before. Al has brought it up in his paper. It gets down to transference. The idea is that any one analyst by nature of his personality and character probably does not evoke the wide range of transferential responses which are possible in the group setting because of the multiobject reality in the group. Now the question is, since transference is an unconscious phenomenon, why would the analyst's character or the multiobjects provoke a wider range of transferential responses? Would not any one analyst over a period of time, since transference is unconscious and repetitious, be projected with the total repertoire of illusions that the individual has within himself by virtue of his history? I am wondering about the bilateral nature of transference. How much of transference is related to the real characteristics of the personality and how much of it is unconscious?

Al: Apparently some analysts evoke all the transferences that the patient needs to work through in an individual analysis. Perhaps this is a reflection of their skill. On the other hand, I have seen patients who have had a single transference to an analyst for the duration of the analysis and they never changed. It is never worked through. I think it is much easier to see multiple transference manifestations in the group.

Irv: The question is why is that so, if transference is an unconscious phenomenon and the one person is merely a screen that the other unconsciously projects onto. Gerry and I talked it over at one point. The thing the group teaches one about transference is that the activity does not attenuate the transference; it does not prevent its emergence, which tells us something about the individual model. If by mere activity transference were attenuated, then you could resolve transference in a week or two and you could cure the person. Even in the activity of people moving and coming and going, as in a group, transference emerges. So that is the other aspect of the problem. Gerry, I was wondering how you see it, about the provocative aspect of reality. If a thing is purely unconscious, does it need a particular character or personality to evoke or bring it out, or what?

Mannie: You ought to be very responsive to Irv.

Irv: What?

Mannie: I was talking to Al. I think Al ought to be very responsive. You are talking about pure unconsciousness. Irv has the belief that a state of pure unconsciousness, a state of absolute lifelessness that is not reality, exists. I do not think it exists. I think this is another one of those self-deceptions.

Mannie: I don't know if that is what Irv is saying.

Al: That is exactly what he is saying. He is saying that transference is pure, exists in a pure state. What we ascribe the title "transference" to exists in a pure state, without reference to any other aspect of any other human being.

Irv: I want to comment on that. I am glad you said that, Mannie. In terms of my own thinking, I have come to this conclusion: When you think of transference existing in pure state and when you think of repetition compulsion in a purely mechanistic way, what happens when you see transference emerging is not that the person just transfers to the other person as if he were a father in a repetitive way irrespective of the situation, but rather that the current situation activates needs and impulses of an earlier infantile nature.

Mannie: If transference is not made conscious, we will never see it. Just as we never see the unconscious in a dream; otherwise we are talking nonsense. We only see unconscious processes as they are manifested through secondary elaboration. We see it by inference only. It is like talking about soul, mind, or ghost. You can never have pure unconsciousness. You can never have the expression or the activity or the projection without the ego being there to enact it. The instrumentality of the human personality is the ego. What kind of ghosts are we dealing with here?

Gerry: Some sort of dualism, Mannie?

Mannie: Dualism? Triple-ism? I don't know, I still want to get Al's reaction. I was addressing myself to Al. Somewhere you have a quotation in the book and maybe it does not represent your point of view, but I would like to hear you, Al, comment on it, that the human being relates to another human being in one way. When a third person is present, he changes; it automatically modifies the situation. You state this in the book with me, our book.[51] Now, you either believe it or you don't. If you believe that the presence of a third party in some way modifies a relationship or has the potential to do so, then obviously it must be conscious awareness of the fact that the third party is there and it must have some effect on how we interact in the presence of the third party. And if it does, then by the nature of our interaction, conscious and unconscious processes, transference and nontransference, must be modified by the reality in which we exist. Either we believe or we do not believe it.

Al: I would say that we are not in pure transference, any of us. Our transference reactions are then contaminated by the reality around us.

Mannie: I would have preferred you said the statement the other way around; that our reactions to reality are contaminated by the transference distortion. You put it that our transferences are contaminated by the reality. This is an interesting formulation. This is where we were a little while ago before the telephone call.

Irv: Are you guys talking about this?

Mannie: Yes, but not specifically about this. We were talking about the concept of lifelessness, of the purity of reaction. Like someone said yesterday at a conference, "You have no right ever to do anything with a patient except let him find himself. You have no right to superimpose anything upon him. He must find himself, be himself." I don't know what that means.

Gerry: That is like saying instead of "No man is an island," "Every man is an island."

Mannie: Yes.

Gerry: I think that Mannie's point is that pure transference not only is unconscious and only inferable from the preconscious and conscious contents, but to say that you have a pure transference is nonsense because it splits the reality of the person.

Mannie: Transference does not exist; human beings exist.

Gerry: I understand.

Mannie: Transference is a shorthand word for a process or a set of processes. Transference is not in existence. Human beings exist and we use the word transference to describe one aspect of their total response, a central quality that we are now paying attention to. You may say that the behavior is transferential and at the same time in the behavior there are pieces of the id that are not transferential. There are aspects of behavior that are physiological. You stop the physiological and transference cannot exist. If you stop the ego, transference cannot exist. Because as long as a human being is alive, you have physiological reactions; you have transferential reactions; you have nontransferential reactions, et cetera. You will have defenses and nondefenses, et cetera. Now, when we focus on one kind or quality of behavior, projection of familiar images, we use a word to describe it, namely, "transference." But that does not mean that there is not a whole spectrum of behavior going on at the same moment. We are enucleating out of an organismic, out of a whole, some single quality. Even under hypnosis, even asleep, the ego does not give up entirely. The heart and the brain do not stop functioning. There may be diminished functioning but the rest of the organism does not drop dead. The ghost, the soul, suddenly separates itself from the body; the unconscious suddenly comes forward and the conscious and all the rest remain behind! What kind of talk is this?

Al: I feel as if I am talking with my ESP friends.

Irv: All right. Let's get back to this in another way. Your point is well taken. Could we say that what happens in an analytic situation or in a group situation is that the presence of the other person, the analyst or the other people in the group, may activate infantile needs which may stir up earlier unconscious, unexpressed fantasies by virtue of the person's history and which he will then unknowingly try compulsively to repeat and gratify in the current situation?

Mannie: What we are saying simply is that the more and various kinds of stimulation you give him, the chances are he will be asked to draw out a whole repertory of responses. In every response the total human being is responding, including those distortions, those projections which we call transferential. Therefore, the more varied the stimulation, the greater likelihood that you will get more varied forms of responses. That is all I am saying. I don't know what anybody else is saying. The analyst has a limited set of roles he can play. He has got to be himself more or less, whether he is quietly himself or loudly himself. Sometimes he is very loud when he is silent; sometimes he is very silent when he is loud. Whoever he is, there is a limited number of roles he can play, a limited kind of provocation he can allow, that he is capable of. The silent analyst, for example, offers a minimum amount of direct stimulation.

Irv: This is based upon the idea that the unconscious comes through and the person repeats earlier needs.

Mannie: It is what Picasso said. Picasso said that you will always have to behave in terms of consciousness because the unconscious is always there in any action, in any reaction. At this moment what I am talking about is . . . this is not pure consciousness even though I am now functioning with executive control, with reason, with feeling. At this moment there are also depths of unconscious feeling, transferential, nontransferential, appropriate, inappropriate, whatever else you want. It depends on where you want to focus at this moment. Do you want to focus on the content, on the process, on the kind of defenses, on the displacement, on the projection? It depends on what aspect of my responding, my function, my behavior you want to focus upon, the thinking, the feeling, the doing; the internal process, the consequences, et cetera. I think this is what Al said a little while ago and I put it in different terms. He said if you have only one other person in relation to you, that the scope of varieties of stimulations, roles, provocations, experiences, is obviously more limited. We ask for free association to be able to tap other aspects of the resources. One other way of getting other aspects of conscious and unconscious behavior might be to stimulate him more. Bellak gives the patient TAT cards in individual treatment. Instead of giving him TAT cards, let's give him people. These are ways of getting him to expose more. Why do analyses stop with passive people who are schizoid and isolated? Because they do not have enough stimulation and activity in order to provide material to work with. The presence of other members in the group provides you with the possibility of the exposure of material of a large variety. If you wait long enough and if you are perceptive enough, if you want to look for every manifestation of every kind of transference projection, probably all of it ultimately will come out in a one-to-one relationship. But you have to live so long. Is this the most efficient and effective way of treating? In analysis we cannot analyze everything. We cannot go on forever. Al's position has always been that what the group does is to facilitate a more rapid appearance of material. It might take longer in the one-to-one. Al, do you have some reaction?

Irv: I am especially interested in what Al has to say, since he has recently been concentrating on transference. You said you gave this paper, Al?

Al: I think the group provokes more reactions with most people. There are some patients who become much more reserved, much more cautious in the group and much less self revealing.

Mannie: Then he is revealing by the fact that he is not self revealing. He reveals another aspect of himself because people are there, i.e., his need to defend himself, to block out, to withdraw. But he may not always give verbal material, you are saying. The question is, Is he behaving differently? And the chances are he is by virtue of the presence of the group. Because when you take him in the individual situation, he is much more verbal. Therefore, the presence of the group is affecting his behavior.

Al: There are some patients that are provoked into verbal acting out in the group and they can only really do introspection in individual sessions. They simply act out in the group. I am talking about exceptions.

Mannie: But that is not really the question Irv is asking. Irv is asking, Is there such a thing as pure transference and if there is such a thing, what happens to it when others are present and why can't it all be handled in the individual situation?

Why have these other people there if it does not really help to have them in the group?

Al: I say there is no such thing as pure transference for the sickest person in the world. There is some contact with reality as long as he is living and breathing. I think that the group provokes both bad sorts of reactions and it provokes very healthy reactions. I find that the provocation of healthy reactions is the wonderful thing about group. It makes me wonder about my own role as an individual analyst. I do not get all these healthy reactions that I can see in the group.

Gerry: Can I introduce a point here? How would we even conceptualize this? Just think of the concept of transference itself. It implies that an unconscious content has been barred entry, because it is traumatic, it is walled off. It is not being experienced and remembered consciously. But this unconscious content is painted onto some preconscious material or content or conscious material as an avenue of expression. The conscious and preconscious contents are the reality coordinates of the repressed unconscious material. So just in saying that there is transference, you cannot say it is pure because the process implies a compound of unconsciousness and consciousness.

Mannie: Transferences do not exist.

Gerry: That is what I am saying. Transference is a logical construct.

Mannie: It is an explanatory principle of behavior.

Gerry: But wait a minute. It is an explanatory principle of a behavior which involves both unconscious and conscious components.

Mannie: It is behavior which we cannot understand in terms of the realities alone. We say something was added. We would then use the word "transference" to describe this.

Gerry: It is not only that you cannot understand it entirely in terms of the reality co-ordinates, but you cannot understand it without them. It does not exist without them.

Mannie: It does exist without them.

Gerry: But how? It does not exist without them.

Mannie: It is an assumption we make. Therefore, we go searching for them. It is another psychoanalytic assumption. This is depth psychology, but the conditioning people would not even look for it in other humans. They would say that it is because of distorted perception. It has no unconscious co-ordinates.

Irv: Let me look at it this way, Mannie and Al. It seems to me that every individual by virtue of the fact that he has a neurosis, has ways of relating in current reality to individuals. These relationships are distorted by virtue of his earlier experiences. Therefore, in a current reality situation he may relate to a person as if the person were a stern father or a seductive mother and because of the fact that he has that unconscious fantasy, he will then relate in a defensive, distorted way.

Mannie: Irv, I asked a question. I want you to answer me before you go on.

Irv: What?

Mannie: Is transference always ambivalent? I asked Al. And Al said, Yes. If this is true, knowing this, "the stern father" is for the birds. You see, the whole concept of how a human being develops is wrong. The child who lies about relating to father may act one way at home and another way with father-figures at school. It is not clean and neat: You have a stern father. He adapts to different kinds of experiences in different ways. Transference by definition implies all manner of feeling toward either parent; the entire continuum.

Irv: This is what I was trying to say in a different way. What I was trying to say is that we never really see or very rarely really see a person seeing the analyst in the exact same way as he saw his father. Rather what happens is that the person has needs which are activated in the analytic situation. When these needs are activated, he may respond in his customary defensive way. He may see the analyst responding to him in a way in which his father might have responded.

Gerry: But the point is, he did not see his father one way. He did not feel about his father one way. He does not see the analyst one way or feel about the analyst one way. At any moment he does not have a pure unadulterated—that is an interesting word—kind of feeling or perception or experience of the other person. It is going to be a mixture of the things that he is.

Mannie: We simplify the situation by focusing upon one emotional quality being expressed in the transference. Then in order to deal with the problems of therapy, Phyllis Greenacre says the primary transference to the analyst is always mother. All others are secondary. She tries to simplify it. This makes for simplification in terms of functioning. Obviously, the patient does have reactions to the therapist as an ideal kind of mother, a healthy person, the person he comes to and says, "Help, help! Nurture me! Feed me!" But the other feelings toward the mother are also latently present. By the way, don't you have patients who have distortions of you in other than motherly ways? There is the father, brother, uncle, grandfather, sister, aunt, et cetera.

Irv: The reason why you get repetitions is that the here-and-now situation in analysis, whether it be individual or group, activates needs or wishes or fears or prohibitions or demands which the person then reacts to. Because of these needs the person then will put the analyst in a particular position which is not realistic. For example, a patient of mine in analysis has the unconscious need to take over, to become the authority, to compete with me in an oedipal sense. He has the hidden fantasy, that is not conscious, that he wants to take my books or sit in my chair. He may then because of that need, which is involved in the power struggle, be afraid of me. He may see me as stern. He may unconsciously perceive me as out to get him and mutilate him and to get after him. This is not because he just simply sees me as a castrating father, but he needs to take over and he reenacts the drama in terms of the repertoire of his earlier perceptions.

Mannie: That is correct. But if that is all he felt about you, he would stop coming. If at the same time you have a woman in the room while he is perceiving you that way, he may feel a slight variation in his experience or in how he behaves. If you have three women in there at the same time and if you have three men, he might feel still differently. What kind of men might provoke differences?

Irv: What activates the transference is a need or demand—

Mannie: What activates the transference is that it is always available as long as he is alive in every piece of his behavior. Nothing activates it. This is part of his total way of life. It is always available. As Picasso says, "Don't worry about the unconscious; it is always there in everything you do." You keep talking about this as some kind of dormant ghost. A hidden animal. Suddenly we kick it in the shins and it pounces on you. An Aladdin's lamp. You rub it and suddenly it manifests itself.

Irv: What you are saying is that the oedipal struggle is always there, but it may not be the primary need activated at that particular time.

Mannie: Always there? It is what we deem oedipal because as analysts we relate it to past history. Let us stop confusing the behavior with ways of categorizing and describing it.

Irv: Gerry is shaking his head. I would like to hear from him what his conclusion is.

Gerry: It is hard to get a word in. It seems to me, Mannie, what you are saying is that the concept of transference which describes a certain set of behavior at a moment, both inner and outer behavior, is the same as unconscious or that we can say that transference is equivalent to unconscious. I would agree with Picasso and say that unconsciousness is always there and unconsciousness is going to express itself, but while transference is unconscious, the unconscious is not transference.

Mannie: Unconsciousness, unconscious processes.

Gerry: All right.

Mannie: Unconscious processes are always present as conscious processes are always present, but living human beings are totalities. If we believe in depth psychology, we believe that the streams of consciousness on all levels are flowing as long as the organism is alive.

Gerry: The thing we call transference is always going on.

Mannie: History is always with us.

Irv: Are all the transferences going on at the same time?

Mannie: In every behavior transference must be present, wouldn't you say that?

Al: Yes, I think so.

Mannie: In analyzing a piece of behavior, it would depend upon what you would focus on in that behavior.

Irv: Wait a second now. There are times when we feel like having sex. There are times when we have an impulse to eat, which is the primary thing. There might be other things going on at the same time.

Mannie: When you feel like having sex, there are real, physiological aspects, ego and historical determinants in that momentary feeling.

Irv: What I am saying, basically, is this: On some level when we are feeling we want sex, there are other aspects there latent, not as predominant. Particular needs are activated within the individual just as there are particular times when hunger is the predominant thing.

Mannie: Certain things take precedence; such as the centrality of hunger, which might be physiological as opposed to psychological or social.

Irv: Let's say there may be a particular time in an analysis when what seems to take precedence in the individual's hierarchy of needs and demands, perhaps, is the oedipal struggle. The oedipal struggle may be there on some level, but not predominant, at the apex of the hierarchy or repertoire at some points.

Mannie: Of course, at some point more infantile needs might take precedence even with regard to a wife.

Irv: Okay. Since needs and demands and impulses are more predominant at some time than at another, what makes for a transference repetition at one particular time or another has to do with the particular sense of needs and demands that are hierarchically predominant in the individual at that time.

Mannie: It has little to do with the kind of experience in the here and now a person is having. The fact that he is now in relationship to a woman with great big breasts does not influence the kinds of needs he feels as opposed to another woman with a flat chest. His need systems operate independent of the experience.

Irv: No. This is exactly what I am not saying. What I am saying is that the analytic situation by virtue of the structure, by virtue of the person's history in the analytic situation, may at one particular time provoke his need to take over. When he has this need to take over, he is going to express it in terms of his history and past and relate in his characteristic way and this is going to shape into transference.

Mannie: Fine. What has this got to do with whether I let him do it or not?

Irv: Let who do what?

Mannie: Whatever it is he is going to take over. I might stop him from doing it. I might confront him with reality. I might say, "Hey, you can't get away with this." He might come up with a new set of defenses. He might respond with acts of hate and go ahead and do it. The fact that I will act or not act in a certain way will influence the direction in which he will do his taking over that you are describing, Irv. It means he is going to be continuously responding to the way in which I react to his expression of needs.

Gerry: I think I agree with that without any kind of problem. I think Irv does. Let's get back to the clinical thing, group versus individual kind of experience. It seems to me that the unconscious necessities are going to be there anyway. They are going to be influenced whether the woman is big-busted or flat, whether the man is one way or another, the men in the group are one way or another. Certainly, when you put a person into a group therapeutic situation, when the group changes, when it is an open-ended group, then you are not going to bring up the same set of central struggles, not in the same way at least, as they come up when you are working individually. You are comparing individual and group therapy. It is beating a straw man because these are different kinds of reality experience, different ways of knowing people. We are looking at gems from a different facet.

Mannie: Right. He will function and express all of this differently in a dream than he will on the couch in your presence than he would in a group.

Irv: Isn't the individual analytic model based upon the notion that the analyst is neutral and silent and that the patient's own pathology will reveal itself and project itself onto the analyst? The analyst does not have to evoke any particular transference. The transference will come out by virtue of the individual patient's unconscious necessities.

Gerry: No! Wait a minute! The model of individual analysis assumed that the more activity, the more flat-chested, big-breasted, stern-looking, soft-looking men, women, and children there are around him in the experience, the less an unconscious specific kind of conflict or repetition compulsion is going to emerge.

Mannie: Exactly. The more you will make what is central to you central to the relationship. That does not mean, however, the others don't exist or that the others will be provoked into relationship. It is what Al said before. If you remain passive, the patient will take on what is central to him and he may leave out all of the peripheral stuff.

Gerry: Which may or may not be good. I don't know whether we can say it is good or bad.

Mannie: It is different! It deals with one kind of relationship. It becomes what Greenacre advocates. If you do not interfere, if you do not promote distortion, he draws upon his own needs more and more. The central needs and the central projections and distortions will come out so that he will ultimately make a mother of you and relate to you as if you were his mother.

Gerry: You then foster a regression.

Mannie: Right. Through your frustration of reality demands you will turn him on himself and do what you suggested, Gerry. He will then draw from himself what are his central systematic operations.

Gerry: This is based on the assumption that to do this is necessarily good and corrective. I do not know whether that assumption is necessarily so. Reality is not so much determined just by our central axis, but by the changing experiences we find ourselves in, the changing world. Perhaps we do better therapy by getting more reactions and less of the person's central reactivity, more of his momentary handling with a lot of changes that are related to the history in the analysis of the group. Because you are putting a premium, putting a value upon regression, on purity, which is even in the last analysis an artifact because you can never get that extreme purity that implies direct unconsciousness.

Mannie: Right.

Gerry: And reality is not so much determined by those regressed, ninety-nine and forty-four one hundredths per cent pure unconscious processes, but much more of our reality is related to here and now.

Mannie: Even from a theoretical point of view, what you get expressed in transference processes are preconscious, not unconscious. If it is unconscious, you may not even see the manifestations of it. Because the controls theoretically are so great. The moment it enters into the preconscious you have already by definition contaminated it by secondary process. The moment it becomes verbalized, it is already secondary process. The moment it becomes structured, it is already secondary process. We are sorting out, that is why we call it analysis. We are analyzing out of a constellation, out of a mishmash, out of a complex piece of behavior, we are analyzing out the determinants. Freud said all behavior has multiple determinants and what we are going to do is to analyze the multiplicity of determination in any piece of behavior over the long range. It is over the long range which makes for cure, for change, for therapy theoretically. The analyst then selects what he thinks is central in the totality of the determinants. He cannot analyze all the determinants; he does not know them. He does not want to analyze them all. It is not necessary or desirable, and life does not provide you with that much time. What he does is select what he thinks is central.

Gerry: As you are talking about it, Mannie, analytic procedure and even the word "analysis" are in a way like inorganic chemistry analysis. Once you take a particular chemical compound you can analyze the specific components, but if you tried to isolate one of the components from the compound, you no longer have the compound. That is what we are saying here. So long as you try to achieve purity of isolation of the person's inner demand structure independent of his reality now and in analysis, it is unreal. When we consider the patient independent of his reality span as a child, it is unreal because transference now is explored and analyzed in terms not only of the reality of history, but the fantasy of history or the transference of the history.

Mannie: Talking about a fantasy of history, I think Irv is struggling with a fantasy of history. He has an assumption about an ideal model of psychoanalysis that Freud neither described nor acted upon. The historical fantasy is this illusion about the nature of the psychoanalytic model, as if this were in fact the open door to the mind. Freud never restricted himself to only one kind of analytic relationship, as you will see if you read his writings.

Gerry: I don't think Irv does that. I did not have that feeling, Mannie. Perhaps I am defending him, but I did not feel he was trying to look for one kind, but that he was rather trying to understand both kinds.

Mannie: But if you talk about there being a special situation in which transference occurs, you are in that kind of model. The fact that you ask this kind of question reflects it.

Gerry: Oh, well.

Irv: In the discussion we had on transference some time ago, we talked about Kohut's article. We discussed what distinguished characterological object relations which are autonomous from those which are ingrained characteristic defensive modes of adaptation that are repetitious in character. Those are modes of relationship which involve the here-and-now active bridging across the repression barrier of some unconscious needs projected on the current situation.

Mannie: Now how does character get formed? This is one of the central psychoanalytic questions. We are dealing here with a theoretical concept which has to do with libidinal energy. Character traits and character structure are brought about through the transformation of psychic energy. This is a theory: that when you transform it, it is no longer loose and labile and no longer transferential. It is now fixed because it is transformed. In psychoanalytic theory, transference is untransformed libidinal energy. But character is transformed libidinal energy. This is metapsychology, this is theory. Did you ever see a piece of libido walking?

Gerry: [sings] "Did you ever see a dream walking? Well, I did."

Mannie: That is the point. I think we are struggling with such theoretical problems here and we are misdefining them. We are taking ideas as if they were facts. Obviously there are certain long range attitudes which cover our behavior in which we are so persistent, consistent, and fixed that the quality of transference that Al has been describing is absent. What do you have, Al, a thousand qualities of transference? It is a lively thing, a labile thing, it is vital, alive, it is active, it is ambivalent, it is filled with varieties of activity. It is not fixed, it is not rigid in the sense that you can hold onto it. It is rigid only in that it repeats. This quality is different from character structure and character traits. Character is a long range persistent attitude. It is not transference. Irv, you get hooked on the formulation somebody puts in the middle of an article and you extrapolate from it the whole theory of psychology, and then you don't know what to do with it.

Irv: I don't think I am as bogged down in this as you think I am.

Mannie: I am bogged down in it. Because I go through this again and again with you and apparently it burns me. Why should it? You might ask that question.

Irv: I think Gerry was right when he perceived my orientation, feelings, and attitudes today when I raised this question.

Mannie: All right. Let's go back over it again. Al, what is your reaction in all of this? How about answering?

Al: What are you so worked up about?

Irv: The question is one of clarification. Could you clarify a little bit the bilateral aspect of transference?

Al: I think it is always there; it always exists. We cannot focus too exclusively only on one aspect. Whenever a patient has a reaction to me, I think it is compounded of a real perception and a transferential one. I think my own reactions are the same. Hopefully they are less distorted and more realistic. But I think there is always a bilaterality of reality, even with the most disturbed patient, and a bilaterality of transference. I don't know what else there is to say about it. I think it is part of the function of the therapist to keep his eye on these four kinds of interactions that are going on between him and every patient, between the patient and any other group member. What answer are you looking for?

Gerry: Could we say that what we want is the pure projection of the patient's endopsychic structure?

Al: I do not think there is such a thing.

Gerry: Then we would have to say, paint us a picture on a blank screen.

Irv: The blank card of the TAT.

Al: I think that is a fantasy. I think the therapist is never a blank screen.

Gerry: I agree.

Al: Even that assumption, it seems to me, is a distortion on the part of the therapist. The therapist has a problem if he assumes that he is a blank screen, for it puts the whole burden of the problem on the patient. It is too much of a trial for the patient; it makes him totally isolated. I do not think it is a therapeutic attitude on the part of the analyst. I still do not know what Irv is really looking for. I really do not get a clear picture of what he wants, or why Mannie is getting worked up here.

Gerry: Down, boy.

Irv: I can try to move into this a little bit more.

Al: Do you understand the question?

Irv: Do you understand the question, Gerry?

Gerry: No.

Al: Try it again, Irv.

Irv: All right. Let's talk about some of the dynamics of this picture if there are some. There must be some. Let's say that I need to enter into a kind of maneuver with Mannie in order to get him to shaft me.

Gerry: Let me use a couple of examples of patients in my group so you can tell us what the question is. David is a guy who has a very compulsive structure and some weakness underneath it. He is a man who came into treatment some years ago in a panic because he was engaged and was going to bring his parents over to have dinner with his fiancee's family, and he practically collapsed in the street. His father had been a man who would pound on the table. He was a salesman and when he came home and did not want to hear anything out of the others or he was upset by the kids, he just pounded on the table and said, "I don't want to hear anything more about it." He would thump and scare the living hell out of the kids. David is a very charming man in the group. He is a person who has a cynical touch to him, but he has a Boy Scout touch too. In the group the other night, Sam, who is a very aggressive, defiant man, has been screwing up on paying his bill and has been in and out of the group and quitting and wanting to come back. We have been letting this go for a couple of months to try to get him to get solidly enough started in his treatment that he would not just run away again. But he pulled the same routine. He started therapy again. He quit during December and he started again in January and he had been here about a week or two when he said, "I can't make it. I haven't got any money; I won't be able to come in. I won't be able to pay the bill." I turned around and leveled it out with him. I said, "You have to stay at least until the end of the month." I said it was his responsibility to our mutual contract to try to work with him; and secondarily, I did not want to hear anything more about the money. He could get the money if he wanted to and he was to get it and pay up by the end of the month or leave treatment and not come back. This was very firm and active for me in these kinds of instances. I don't do this often. Once in a while it comes up. David reacted to this immediately with recollections about his father. He was terrified during my firm and assertive pressure on this other member of the group. He said, "Jeez, I never expected you to be . . . I never saw that in you." And yet, he had been calling me a stone; he had been calling me the "Fat Mac," and all these little snipey things with a lot of hostility all along the line. But we were never able to get him to see this kind of transference in terms of a father until something I actively did provoked a very strong feeling and a very strong recollection of its origin in the family. Now, in the one instance here is a man who has been in the group for a long time and I have been relatively neutral, as he sees it, and there is manifestation of transference feelings and distortions which have been there and noticeable and have been analyzable for others, but not too deep in his own feeling about himself. But in the other instance where I acted very much as he said, "It was just like my father pounding his fist on the table." I had done something much more assertive and aggressive with this other patient than is characteristic of the way things go in the group and to this he reacted.

Irv: Okay. That is a very good example of where your behavior provoked a recollection and a feeling, affect related to the father. But let us take a situation wherein the analyst is somewhat neutral, not active, and all of a sudden the patient comes in and is scared to death of him, sees him as stern, mean, and angry, even though the analyst, as far as he knows, has not been mean, stern, or angry. What about a situation like that? Where is the bilaterality there? This is the question. In other words, here you have something you can definitely show bilaterality. But what about when the patient experiences during the analytic hour the tremendous sternness and anger of the analyst and may even end up with fantasy that the analyst is going to come over and beat him?

Al: You really know of any analyst who is neutral? Have you experienced your own analyst in therapy as a neutral screen?

Irv: I would say, relatively neutral. Nobody is neutral. I mean silence in itself is not neutrality. Silence is an activity, a very powerful activity, the analytic silence. But the point is, not everybody reacts to analytic silence in the same way. People react in terms of their characteristic mode and in terms of what feelings it stirs up.

Al: What is the question then? Gerry, having stated—described these two men in the group . . . ?

Gerry: I was only trying to provide him with an example. I don't have a question. I see the situation as one where my side of the bilateral exchange was relatively strong and noticeable and his response was both to the reality of my firmness and to the transference thing of his feeling about his father.

Al: Yes.

Gerry: And in the other instance? That is, any time prior to that in the group, he has had the same feelings in regard to me that are transferential from the father and he has had certainly some of the same minor provocation in my assertiveness or aggressiveness in much less noticeable ways. I was only saying these are two situations where both of them were bilateral. The one was a much more noticeable thing than the other. I tell you, the way we know the bilaterality of it is that at the same time as he says, "That is my father pounding on the table," another in the group saw it as "That is good; Dr. McCarty is not being unrealistic and aggressive. He is just being firm. Sam needs that because Sam is just screwing around. It has to be fish or cut bait with him because he is just mucking up with himself and mucking up group time." They did not experience me as being abusive or tyrannical or anything else. They thought it was good. I was being nice in their eyes.

Irv: I see it exactly as—

Gerry: At the same time, other times previously, David has seen me as a stone, as a cold and unfeeling man, and has reacted without much feeling but in a hostile and pouty way. Others in the group have said I was quite friendly. So that tells us that in both instances I am doing something. In one I am less active and in the other I am more active.

Irv: What about the example I give where the patient on the couch all of a sudden becomes terrified of the analyst and starts to bring up fantasy material that the analyst is going to come over and beat him up, but—

Gerry: Yes, but you are assuming that this material comes up. You are assuming, as Mannie has said many times, that the illusory material that is bubbling up, is coming up in a relatively neutral situation because the defensive structure has been eroded and it is a pure unfolding from within, an eruption of a volcano.

Irv: All right, now where is the—

Gerry: I would say that if we could examine it, that very probably the behavior of the analyst during that period of the analysis, the last few days of it or the last week of it, has been equally strong and feelingful, as has been the patient's reaction.

Al: Is there anything transferential on your part, Gerry, in your reaction to these two men?

Gerry: In this particular instance?

Al: Yes.

Gerry: I don't know. I suppose, of course, there is. Let's see—what is the transferential thing in my relationship with Sam? Who is this defiant, mouthy, critical guy? I think that in terms of him he is the kind of person who is like, has qualities like my own, where I have been very nasty and biting with authority, with my father. So what he was doing with me was very much what I used to do with my father and did with my own analyst. Sam came in to the group one night and took my chair. I went out to get a drink of water and told the group to come in; and he is sitting in my chair looking at me and laughing. I just waved a finger at him and he jumped up and he was mad as hell. He moved, but, boy, he hated me because I was so unreasonable and such a son-of-a-bitch for booting him out of my chair. So my own transferential feeling would be that I was perhaps identified with him in some sense as I was being my father, with myself too. I was getting tough with myself, with him. So that in this situation I thought it out pretty clearly over a period of time. I have been watching this work and I thought, "Well, here we go again, what is the best thing to do here?" Usually I do nothing. I would wait and try to explore and then try to get the group to interact. I thought maybe I really needed to get firm with him right now and perhaps in saying I needed to get firm, there was a little bit of the element of my father, when I was a teenager, getting firm with me and picking me up by the shirtfront ready to belt me and saying, "No, I won't belt you, but. . . ." You know, this sort of confrontation. Knock it off! This is what my father did with me.

Al: You identified with Sam.

Gerry: I think I was identified with him, yes. And with David I think he is perhaps a little more like my father. He is Jesuitical, if you fellows know what I mean by that. It is a very snobby attitude about self, very aloof. I have a lot of it too. So perhaps it is also identification in there as well. But I think there is also a feeling about it that he is like the father, that he is critical, that in being critical of others, he is also shooting himself down. So I would say there is a little bit of both. Both men have a lot of similar characteristics. Both can be, in one sense or another, myself or my father.

Irv: All right now, wait a second. There are ways in which you could have handled that situation. You were firm and you set limits with that patient. What are the other ways in which you could have handled it? I suppose you could have been very mousy about it. That would be one way, huh? Or you could have just told him to get out. You could have kicked him right out. Or you could have said, "I will give you six months to handle it." But it seems to me that—

Gerry: What we are getting at though, as I expressed—

Irv: You had a lot of feeling. . . .

Gerry: I expressed a lot of feeling.

Irv: You were disturbed about it when you spoke to me because I came in the next day. . . .

Gerry: I was disturbed about the fact that I actually, instead of just being neutral in my tone, I put some feeling into it.

Irv: You were in some struggle, but I thought that the struggle primarily was that here you were in danger of losing a patient. In other words, losing income, losing money, losing some security, some narcissistic supplies.

Al: Irv, remember there is a four-way process going on here of seeing reality, probably on both sides and both making distortions. What is the question? I still don't understand the question that Irv wants to ask.

Irv: We largely think of a person's neurosis or a person's symptomatology as being inner determined.

Gerry: You largely think that.

Irv: All right. But a person brings this out. Let's say I do what I do with Mannie over and over again. And so, Mannie gets into the act, but I have a need to do it apparently. Now maybe he has a need reciprocally to act out with me. You do not do the same thing. At least, you don't draw his fire the way I do. Now, perhaps if he would not behave the way he does, maybe I would not express my problem this way. Maybe I would express it another way.

Gerry: I think you would.

Irv: Maybe I would. I suppose this is what we are learning.

Gerry: No maybes about it. You do not repeat and repeat and repeat a thing unless you get some gratification and some frustration, unless someone else is also going to do it. If he doesn't, you go off and try something else.

Irv: Okay. Does that mean, then, that a person will shift symptoms if he does not get the response he is looking for in the environment?

Gerry: But that is the whole theory of the regressive procedure in analysis. If he does not get the gratification, he shifts to another and another and another and goes through the repertoire of his procedures of trying to get gratification and none of them work, the building collapses, and he starts to try to find new ways.

Irv: Yes.

Gerry: But he will never find a new way or another old way unless he stays in treatment. He is not going to stay in treatment unless there is in some sense a situation for trying it out, unless the other persons involved express their ideas in some way. The notion of Menninger of the analyst not saying a word is even unreal. Even if he does not say a word, he is doing something; very direct and very gratifying to the person. I think that we talk about depriving him of a gratification of a neurotic demand as if it could be done, but I just do not think it can be done for long if a person is alive and in a contact with other people.

Al: What is the question?

Gerry: I think the question goes back to the one we have heard so much before: Can we have a pure transference, a pure endopsychic structure being expressed without it being interdependent upon the outside reality, the personal reality?

Al: I doubt it. I think the whole question is one of purity. Maybe that is the question, the question of purity, of absoluteness, of finality, of individual analysis being perfect and group analysis being less than the perfect analysis that Irv wants to achieve.

Gerry: Maybe we should not use that word "perfect." Irv feels abused on that. We gratify him with that "abuse." But perhaps purity implies some rating on a scale of good/ better/best; something from some moral evaluation, I think. Maybe we ought to say it in some less emotionally loaded terms such as complexity, simplicity.

Irv: Let's put it this way. Let's take TAT cards. A person looks at the TAT card with the boy looking at the violin and projects the story of this boy looking at the violin; he is plotting to kill his father. Someone else looks at it and says this boy is wishing he could go out and play with his friends but his mean mother won't let him go out and he is angry at her. Now, where is the bilaterality in these projections? Why does one say he is plotting to kill his father and the other one say that his mother is mean and does not let him go out and play?

Gerry: Because each of the boys has a history which will influence and determine the shape and color and texture of the painting of reality that they make. But that does not mean that there is not any reality out there, which also stimulates them to produce.

Irv: Okay, now, what stimulated this. . . .

Gerry: In one gulp you take a piece of granite out of the quarry and set it on a corner of the street. One sculptor is going to come up and he is going to make a "Napoleon on a Horse," and the other one is going to make "Transcending." Both of them are being stimulated by the chunk of marble and the current realities of the world and the color of the marble and the texture of it and by their own history and their interests.

Irv: I agree, but the point is, I am trying to understand—

Gerry: If there is no marble there, neither one of them is going to make anything!

Irv: But here is a guy looking at a violin and one guy turns it into a plot against father; he is going to murder his father; and the other guy turns it into a mean mother that is preventing him—

Gerry: So what?

Irv: So I am saying where is the bilaterality? Where is the provocative aspect?

Gerry: The provocative aspect is the piece of marble or the boy with the violin. Here I am; what will you do with me?

Irv: Okay.

Gerry: I am presenting myself to you; I am teasing you.

Irv: So where is the bilaterality?

Gerry: Why did you, as the therapist, why did Murray in gathering up the TAT cards select the boy with the violin picture instead of some other picture?

Irv: I don't know.

Gerry: Don't you think he had a reason for selecting that?

Irv: Probably stimulates and provokes certain essential conflicts related to being forced to do something in that kind of situation.

Gerry: I mean, it isn't forced.

Irv: But it involves this kind of thing. How did the parents handle such situations? What sort of experience did they have?

Gerry: I have had a lot of TAT responses of that kind which had nothing to do with force, where the kid finds an old violin that belonged to father and grandfather up in the attic and he wants to learn and become accomplished and master the instrument.

Irv: All right. All right! But it involves this whole thing of training, that can be one-dimensional. It evokes a lot of ideas and feelings. Now the question is, where is the bilaterality?

Gerry: Bilaterality in this problem we are in right now is that to you reality dimensions, reality considerations, reality frustrations are, in a sense, demands, controls. Here we go back again to that damn struggle we have been through a million times. I think it is one that you and Al have, by the way, and I don't hear it out of Mannie; which is, How come we have to be frustrated and deprived and have our archaic inclinations blocked or impeded by reality? Let's throw out reality.

Al: I have a slightly different idea about what Irv is looking for.

I think Irv has the feeling that an individual analysis lets the therapist be more neutral, less provocative, less involved; the blank screen or TAT card.

Gerry: But why, Al?

Al: But that in the group, patients respond. The therapist may be more responsive and if he is not, how can the patient's real transferences come out and be worked through?

the good guy today until I get myself in a position to get clobbered.

Mannie: It is five minutes after eleven.

Irv: Gerry was five minutes late then.

Gerry: I was five minutes late. I slept in.

Irv: I want to tell you, but maybe you have already seen it in the *International Journal of Psychoanalysis.* I just got the October issue. There is a review of your book. Are you familiar with it?

Mannie: No.

Irv: It is under "Shorter Reviews," page 609, and it is entitled, "Recent Books on Group Psychotherapy." The person who did the reviewing does not give his name so we don't know who it is. He reviews Klapman's book, Bion's book, and then he reviews, *Psychoanalysis in Groups* and the Kadis, Krasner, and Foulkes's book. But it is apparent from looking over what he said, he has not understood your book.

Gerry: Irv said this as he handed it to me. But I think there is one thing he is not referring to that is significant. That is, he gave about three sentences to a paragraph on each of the other reviews, but he spent most of the time, almost a column and a half, on your book.

Irv: Yes. He spent most of the review on your book, but it is the most uncomplimentary part.

Gerry: But he is talking about their book. As Mannie said, "Call me anything but call me."

Irv: I want you—

Gerry: What would it be like if he had not included it?

Irv: He says, "The use of the term psychoanalysis and group psychotherapy can be justified despite the fact that the authors, as in this case, are not accredited psychoanalysts."

Mannie: That is the part I like best.

Irv: You like that the best?

Mannie: Yes, because that is the line that bothers you most.

Irv: Who, me? It doesn't bother me.

Mannie: It is the only line you could find in the whole thing that made any sense to you.

Irv: No. I told you the whole thing.

Mannie: Accreditation! We are back to that again.

Irv: I told you the whole thing.

Mannie: We are back to that again.

Irv: Oh . . . nuts to you.

Mannie: It is true we are not accredited.

Irv: By whom?

Mannie: By the American Psychoanalytic Association.

Irv: You are accredited by the International Psychoanalytic Association and Al is accredited by the Academy of Psychoanalysis.

Mannie: But by the American Psychoanalytic we are not accredited. This person who wrote it is a member of the American Psychoanalytic.

Gerry: Yes, but the point both you guys are missing is the one that is important. That is, he spent more time trying to shoot you down. Some of these people he shot down in one sentence. He spends a lot of time trying to shoot you down. This is the only one where he says, They are not accredited.

Mannie: It is a way to shoot us down, the *ad hominem* argument.

Gerry: Sure.

Mannie: It has nothing to do with the value of the book but this is the one thing that Irv picks out. Irv knows this, that we are not accredited by the American Psychoanalytic Association. We cannot accreditize him; he will always be unaccredited by them. He cannot accept the role of being a bastard.

Gerry: Especially of bastard parents.

Mannie: Yes, indeed.

Gerry: Irv, you started out all right, what happened?

Irv: Oh, I think he is a son-of-a-bitch, that's all.

Mannie: I know. I am an illegitimate son-of-a-bitch.

Irv: I think that this statement, even from the orthodox point of view, is inaccurate; because, Mannie, you are a member of the International and if you are a member of the International, that makes you accredited.

Mannie: Not by the American.

Irv: But this is written probably by an Englishman. I doubt that this was written by an American.

Mannie: Maybe. You cannot tell, you don't know.

Irv: The point is, this is the official journal of the International Association and they say here you are not accredited when you are a member. So that even from that point of view they are wrong.

Mannie: What do you think I ought to do? Write them a letter?

Irv: This guy who wrote this stupid thing did not sign his name, so I don't know who wrote it. Yes, I would think so.

Mannie: You could certainly write a letter to the President of the United States.

Irv: I would do that too.

Gerry: Oh, Mannie, you are all right!

Mannie: I could complain.

Irv: What?

Gerry: How about a copy to the secretary of war?

Mannie: Right. Gerry, you are helpful too. Are we going to beat our gums about this again? I think we need a holiday, Al. [guffaws from Al, Mannie, and Gerry]

Irv: What is going on, you guys?

Gerry: I think Irv had a lot of feeling. He wanted to tell you about the review. You were kind of irritated about it when you handed it to me.

Irv: I was irritated by the review because—

Gerry: I was not when I read it, interestingly enough. I thought, "Now why did he get in a stir about it? It is not really a bad review."

Irv: The review, to me, indicated that this person had not read the book. Whoever reviewed it had not really read the book, just like Aaron Stein's review of your book indicated that he really had not carefully read it. It just bothers me when people write reviews and they don't read a book, that is all. If people are going to review something, they ought to read the thing they are reviewing and know what is going on.

Mannie: I agree with you, Irv, but you are screaming for justice in the wilderness. You are all alone in the wilderness yelling for justice.

Gerry: I think I know what the problem here is though. I read Erich Fromm's article, "Humanism and Psychoanalysis," that he read at the dedication of the building for the Institute of the Mexican Society.[17] And at one point he said something about knowing and loving the stranger, that this was getting in touch with humanity in one's self. I think that Irv is beating the stranger here.

Irv: Who is the stranger?

Gerry: Your unconscious, the element that is not acceptable to you.

Irv: I can't take injustice, that's all.

Gerry: But it is your injustice that you hate so.

Irv: Maybe, maybe.

Gerry: Because the point I was getting at here that Fromm made is the injustice you see them perpetrating is a part of what it is to be human. You are that way too, but you never say you are. It is the same thing I was talking about yesterday.

Irv: It may be clear—

Mannie: I can see that Irv reads every book he reviews and even those he does not review.

Gerry: There is no question that he reads them, but if the person's point of view is strange to his own, he says they did not read it.

Irv: Oh, no. Oh, no. I don't mind someone reading a book and taking a blistering position on the book. You can tell from the review that one has read the work.

Mannie: Like the way Al and I read Whitaker and Malone, *The Roots of Psychotherapy.*

Irv: That's right.

Mannie: We read it with a fine-tooth comb. We spent two full years reading that book, word for word. There was hardly a word we did not discuss.

Irv: I will give you an idea. I will tell you what angered me here. I read this thing quickly. He is referring in this review to the alternate session and how you said that the alternate session is a must for effective treatment. Then he says no clear theoretical basis is given for the treatment as a whole or for this particular practice. Well, didn't he read the chapter on the alternate session?

Mannie: No.

Irv: So, in the first place, you wrote a big chapter on the alternate session, giving the theoretical rationale, the clinical rationale and how it is utilized. He makes the statement that no clear theoretical basis is given for the treatment as a whole or for this particular practice. Then he goes on to make reference to the writing of Bion and Ezriel whose working principles would not encourage such a procedure. He indicates that you have not studied these writers, who are held by many group therapists to have made some of the most profound observations in the field. He is giving the implication that you have indicated that Bion and Ezriel use alternate sessions, which they never did.

Gerry: I don't think he says that at all.

Irv: What did it say to you?

Gerry: He says that reference to—

Irv: This is all in the context of the alternate session. This is all about alternate sessions. Then he brings up Bion and Ezriel.

Gerry: Yes, but he says that the references to their writings would indicate that they have not studied those writers. He is talking about all that. That is his point of view.

Irv: "References to the writings whose working principles would not encourage such a procedure indicate that the present authors have not studied these writers." Now, what is he saying here? Maybe it is obscured, but to me he is saying that if they had studied Bion and Ezriel, then they would not have an alternate session.

Gerry: He is saying that if they studied Bion and Ezriel, then when they gave their theoretical position for the alternate session, they would have been able to clarify their position comparatively to that of Ezriel and Bion.

Mannie: I would like to shift this a little bit.

Gerry: But I don't think that is an issue.

Mannie: I would like to get to the issue. I do not think the review is the issue. I have a feeling Irv is saying that you are threatened in your theoretical orientation to the work you do.

Irv: Not at all.

Mannie: Don't you have a theoretical orientation? Do you feel that last Saturday at San Francisco* I outlined a theoretical basis for including the alternate session in our formulation?

---

* The previous week Drs. Schwartz, Goldberg, and McCarty gave an all-day workshop at the annual meeting of the American Group Psychotherapy Association.

Gerry: Yes, but Mannie, I do not know if you did so well in the book as you did when you presented it there.

Mannie: Did you feel that you got it when I presented it?

Gerry: What?

Mannie: The theoretical formulation.

Gerry: I thought your conceptual frame was wonderful and I thought it was done well, and I know that is what Al and you have been saying, I don't have any question about that. I am only saying that this person is reviewing a book.

Mannie: What I want to know is why Irv is so threatened. Suppose someone reviews it and disagrees? Isn't there room for disagreement or challenge?

Irv: I am not threatened by someone disagreeing. I am angry about the injustice of somebody panning something when he apparently does not understand it.

Gerry: Listen, Al and Mannie have panned it themselves in certain ways; and they are saying that they have taken certain of their older articles and re-edited them. I do not feel that Mannie and Al have as much of an emotional attachment to their written words, or even the best-spoken words, as you do to the written or spoken word.

Irv: I, myself, don't think the book is that good a book. I think the book could have been better. I have stated it before.

Mannie: You are too defensive about it.

Irv: It isn't just your book. It is the general feeling I have about people making all sorts of categorical statements without knowing what they are talking about.

Al: I agree with Irv.

Irv: This is a general principle. There is just too much of it going on in the profession. I don't care for it.

Al: I think you are right, Irv. I like your position.

Irv: Great, Al.

Al: I think there is too much categorical nonsense going around.

Irv: How can you have a book where you devote a whole chapter to the alternate session, its use, its theories, rationale, et cetera, and then this person writes that no theoretical statement is made about the alternate session? How can he say that? I don't know, unless he does not consider that chapter a theoretical statement about the alternate session. I just do not understand.

Gerry: I can understand what he is saying. He is saying that the theoretical statement which they give and the rationale they give do not coincide with a theoretical premise in psychoanalytic liturgy.

Irv: Well, let him say that then.

Gerry: He is. He is writing to the members of the orthodox psychoanalytic group and he is comparing Mannie and Al's theoretical presentation, which is quite anti-orthodox, with the orthodox position. What he is saying is, How do they defend, explain, or explicate the use of the alternate session in regard to specific premises of psychoanalytic theory? I don't know that they have done that. They gave a rationale for it, a good one, and a theoretical basis of how it affects character and character defenses, but maybe not sufficiently for him in terms with which he is happy. Irv, you did the same thing when you wrote a review on some book and you said, "What do you think?" I said, "Well, you are offering a lot of opinion; I don't know how it stands as a review."

Irv: I wrote a review of Johnson's book. I really indicated what he wrote. Then I just made one or two statements about my point of disagreement with his over-all philosophy; but I did not misrepresent him. When I clearly differed from him, I indicated that it was my point of difference. It is the misrepresentation that bothers me.

Gerry: Maybe I am wrong.

Irv: However, Stein writes a review and he misrepresents, showing a lack of understanding. If a person is going to read a book, let him understand the author's point of view. If he wants to take a point of difference, let him clearly indicate that this is his point of difference. That is the position I take. Maybe I feel so bad about this because I have been misrepresented at times.

Mannie: You have been terribly misrepresented and the world is unfair to you.

Irv: Right.

Mannie: It is so unfair to you that you are angry with anyone who is indecent.

Irv: That's right.

Mannie: And you are holier than thou.

Irv: Right.

Mannie: You would not be unfair to anybody.

Irv: To anybody, nobody. I would not even step on a cockroach. I am a nice guy.

Mannie: You are a nice guy and the world is filled with injustice. But why are you beating your brains out?

Irv: Oh, you are the most exasperating person I have ever met!

Gerry: What is that, Mannie?

Mannie: What constructive purpose can this energy that Irv is devoting to this serve? You have to go beyond it. You cannot keep on reviewing and rehashing all the terrible injustices. This is the nature of the world, the way of the world. Let's transcend it by doing a better job next time. Let's not complain constantly about the injustice unless you want to change the world. That is different. Then, we have to organize a plan. Let's have an idea of where we want to go and how we are going to get there. Let's not spend the rest of our lives beefing about it. I do not see any value to it. The reviewer is not right. We are analysts. But, look, he has a right not to be right.

Gerry: That is the point I made on the basis of reading Fromm. That is why I said that Irv is not beating the man that wrote the review, but the injustice within himself that he does not say he has.

Mannie: For the rest of his life? Irv is a tremendously talented man with a lot of energy, a lot of information, a lot of creative capacity, spending it all fighting injustice. The reality will not be altered one bit by all of this.

Al: But that's what we did with Whitaker and Malone.

Mannie: No.

Al: We did not have to spend three years beating ourselves against this injustice.

Mannie: That is correct.

Al: We could have said something constructive, more constructive.

Mannie: The time we wasted was the time in writing the article,[41] not in having spent the time together in analyzing it and going over the book with one another and learning a common language. That was very constructive and very useful. It served a catalytic purpose. We should have gone beyond it. Al, I want to hear your thought. What is the analytic solution, what is the dynamic solution of the problem? I am asking Al to give us a theoretical solution of the problem because you took a position encouraging Irv.

Gerry: I took that position?

Mannie: No, Al did. I share his feelings about the values. I do not think he has a monopoly on decent values. I do not think you have. I think I have good values too. But I am not going to *kill* myself over it. I am going to try to teach those values, to produce, to fulfill myself the best I can in a sometimes lousy world. That does not give me a plan about how to change this world.

Al: This gives me a good entry to make the following proposition; namely, maybe Mannie and I ought to stop feeding for a couple of months.

Irv: Stop what?

Al: Feeding you guys for a couple of months; and you use the next couple of months, give up our meetings and draw up the first draft of the book. That would be productive and creative. You will not have our breast for two months. So you guys can assert your creativity, your independence, and your protest.

Irv: Here is what we had planned on the thing.

Gerry: I think we want to respond to that before we go on. I want to make a point here. Irv started by pointing out how I was in the doghouse because I was the one who was late and who slept in, but he said it won't last long, and it sure didn't.

Irv: Right.

Gerry: You created it for yourself.

Irv: All right.

Gerry: You can't stand prosperity.

Irv: That's true.

Gerry: Ha, ha.

Irv: We are going to get to the book. We are going to get to it. But I think that there is a lot of work there, a tremendous amount of work. It takes about a half an hour, I think, just to read one of those typescripts, doesn't it, Gerry? I mean, to really read the thing.

Gerry: Yes.

Irv: You figure it out. You have a year's typescripts to read even if you do just one year.

Mannie: Let's knock off for a couple of months, Al was saying. I hear you are not responsive to this. Al is saying, let's knock off a couple of months and just spend whatever time you would use, the money and whatever else is involved in working on this thing and getting it out.

Gerry: I think—

Mannie: Let's see if we can come out with a better book that reflects the attitudes that you will be prouder of.

Gerry: I think this is a good point of view, but my own reaction when Al said it was, "Oh, he is getting rid of us. He is going to throw us out." The kind of a feeling of your father saying, "It's time to go out and get a job."

Irv: I was thinking about it myself this morning on the way down. I was thinking, "I wonder how long we are going to continue meeting together." But then I have the feeling I do not want to break up our relationship. Even if we don't meet as we have been meeting, it is a kind of working relationship that is so enjoyable that I would not want to lose it altogether, you know? I want to keep our association going.

Al: I would miss you guys.

Gerry: What?

Irv: He says he would miss us. Well, we would miss them, too.

Gerry: I have no doubt about it.

Irv: I think people do have to get together and talk and share ideas. Now, maybe we have been too much on the taking side of it.

Al: I think you can be on the feeding side of it. There must be a population in your community that you could draw upon where you can be the feeders.

Irv: Do you know what happened to me at a local psychiatric clinic? Did I tell you? They called me in there for five lectures. Last Monday was supposed to be the last lecture and I started out by saying, "I guess this is my last talk," and I said, "Frankly, I am frustrated by the experience because I was mostly in a position of lecturing to you and there was not much opportunity for interchange." So now they want to keep going. They started off with five sessions and they were kind of hostile and formal. Now they are friendly and want to keep going.

Mannie: Great.

Gerry: Irv, I think it is wonderful; you are doing a good job. But that is the domain of medicine, in their eyes. You have to have that clear in your own mind in order to continue to do the justice to them and to yourself.

Al: You are avoiding the question of your separating yourselves from us, and the book.

Gerry: I don't think so, Al. Because you asked, isn't there some forum here where we can be giving instead of just taking, from you. Irv is talking of a place where he can give. And I have taken on a teaching of a couple of people and trying to get a group therapy program set up out at a residential school. I think we are giving.

Mannie: Now that you got that one off, let's go back to the issue. What do you think about Al's suggestion?

Irv: Ahhhhh . . .

Gerry: I think it is a good one. Perhaps if we deprive ourselves of our opportunity to do what we are doing, we can make something out of what we have done.

Mannie: What shall we set as our next date? May first?

Gerry: No. I think we should not set a next date until we have a draft. Until we have mailed you a draft. Then we will meet the next Saturday.

Al: Great, great.

Mannie: All right with you, Irv?

Irv: It is fine by me. I have a little reluctance, I admit.

Mannie: That was the most definite, the most positive solution I have heard in a long time.

Irv: I am interested whether or not you talked this over beforehand or whether this was just something spontaneous that Al threw out?

Al: We talked it over beforehand. We have talked about it for a long time because for a long time we have felt your excellence and your competence and the feeling I had is that I would put you up against many of the analysts that I know in New York.

Mannie: I also recall that when we were giving the seminar in San Francisco, I said, "Next time you two do it yourselves. You don't need me for it."

Irv: That's the whole thing, Mannie. Maybe we have reached the point where this kind of student-teacher need may be lessening, but what about the association? What about the relationship? What about the fact that people do get together and talk and share ideas?

Mannie: We will give you a membership card.

Irv: What kind of membership card?

Mannie: We will organize. Let's incorporate.

Al: Well, we can do this. We can have irregular dates with one another and just chew the fat.

Irv: That is what I mean. Hey, what about this once a month? I agree with this position on the book. Let's get the book going.

Mannie: Let's hold any decision about the future until we have gotten through this phase of it.

Gerry: Let's cope with, let's learn to do something with what exists. Then let's talk about where we go from there. That is what I was saying.

Irv: Well, let me feed on one thing that I wanted to ask you a question about, a question I brought up last week. I set a limit on Rose. I told her that she had to make a choice.

Mannie: All right, pick it up.

Al: I predicted you would do this, Irv.

Irv: What?

Al: I predicted that you would do this. Irv, it isn't that I don't want to hear about Rose, but I said to Mannie, "As soon as we say this to you, that you are going to come up with a demand for a feeding."

Irv: All right, so I will.

Al: Okay.

Irv: I found out from Rose something very interesting. . . .

Mannie: Can't we use these last fifteen minutes more constructively?

Irv: I just want to ask you one question.

Gerry: Just one, fellows? Ha!

Irv: No. I just want to ask you one question on setting a limit. The question is this: I have told Rose that she had to make a choice between giving up this boyfriend or treatment. Incidentally, she brought up an association that she had. She did not walk until after she was eighteen months of age, which is significant. Now, this all ties in with what we are doing here right now.

Al: I am impressed by how much in the last two or three meetings Irv and Gerry pass us by. They really carry on the dialogue and do very well. It is an illusion that we are feeding them. They really feed each other.

Mannie: Maybe we feel rejected that they really have not been feeding on us? Maybe that is why we are quitting?

Irv: Hey, you two are going to make me feel bad. What do you mean, quitting?

Gerry: Last week you, Mannie and Al, brought something up. You asked why I was so quiet, but I find it very hard to cope with this kind of thing that was just happening right here. They wanted to talk about this idea of terminating, ending, this kind of an exchange. Perhaps they are not talking about not having a different kind but ending this kind of relationship. And you kept going at this in this way. And I got exasperated last Saturday in the same way. I think I felt that right here, now, Mannie and Al after trying three or four times to cope with that, sat back and said, "Well, we will have to wait until it plays itself out." I think I sometimes feel that way. You ask how come I don't bring up the issues. And there are a lot of issues, sure. But it is very, very difficult sometimes; not other times. But there are times when you are going to get that point across whether it comes hell or high water. And I think that is good. It will probably stand you in good stead.

Al: I think you two have the capacity for a kind of exchange in helping one another that Mannie and I have. And Mannie and I are trying to get you free of the fantasy that you need to maintain a hierarchical relationship with us when I feel you are peers with us, and that you are peers with one another. You can help one another. You are peers, fundamentally, and somewhere we have not been able to resolve the vertical vector with us.

Irv: I think there is a great deal of truth to this. For example, as in the summers when we break off contact, we use our own resources, solve our own problems. We don't come running. Occasionally, something comes up that I might mention to you, or you might mention to me, Gerry.

Gerry: That's right.

Irv: But I think there is a temptation, when there is a resource around and available, and the temptation is to use it.

Gerry: There is no question. One of the things about it is, I think it has been a very growing thing for us. When we started, we needed it a lot. Certainly we have learned a great deal in the process. You hate to give up something that is so good. If there is any rationalization you can have for dependency, you are going to grab it.

Irv: I hate to give it up.

Gerry: But I think this issue with Rose, I think you knew what you wanted to do and you knew what was right to do. Bringing it up here—

Irv: I already did it.

Gerry: Yes, you already did it. It was just a rationalization to grab hold again.

Irv: Except for this one area, and it is probably a big area, that I have to resolve. That is the whole area of control over patients. Like this issue of having alternates in the home, this issue of patients socializing with one another outside the treatment setting. I wanted to explore more my own anxieties and my own reluctance and maybe work through this, because I figure I am a little too rigid. I don't know, maybe just you and I talking about it ourselves can resolve this particular problem.

Gerry: I think we have, to a large extent. You just do not want to admit you have. Actually, in the practical situation you do handle it well, but most of the time you do not want to give yourself credit for it. I don't always want to give myself credit for what I know and can do, and I want to keep that vertical vector that Al is talking about here. In a sense, it is a time when they are having to say to us, "Look, you are grown." I guess when you get to the end of adolescence the parents recognize the need for separation and the kids do, but neither one really wants to give up the relationship.

And no matter who makes the decision, it feeds the, let's say, the resistance of the other. If the child decides to go, the parent feels lost or left. And if the parents say it is time to go, then the child feels kicked out or left. You have that kind of feeling. There is no way to get away without it.

Irv: Right. Yes, I have the kind of feeling I think I had when I had my last analytic session and when I was driving home; no, driving to the office. I said "home" because my office then became home. And I was leaving for home, leaving my last session with the analyst. I happened to turn the radio on and they were playing graduation music. [He hums "Pomp and Circumstance."] You know that one? The tears were just rolling down my face and I felt kind of wobbly. It was really—

Gerry: I would have to say I was stunned. I don't know what I was stunned by. . . .

Mannie: Irv, any time you want to have a get-together with the four of us, play the drum while we get our harmonicas and play that song, we will be happy to do it. What do you say, Al?

Al: Sure.

Irv: Hey, but don't. For example, let's say in your training institute or in most analytic or professional groups, when a person graduates, don't they have an association where he participates together with the others in scientific papers and associations and things like that?

Gerry: Like when you go to junior high school, you always come back to see your sixth grade teacher or the fifth grade teacher.

Irv: Aw, no, wait a second. Just take a look at the—

Al: Reality?

Gerry: That is what they are saying. You visit. Isn't that what you said?

Al: It is true, Irv. I think you know that there is a professional association at the Postgraduate Center. There is a society that the analytic students at Flower join, where they can continue some kind of peer relationship. I think it is not just a question of the certificate. There is an exchange.

Irv: There is some reality involved although it probably is a symbiotic gratification as well. Because everybody has ties. Everybody has attachments.

Gerry: They do. You know you go back to the tenth anniversary of your graduating class, go back to the alma mater for the homecoming. You go home at Christmas or holidays.

Irv: Nobody severs completely, nobody completely exists alone.

Gerry: Why should they?

Irv: I don't think they should. I think it is the nature of the human relationship.

Mannie: I was just saying to Al that your corporation will save a hundred dollars a week now.

Al: How so?

Mannie: You won't be paying the telephone, paying our fee. It's about a hundred dollars a week, isn't it?

Irv: I don't know. What is it costing us, Gerry?

Gerry: The—

Irv: Gerry is the financial expert.

Gerry: I would say it costs us somewhere between ninety and a hundred and ten dollars.

Mannie: That's what I said, a hundred dollars a week. You ought to be able to have some fun on a hundred dollars a week.

Irv: Well, it will go to taxes anyway.

Gerry: No, it won't go to taxes.

Mannie: Make a contribution to some charitable organization. Found a foundation for training, a foundation of your new service. What is it called, the Northwest Psychological Services?

Irv: Listen, do you guys really think?

Mannie: Sure!

Gerry: Yes!

Irv: Are you really saying that our hierarchical relationship has ended and that we will work on the book? Then we will get together about that and we are really not going to be seeing each other like we have been? Is that what you are saying?

Gerry: Yes.

Irv: Why, I am getting tears in my eyes.

Gerry: [singing] "I'm laughing with tears in my eyes."

Al: Or we can do this. You can form a Northwest Group Psychotherapy Association and we will join it, come out once in a while.

Mannie: What we are saying, Irv, is that we don't know what the future will be. Let's not make a commitment here. We have a commitment now only that we will finish the book. Beyond that, *Quién sabe?*

Irv: What does that mean?

Mannie: "Who knows?" "*Che sera, sera.*" Do you want to hear another song?

Irv: No. We ought to get up and sing a song together.

Mannie: Al, Irv is an expert on movie cowboys. You should see his left knee. He has a trick knee. He can make that knee do the twist—or is it the right knee? That one you, Irv, stick over on the side and shake it back and forth.

Irv: I think that separation is a hard thing, but with it comes a self-reliance, an autonomy, a looking on one's own resources.

Gerry: But I think that separation is not really separation, because when you can make a separation, you can get in touch.

Irv: You mean, if there is a potential for getting in touch, then you never really separate?

Gerry: No, I don't say that, not that, at all. I am saying that only when you make the separation from the vertical vector of the authority and sort of get in touch with the authority in yourself, you are in a position to confront other people, strangers as well as friends or acquaintances or people you know, and get in touch with them. Now, instead of re-enacting some kind of a magical position with the parents so that it is really only after we can somehow get free of the feeling of wanting to stay the child with Mannie and Al, that we could get to know Mannie and Al, because that is the only time we get to know ourselves.

Irv: I think there is a lot of truth to that. In other words, this is the essence of that article on small talk, the article I think I discussed with you. Those people who cannot make small talk are so eager in their relationship, in the unconscious need to get symbiotic gratification, that they really can't meet the other person or talk to him. That is what you are saying.

Gerry: That is right, yes. That you can get in touch only once you have gotten in touch with yourself. But I still don't like to say goodbye.

Irv: I don't either.

Al: Just *au revoir*, fellows.

Irv: Okay, oar reevwar and we will get—

Gerry: Oh 'voir.

Irv: We will get this book shaped up and send you the manuscript and then we will talk about it.

Mannie: Remember, if you want to talk to us again, you had better
finish the book!

Gerry: Yes, that's right.

Irv: Hey, you guys aren't imposing a limit by any chance, are
you?

Gerry: I did, I did.

Mannie: I will be watching for the manuscript in the mail.

Irv: All right, guys.

Gerry: Goodbye now.

Al and Mannie: So long.

References

1. Ackerman, N. *The Psychodynamics of Family Life*. New York: Basic Books, 1958.
2. American Telephone and Telegraph Co. Advertisement, *American Psychologist*, **22**: April, 1967.
3. Alger, I. and P. Hogan. "The Impact of Videotape Recording on Insight in Group Psychotherapy," presented at the Twenty-fourth Annual Conference, American Group Psychotherapy Association (AGPA) New York, 1967.
4. Bell, J. Personal Communication, 1967.
5. Bibring, E. "Methods and Techniques of Control Analysis: Report of the Second Four Countries Conference," *International Journal of Psycho-Analysis*, **18**: 369, 1937.
6. Bion, W. R. *Experiences in Groups*. New York: Basic Books, 1961.
7. Brill, A. A. "The Only or Favorite Child in Adult Life," in *An Outline of Psychoanalysis*, edited by J. S. Van Tesslaar. New York: Random House, 1925.
8. Colby, K. M. *A Skeptical Psychoanalyst*. New York: Ronald Press, 1958.

9. Committee on Psychiatry and the Law. "Confidentiality and Privileged Communication in the Practice of Psychiatry," Report No. 45. Group for the Advancement of Psychiatry, p. 93, June, 1960.

10. Ekstein, R. and R. S. Wallerstein. *The Teaching and Learning of Psychotherapy.* New York: Basic Books, 1958.

11. Ezriel, H. "A Psychoanalytic Approach to Group Treatment," *British Journal of Medical Psychology,* No. 23, 1950.

12. Fenichel, O. *The Psychoanalytic Theory of Neurosis.* New York: W. W. Norton, 1945.

13. Fleming, J. and T. Benedek. *Psychoanalytic Supervision.* New York: Grune & Stratton, 1966.

14. Foulkes, S. H. *Therapeutic Group Analysis.* New York: International Universities Press, 1964.

15. Freud, A. *The Ego and the Mechanisms of Defense.* New York: International Universities Press, 1946.

16. Freud, S. *Collected Papers, Vols. I-V.* London: Hogarth Press, 1950.

17. Fromm, E. "Humanism and Psychoanalysis," *Contemporary Psychoanalysis,* 1, 1, 1964.

18. Gill, M. M. *Topography and Systems in Psychoanalytic Theory.* New York: International Universities Press, 1963.

19. Gladfelter, J. "The Use of Videotape Recording for Supervision of Group Psychotherapists," presented at the Twenty-fourth Annual Conference, American Group Psychotherapy Association (AGPA), New York, 1967.

20. Grotjahn, M. *Psychoanalysis and the Family Neurosis.* New York: W. W. Norton, 1960.

21. Guntrip, H. *Personality Structure and Human Interaction.* New York: International Universities Press, 1961.

22. Hulse, W. C. "Communalization as an Active Group Psychotherapeutic Process," presented at the Eighteenth Annual Conference, American Group Psychotherapy Association (AGPA), New York, 1961.

23. Johnson, A. M. "Sanctions for Superego Lacunae of Adolescents," in *Searchlights on Delinquency,* edited by K. R. Eissler. New York: International Universities Press, 1949.

24. Jung, C. G. *Memories, Dreams, Reflections.* New York: Random House, 1961.

25. Kovaks, V. "Training and Control-Analysis," *International Journal of Psycho-Analysis*, **17**: 346, 1936.

26. Markowitz, M., E. K. Schwartz, and Z. Liff. "Non-didactic Methods of Group Psychotherapy Training Based on Frustration Experience," *International Journal of Group Psychotherapy*, **15**: 220–227, 1965.

27. Menninger, K. *Theory of Psychoanalytic Technique*. New York: Basic Books, 1958.

28. Mittelman, B. "Motility in Infants, Children and Adults: Patterning and Psychodynamics," *The Psychoanalytic Study of the Child*, vol. X. New York: International Universities Press, 1954.

29. Munroe, R. L. *Schools of Psychoanalytic Thought*. New York: Holt, Rinehart & Winston, 1955.

30. Pelz, D. C. "Creative Tensions in the Research Development Climate," *Science* **157**: 160–165, 1961.

31. Reich, W. *Character Analysis*. New York: Orgone Institute Press, 1949.

32. Saul, L. J. "A Note on the Telephone as a Technical Aid," *Psychoanalytic Quarterly*, **20**: 287, 1951.

33. Savage, C. "Countertransference in the Therapy of Schizophrenics," *Psychiatry*, **24**, 1, 1961.

34. Schwartz, E. K. "Group Psychotherapy: The Individual and the Group," *Acta Psychotherapeutica*, **13**: 142–149, 1965.

35. ———. "Non-Freudian Analytic Methods," in *Handbook of Clinical Psychology*, edited by B. B. Wolman. New York: McGraw-Hill, 1965.

36. ——— and H. M. Rabin. "A Training Group with One Non-Verbal Co-Leader," *Journal of Psycho-Analysis in Groups*, **2**: 35–40, 1968.

37. Schwartz, E. K. and A. Wolf. "On Countertransference in Group Psychotherapy. *Journal of Psychology*, **57**: 131–142, 1964.

38. ———. "The Interpreter in Group Therapy: Conflict Resolution through Negotiation," *AMA Archives of General Psychiatry*, **18**, 186–193, 1968.

39. ———. "Psychoanalysis in Groups: Resistances to Its Use," *American Journal of Psychotherapy*, **17**: 457–464, 1963.

40. ———. "The Quest for Certainty," *AMA Archives of Neurology and Psychiatry*, **81**: 64–84, 1959.

41. ———. "Irrational Trends in Contemporary Psychotherapy:

Cultural Correlates," in *New Directions in Mental Health,* Vol. II, edited by B. F. Riess. New York: Grune & Stratton, 1969.

42. Silverberg, W. V. *Childhood Experience and Personal Destiny.* New York: Springer, 1952.

43. Szasz, T. "The Uses of Naming and the Origin of the Myth of Mental Illness," *American Psychologist,* **16,** Feb. 1961.

44. Szasz, T. "The Concept of Transference," *International Journal of Psycho-Analysis,* **44:** October, 1963.

45. Vaughn, W. Personal Communication, 1961.

46. *Washington Square Journal* (New York University) **12:** 1, January 12, 1967.

47. Whitaker, D. S. and M. A. Lieberman. *Psychotherapy through the Group Process.* New York: Atherton Press, 1964.

48. Wolberg, A. R. "The Psychoanalytic Treatment of the Borderline Patient in the Individual and Group Setting," in *Topical Problems of Psychotherapy,* Vol. II. Basel: Karger, 1960.

49. Wolberg, L. R. *The Technique of Psychotherapy.* New York: Grune & Stratton, 1968.

50. Wolf, A. "Psychoanalytic Group Therapy," in *Current Psychiatric Therapies, Vol. IV,* edited by J. Masserman. New York: Grune & Stratton, 1964.

51. Wolf, A. and E. K. Schwartz. *Psychoanalysis in Groups.* New York: Grune & Stratton, 1962.

52. ———. "Psychoanalysis in Groups: The Alternate Session," *American Imago,* **17:** 101, 1960.

53. Wolf, A., E. K. Schwartz, G. J. McCarty, and I. A. Goldberg. "Training in Psychoanalysis in Groups without Face to Face Contact," *American Journal of Psychotherapy,* **23:** 488–494, 1969.

Index

A

Ackerman, N., 142
Acting out, 249, 250
Adler, A., 142
Adolescents, 124, 126, 127, 128, 131, 150
Alternate sessions, 2, 35–52
Analytic contracts, 209–215
Analytic group therapy, 13
Anxiety, 69
Associational flow, 81–93
Audiovisual aids, in psychoanalytic training, 28
Authority, 10
Authority vector, 19

B

Bellak, L., 314
Benedek, T., 29
Berman, Leo, 255, 256
Bibring, E., 29

Bilateral resistance, 22
Bilateral transference, 243
Bion, W. R., 81, 282, 342
Borderline patients, 187–208
Brill, A. A., 142
Burrow, Trigant, 1, 5, 6

C

Cognitive content, of psychoanalytic training, 32–34
Colby, K. M. A., 211
Collected Papers (Freud), 109
Concepts of Personality (Wepman and Heine), 296
Conformity, 95–109
"Conjoint Family Therapy" (Jackson), 248
Control analysis, 209, 223
Countertransference, 19, 30, 79, 88, 196, 205, 209, 221, 222, 223, 234, 240, 248–249, 250

D

Deutsch, Martin, 290
Displacement, 65
Distortion, 65
Dreams:
  analysis of, 10, 213–214
  regression in, 149
Dyadic psychology, 148
Dyadic therapy, 286

E

Eissler, Kurt, 77
Ekstein, R., 29
Electronic devices, in psychoanalytic training, 28
"Epitaph for an Age" (Krutch), 26
Ezriel, H., 81, 280, 282, 342

F

Face-to-face cues, 217–236
Fairbairn, W. R. D., 283
Family dynamics, 142
Fenichel, O., 109
Ferenczi, S., 4, 61
Fleming, J., 29
Flexibility, of therapist, 25
Flight into health, 103
"Focal Conflict Group Therapy" (Whitaker and Lieberman), 81
Foulkes, S. H., 81
Free association, 10
Freud, Anna, 303
Freud, Sigmund, 4, 5, 59, 78, 98–99, 109, 142, 207, 209, 281, 323, 324
Fromm, Erich, 175, 340, 341

G

Garma, Angel, 148
Gill, M. M., 305
Greenacre, Phyllis, 244, 318
Grotjahn, M., 188

Group for the Advancement of Psychiatry, 21
Group therapy:
  alternate sessions, 2, 35–52
  analytic, 13
  limits of, 15
  nature of, 6–22
  nonanalytic, 13
  patients to be excluded from, 15
Guntrip, Harry, 283, 287

H

Hallucinations, 282
Horney, Karen, 283, 287
Hulse, W. C., 133
"Humanism and Psychoanalysis" (Fromm), 340

I

Individuation, of patient, 73–80
Interaction, 81–93
Intrapsychic exploration, 6
Intrapsychic processes, 11, 59

J

Jackson, Don, 248, 250
Johnson, A. M., 111
Jones, Ernest, 4
Jung, Carl G., 4, 5, 282

K

Klein, Melanie, 76, 148, 283, 287
Kohut, H., 296, 298, 299, 301
Krutch, Joseph Wood, 26

L

Lateral transference, 169–175, 250, 252
Libidinal energy, 324
Libido theory, 304
Lieberman, M. A., 81, 282, 283, 291
Limits, 15
Lindner, Robert, 142

M

Marathon group sessions, 14
Menninger, K., 29, 211, 332
Meyer, Adolf, 242
Mittelman, B., 68
Models, of patient, 73–80
Monadic psychology, 148
Monroe, Ruth, 109
Moreno, J. L., 1, 81, 263
Mother relationship, 147
Mother transference, 198
Multilateral transference, 243
Multiple interaction, 6, 8–10
Multiple reactivities, 10
Multiple supervisors, 219

N

Neuroses, inhibition of, 11
New York Medical College, 4
Nonanalytic group therapy, 13

O

Oedipal derivatives, 146–153

P

Partipotence, of patient, 24
Peer vectors, 10
Pelz, D. C., 15, 21
Perls, F. S., 81
Phenomenology, 304, 305, 306
Postgraduate Center for Mental
   Health, 4, 29
Prenatal ego, 148
Pre-oedipal derivatives, 146–153
Pribram, Karl, 290
Psychoanalysis and the Family
   Neurosis (Grotjahn), 188
Psychoanalytic Study of the Child,
   The (Mittelman), 68, 142
Psychoanalytic training, 27–34
Psychodrama, 1

R

Rangell, Leo, 296
Rascovsky, 148
Reactivity, 8
Regression, 75, 76, 77, 149, 212,
   213, 214, 301
Reik, Theodor, 175
Repetition compulsion, 61
Resistance, 10, 146
Rituals, 95–109
Roles, of patient, 73–80
Roots of Psychotherapy, The
   (Whitaker and Malone), 341
Rosen, John, 60

S

Savage, Charles, 196
Schilder, Paul, 1
Schizophrenics, 77
Schools of Psychoanalytic Thought
   (Monroe), 109
Schwartz, E. K., 29, 81
Seitz, Phillip, 296
Sex, and violence, 111–122
Sexual fantasy, 101–105
Sibling relationships, 140, 141
Socialization, 54, 57, 60, 67, 70, 71,
   164, 167
Strupp, Hans, 196
Sullivan, Harry Stack, 76, 283, 287
Supertransference, 33, 224
Supervision, in psychoanalytic
   training, 29–30, 223, 237–258
Szasz, Thomas, 75, 279, 283

T

TAT cards, 314, 333, 334
Telephone, in psychoanalytic training, 27–29, 30

Termination, 337–355
Tetradic psychology, 148
Therapeutic pressure, 242
Tradition, 95–109, 123–143
Transference, 10, 30, 60, 76, 77, 169, 209, 213, 232, 248–249, 250, 252
Transference neurosis, 16, 58, 63, 64, 65, 66, 214, 243, 244
Transference theory, 279–308, 309–335
Treatment setting, 259–277
Triads, 6, 8
Triangular psychology, 148

V

Violence and sex, 111–122
Visual cues, 240

W

Wallerstein, R. S., 29
Wender, Louis, 1
Wepman, Joseph M., 296
Whitaker, D. S., 81, 282, 283, 284, 289, 291, 341
Wolf, A., 29, 81, 210
Wolberg, A. R., 111
Wolberg, L. R., 223